THE BIRTH OF SOLIDARITY
The Gdańsk Negotiations, 1980

THE BIRTH OF SOLIDARITY
The Gdańsk Negotiations, 1980

Translated and introduced by
A. KEMP-WELCH

St. Martin's Press   New York

ISBN 0–312–08187–1

Library of Congress Cataloging in Publication Data

Main entry under title:

The Birth of Solidarity.

Bibliography: p.
Includes Index.
1. NSZZ "Solidarność" (Labor organization)—History—
Sources. 2. Labor policy—Poland—History—Sources.
3. Collective bargaining—Poland—History—Sources.
I. Kemp-Welch, A., 1949–
HD8537.N783B57   1983   322′.2′09438   83–8704
ISBN 0–312–08187–1

Contents

Preface

This book presents a full text of negotiations between a Polish Government Commission and the Interfactory Strike Committee at the Gdańsk Shipyard during August 1980. The proceedings were transcribed from tape-recordings by Mirosław Chojecki and published by Solidarity in Warsaw to mark the first anniversary of the Gdańsk Agreement. In translating, I have adopted his rule that 'only the most evident lapses in the use of language' should be corrected. The text is followed by an important mémoire on the role of experts and the 'working group' which met in private between the plenary negotiations. It was prepared especially for this volume. Finally, a word of acknowledgement to my wife for her help with the translation.

A. K.-W.

Introduction

Our actions will astound the world.
Lech Wałęsa

The Gdańsk negotiations of August 1980 were unique in history. For the first time, workers were accepted as equal partners to negotiations with a communist state. They led, moreover, to the granting of independent trade unions – the future Solidarity – the right to strike, and other concessions unknown within a Soviet-type system. These events were unprecedented, yet to describe them as 'revolutionary' seems not entirely appropriate, for two main reasons. In the first place, the strikers' demands, though radical and far-reaching, were also limited: they did not seek to take power but to bring it within legal jurisdiction. Thus the rule of law and freedom of expression were called for, but not the abolition of censorship, political pluralism or change in Poland's international alignment. In so restricting the scope of their demands, the strikers sensed with uncanny accuracy the boundary between what could and what could not be granted. Secondly, the strike was peaceful throughout. The occupation of the shipyard has a rich iconography, but flamboyant episodes from the past –when workers sallied forth to attack public and Party buildings – were absent. Instead, the strikers remained strictly within the workplace, knowing full well what might befall them if they ventured out onto the streets. Their watchwords were prudence (*rozwaga*) and solidarity. For their part, the authorities also avoided violence. At the last moment, the Party's Central Committee decided to end the occupation by agreement, rather than by force. The outcome of negotiations was thus a compromise which could plausibly be presented at the Final Ceremony as a 'victory for both sides'.

One of the most intriguing aspects of negotiations was the use of language by the Strike Presidium. For the first time, workers found their voice and started to speak independently of the state. In the past, as Adam Michnik has suggested, 'Stalinism succeeded in imposing false solutions because it succeeded in imposing its own language.'[1] The technique still worked in the early 1970s, when the Party leader Gierek held a renowned 'debate' with strikers in the Szczecin Shipyard: 'Gierek won hands down, just by using language which had no grammatical rules for concept-formation separate from the activity of the communist party.'[2] But now in Gdańsk, the strikers emancipated themselves from the official sphere and started to create a 'cultural space' of their own. At first this took the form of delimiting the 'political' realm, by constant assertions that they were 'social activists, interested in social questions'. Later, their spokesmen grew in confidence and started to echo, but not to adopt, the alternative language most readily to hand, that of the Catholic Church, not in any denominational sense, but simply as the repository of Polish culture for all citizens over a thousand years. In the final phase of negotiations and in the Solidarity stage that followed, workers emerged as autonomous social beings, expressing themselves[3] and acting in ways that were distinctively their own. This 'coming of age' in 1980 is thus best understood as the culmination of a process whose roots lie in the experience gathered over the entire duration of the post-war state.

Under Stalinism,[4] Polish workers were declared the new rulers of the state, while simultaneously deprived of institutional means for self-defence. Political channels were steadily reduced to a monopoly exercised in their name by a 'Polish United Workers' Party'[5] formed in 1948, and trade unions were amalgamated into a single Federation the following year, completely dominated by the state. Socially divisive wage systems, such as piece-rates, were perpetuated and new methods of 'socialist competition' such as shock-working (Stakhanovism) were introduced. The working class split rapidly into a 'labour aristocracy' of better-paid workers in strategically important industries, and an underpaid and sometimes impoverished majority. Social differentiation confirmed this picture.[6] Preferential access to further education and above all through the Party gave unprecedented possibilities for advancement, again for a minority of workers. We may concur with the suggestion made for the comparable phase in Soviet economic development: 'The Bolsheviks never tried to fulfil the Marxist promise that the workers would rule. But they did fulfil a simpler and more comprehensible promise of the revolution – that workers and peasants would have the opportunity to *rise* into the new ruling élite of the Soviet state.'[7] Unlike neighbouring Bohemia and East Germany, Poland had no working-class disturbances in 1953.

After Stalin's death, the Polish Party passed resolutions on 'the restoration of Leninist norms' but most practices remained the same. Bread shortages continued to be blamed on hostile 'kulaks', who allegedly preferred to hoard grain for their own pigs than to sell it to the population. Work norms began to be tightened to cut costs, without consulting the workforce. In the first attempt to defend their interests, workers at the Cegielski[8] Carriage Works in Poznań – the second largest enterprise in Poland – looked to pre-war means of protest.[9] But trade unions no longer existed as an instrument for their protection and other bodies, such as the Work Inspectorate, were not independent of management. Even so, their original protests were directed through the 'normal channels' and the first of three delegations was sent to Warsaw, without results. Instead, a 'regulation' of norms was announced at the beginning of 1956 and protest stifled by hints of a compensating wage increase. The dethronement of Stalin in the following month aroused great interest amongst the factory *aktyw* (the speech was read at 'open meetings' of the Party) and there were rank-and-file pressures to democratise political life. But the basic concerns of the workforce remained welfare: supplies to the market, 'hidden' inflation (by changing a brand of product or just its name), shortages of coal, the cost of imported medicines, inadequate housing, as well as the question of norms and poor organisation of work – leading to stoppages due to shortages of raw materials and parts. The factory authorities attempted to dismiss these demands as 'provocations'. Later the Director promised to clarify them within seven days. He did not do so. Workers' patience with the 'normal channels' was gradually exhausted. There were stoppages in early June. Strike preparations were set in motion.

To head off the strike, the central authorities dispatched a high-level delegation, including the Minister of Machine Industry and the Chairman of the Trade Union Federation, to the factory. After a mass meeting with the workforce on 27 June, it withdrew, announcing that matters could be resolved at local level. The meeting, in which many Party and union officials took part, then decided on a march to the People's Council, which stood next to the regional Party headquarters, in the centre of town. Its purpose would be to put pressure on the authorities to send the Party First Secretary or Prime Minister to Poznań to settle their grievances. Early on 28 June, about 80 per cent of the workforce (including Party members and officials) marched into town. A delegation went into the People's Council to present their demands. The protest was joined by workers from other enterprises *en route* and by citizens: 100 000 in all, appealing to the authorities to listen. The senior officials present – including Edward Gierek, who had arrived in Poznań as part of a five-man delegation the night before – made no attempt to find a peaceful solution. Rumours of arrests spread. Part of the crowd went to the prison to release those held there. The police headquarters was unsuccessfully attacked. A tank division, on manoeuvres in the vicinity, was called in 'to restore order'. The ensuing battle left 75 dead and 900 wounded. The great majority of victims were very young: seventeen to twenty-one years old. They included a few soldiers: Gierek spoke at their funeral. The Prime Minister, Cyrankiewicz, now arrived in Poznań. His proclamation to the populace stated that 'imperialist centres and the reactionary underground hostile to Poland are directly responsible for the incidents, and are burdened with the blood spilled, in Poznań'. He promised to 'cut off the hand' of those 'provocateurs' and 'diversionists' who dared to challenge 'people's' rule.[10]

Identical phrases were used at a special session of the Soviet Communist Party on 30 June. Noting that the US Senate had recently allocated huge sums to be spent on 'subversion behind the iron curtain', it stated: 'the anti-people's demonstrations in Poznań were clearly financed from this source'.[11] The Soviet process of de-Stalinisation was abruptly halted. But the Polish Party drew the opposite conclusion: 'All attempts to hamper the process of democratisation as a result of the Poznań events would be erroneous and politically harmful.'[12] Democratisation, though, remained undefined. While there was a vague commitment to grant some of the rights of factory councils promised in 1945, those of enterprise directors to direct and the duty of unions to transmit directives downwards, and compliance with them upwards, remained unimpaired. Even this modest programme, accompanied by wage rises and investment in housing, was bitterly contested in the Party hierarchy. The Stalinist conservatives sought to engage Moscow more actively, but reformist leaders broke the communist taboo by 'going public' with some points at issue.

Workers' Councils began to be established at factory level. Amongst their principal demands was the reinstatement of Władysław Gomułka who had become a popular hero since his dismissal as Party Secretary in 1948 and his later imprisonment as a 'nationalist deviationist'. The first act of the Eighth Party Plenum, which met on 19 October 1956, was to coopt him onto the Central Committee. Proceedings were then suspended while Polish leaders, including Gomułka, received an uninvited Soviet delegation, headed by Khrushchev. After acrimonious exchanges, which lasted until the folllowing morning, the visitors withdrew. Soviet troops which had been advancing on the Polish capital were ordered back to barracks. The Eighth Plenum resumed with a long address by Gomułka.

His speech and the programme it elaborated caused a national sensation. Gomułka castigated Stalinism in every sphere: shortcomings of the Six-year Plan (1950–5); the disaster of collectivisation; the Party's isolation from its roots – the working class – and from society as a whole. The economy should be revived partly through workers' self-management; collective farming should be voluntary; the Catholic Church should be allowed to propagate its doctrines: 'It is a poor idea that only Communists can build socialism, only people holding materialist social views.' He noted the 'animating social current passing through the whole society . . . silent and enslaved minds begin to cast off the poison of mendacity, falsehood and hypocrisy'. 'The clumsy attempt to present the painful Poznań tragedy as the work of imperialist agents and provocateurs' had been 'very naive politically'. Finally, relations with the Soviet Union should be based on sovereignty, equality of rights, and full independence.[13] The speech was broadcast live and stayed long in the popular memory. It was quoted extensively during the Gdańsk negotiations.

The gains of 'October' were fourfold. First and most prominent of these was the degree of social solidarity shown by the population at large in the face of an impending Soviet *coup*. Although there were incidents of hooliganism in Warsaw and demonstrations which threatened to get out of hand in certain other cities during the weeks which followed the Eighth Plenum, the general atmosphere was of calm determination, which together with the firmness of Gomułka and his supporters in the Party leadership, helped to bring about a peaceful outcome. For a unique moment, the Party leadership and population were united. A second gain was the genuine attempt by the new leaders to rein in the security services and bring them under Party control. The more notorious torturers of the Tenth Section were tried and sentenced. Poland had neither political prisoners nor the usage of the special riot squads for a decade. A third was the effort to regularise relations with the Soviet Union and place them on a more formal footing. Gomułka led a delegation to Moscow in mid-November, which reached an agreement over the conditions under which Soviet troops would be stationed on Polish soil. In return, the Soviet Union assisted the Polish economy with long-term credits and grain deliveries, and agreed to further repatriations of Polish families. Although this did not mean restoration of sovereignty, it did at least introduce an element of reciprocity into relations. Finally, there were important concessions to society.

For the peasantry, October signalled a spontaneous de-collectivisation, during which 85 per cent of existing cooperatives were disbanded within four weeks. Though the Eighth Plenum noted that 'the idea of collectivisation is still necessary,' the practice had been abandoned. The Church, too, obtained important benefits: religion could again be taught in schools, churches could be constructed and priests, bishops and Cardinal Wyszyński were released from detention. Even the intelligentsia, whose actions had helped to prompt October, enjoyed greater cultural and intellectual licence for a while. Paradoxically, the class which had done most to anticipate October, gained the least of all from it.

For workers, 1956 meant the opportunity to gain some measure of control over their own destiny. In part their aspirations were material and were met by an average growth of real wages of 5 per cent each year until 1960. But hopes were also placed on a reform of management, particularly by skilled workers in large enterprises who shared with technical specialists a desire to cut through the obstruction and incompetence of local Party and union officials. The latter retaliated by delaying the formation of Workers' Councils which were supposed to circumvent them. Similar blockages appeared in high politics. An advisory economic council under Oskar Lange presented a report on radical economic reform in May 1957. It envisaged thorough-going decentralisation based on enterprise autonomy and the profit motive. Had it been adopted, the 'model' would have put Poland at the forefront of economic management and planning. Instead, it was shelved. Workers' Councils, thwarted both from 'above' and from the side, were steadily emasculated. As they failed to perform any real functions, workers lost interest in them and they were reintegrated into the existing structure, without much protest.[14] The economy grew slowly and there was even slower increase in real wages: 8 per cent over the 1960s.

The 'retreat' from October is often analysed in terms of Gomułka's own temperament. One commentator refers to 'his mistrust of the spontaneity that brought him back to power' and calls his programme 'essentially a conservative concept, based on a compromise between doctrinaire orthodoxy and a recognition that popular attitudes and prejudices had to be taken into account'.[15] One might put this in the broader terms of popular psychology: Gomułka was a repository of national hopes, which ignored much of his past (the 'first term' from 1944–8, for instance) and was partially at least a misidentification. One lesson workers learned – and were to have reinforced during the winter crisis of 1970–1 – was not to take the promises of political leaders on trust. And there was a further lesson. In 1956, hopes for the future, as analysis of the Stalinist past, rested on individuals. They would more profitably have concentrated on institutions.

Before this was fully assimilated, there were two further attempts to change the polity. Both came from the intelligentsia and both failed, yet the experience of each was, in different ways, formative for the social movement that developed later. One, the 'Znak' group, announced its appearance in the immediate aftermath of October. It offered full support for Gomułka's pro-gramme in exchange for political concessions: the right to run discussion clubs for Catholic intellectuals; the return of the weekly newspaper *Tygodnik Powszechny* (given to the pro-government 'PAX' in March 1953) and the monthly *Znak* (shut in 1949) and the admission of five members to the *Sejm* following elections in January 1957. These activities had significance out of all proportion to their scale. In effect, they were the only example of political pluralism in the Gomułka period. They could not, however, be described as oppositional; they styled themselves 'neo-positivists'. While making clear their rejection of Marxism, the 'Znak' group sought every opportunity for understanding rather than conflict.[16] They aspired to play the part of mediator between the Party and the population, a role continued by one of their most prominent members, Tadeusz Mazowiecki, during the Gdańsk negotiations.

A second group were the 'revisionists' within the Party who called for its democratisation. They saw no contradiction, in principle, between Leninism (including single Party rule) and liberty, but considered obstacles to reform of the communist system to lie in the 'dogmatic' and Stalinist office-holders which dominated it. Their intention was to restaff the apparatus. After October, an intellectually outstanding 'revisionist' literature was published, ranging across philosophy, economics and sociology,[17] to the broader fields of history and literature. The *apparat*, however, remained unmoved. Moreover, it was steadily removing the revisionists. The dénouement came in 1968, when the most cynical and primitive elements of the Party and police apparatus launched a campaign against Jewish Communists and citizens, forcing many from office and into exile.[18] These 'March events' and the destruction of the Czechoslovak reform movement, five months later, put paid to revisionism. For many of the younger generation, caught up in the repression of the universities, these events were formative: no longer was the Communist Party regarded as a potential vehicle for democratic change. Its impulse would have to be found elsewhere.

After 1968, the fall of Gomułka was only a matter of time, yet there was little anticipation of the dramatic circumstances of his departure. In 1970, Polish workers erupted onto the political stage. They did so neither as surrogates – as a Party professedly ruling in their name – nor as the allegedly 'angry force' dispersing student demonstrators two years previously, but as themselves. This assertion of identity was indicated by their first political action: by-passing existing institutions such as the Party and trade unions, they elected independent Strike Committees often including Party members. From this moment on, compromises might follow, apparent advances or bloody defeats, but there could be no going back. The Party began to lose both its mass base and the constituency it claimed to represent.

The uprising began in the Gdańsk Shipyard on Monday 14 December.[19] Three thousand workers assembled spontaneously in front of the Director's office to protest against increases on basic prices announced over the weekend. Receiving no satisfaction – the factory officials quite reasonably blamed higher authorities – about a third of them marched out onto the streets, heading for the city centre. Some sang the *Internationale*. A delegation entered the provincial Party headquarters, but found that the First Secretary had left for a Central Committee meeting in Warsaw. One of his subordinates was instructed to address the crowd. While he hesitated, rumours spread that the delegation had been arrested. Scuffles broke out and a police vehicle was overturned. Part of the crowd marched off to the Northern Shipyard to ask for support; similar appeals were made at Gdańsk Technical University and the radio station, both to no avail. The mood changed in the late afternoon. Demonstrators broke through a police cordon around the Party headquarters, this time throwing stones. Windows were broken. There were attempts to set the building on fire. Riot police and the army then moved in. The crowd was pushed back towards the main railway station. The first deaths occurred. Disturbances ended by 10 p.m. At the Central Committee meeting, Gomułka did not mention the uprising, though news had reached the capital by 1.0 p.m.[20] A smaller group of Politburo members and military leaders secretly decided the response: terror. The Gomułka era thus came full circle: the leader brought to power with overwhelming public support, dissipated that trust and eventually resorted to force against an unarmed population.

The following morning, Gdańsk Shipyard workers again marched towards the city centre, joined *en route* by workers from other enterprises. As at Poznań in 1956, the prison was attacked, but the assailants were beaten off. The crowd, now numbering 10 000, attempted to set the Party headquarters on fire. It was soon in flames. About an hour later, the military received authorisation to shoot. Armed forces occupied Gdańsk that evening. Meanwhile, the 'Paris Commune' Shipyard in neigh-bouring Gdynia had declared a general strike. Tanks appeared on the streets. On the orders of Politburo members Kliszko and Loga-Sowiński (Chairman of the Trade Union Federation) they took up positions outside the shipyard, to 'prevent vandals' from damaging public property. That evening, a further Politburo member, Kociołek, appealed on local radio for a return to work. Management made unavailing efforts to rescind this announce-ment, fearing the worst. When the first shift arrived next morning a large number of them were massacred at the railway station.[21]

Next day, demonstrators once more assembled in the Gdańsk Shipyard and, ignoring warnings from the Director, began to march out towards the centre. Those in front were shot dead outside Gate Two. The corpses were carried inside. A Workers' Committee was elected and demands drawn up: substantial wage increases and restoration of old prices; that those responsible for the catastrophic state of the economy be brought to account; and the withdrawal of the armed forces. The revolt spread along the Baltic, from Elbląg in the east, to Słupsk and Szczecin[22] in the west. Wildcat stoppages were reported from Silesia, Poznań (again the Cegielski Works) and the Warsaw car factory. A general strike seemed imminent. Soviet leaders called a halt at this point. According to Gierek, speaking soon afterward, 'Comrade Brezhnev telephoned Comrade Gomułka, at the height of the present crisis, to say that it should be settled politically, by persuasion.'[23] A letter followed. Gomułka had a stroke and was removed to hospital on 19 December. Gierek became Party Secretary.

He came to power with none of the advantages enjoyed by Gomułka in 1956, yet he managed to gain public trust, albeit of a more qualified variety. This was largely a personal achievement. In part, it rested on subterfuge. His personal biography was doctored to advantage. Inconvenient facts, such as his arrival in Poznań the day before the massacre of 1956, were censored. His presence in Gomułka's Politburo was explained away – not implausibly – by stating that this ceased to be a discussion forum. In Gierek's words: 'Comrades, there was little the Politburo could say, or at least some members of it: if they tried to raise an issue they were isolated or reprisals were taken against them.' He further claimed to have opposed the December price increases and to have stormed out of the meeting. But these alibis were secondary. He based his call for trust principally on an appeal to class instincts. In Szczecin on 24 January 1971, he stated

> I appeal to you, as I did to the miners in Silesia: help me . . . You, cannot suspect me of bad faith. I am a worker, the same as you. I worked at the coal face for eighteen years. I don't need lessons from anyone about the problems of the working class. All my family work down the mines. All of them! I have no relatives in high places.[24]

This was accompanied by hints of intervention (quite contrary to Brezhnev's statement) such as 'the fate of our nation is in the balance'. The appeal worked. As one strike delegate put it: 'Comrade Edward is the right kind of man. Let's give him a year or two at least, and then look at the results.' It was successfully repeated in the Gdańsk Shipyard the following day.[25]

Gierek offered Polish society a new deal under which both sides conceded something.[26] The population agreed to abandon its 'political' aspirations, such as the election of factory councils not controlled by the state. Even in Szczecin, where this was most advanced, activists of 1970–1 were steadily removed and the autonomy of councils obliterated.[27] For its part, the state reduced its ideological demands on Polish society: 'there were no longer debates about Marxism or communism, only discussion about productivity'.[28] There followed a 'dash for growth', largely funded by Western capital. Average living standards rose annually by 5 per cent, while well-placed groups (miners, shipbuilders, functionaries, the military and police) did better still. Compulsory deliveries by peasant farmers were abolished; there were further concessions to the Church and the usual promise to widen cultural freedoms. Efforts were made to involve specialists in government, through, for instance, a comprehensive report on educational reform.[29] A wave of optimism was engendered and it was widely felt, as it had been in the late 1950s, that the population as a whole might start to profit from the communist system.

By 1975, strains started to appear. Meat shortages in March leading to strikes in Łódź and Radom and intellectual protests against proposed changes to the Constitution,[30] were ominous signals of a coming crisis for the Gierek leadership. Moreover, the extent of Western indebtedness had now reached a serviceable maximum, requiring a radical restructuring of economic policies.[31] By June 1976, the government was reaching the end of an import-led investment boom, with still little in the way of consumer output to show for it. No longer able to afford the 12 per cent of GDP being spent on food subsidies–a legacy of the previous political crisis – it announced basic price increases of 40 per cent. The response was instantaneous and nationwide. In Radom, demonstrators occupied the Party headquarters, running down the red flag. At 'Ursus', near Warsaw, workers blocked the railway line, imprisoning the express from Paris for several hours. In Płock, the army was incited to defect.[32] The Prime Minister withdrew the price increases that evening. Repression followed. Thousands of workers were forced to 'run the gauntlet' of policemen wielding batons, brutally treated in detention, dismissed, demoted or imprisoned. This violence was met by new forms of resistance to repression.

A great source of stability in post-war Eastern Europe has been the inability of different social groups or classes to act together. Atomisation appears essential to the system. The assault upon the Polish intelligentsia in 1968 was received with indifference by the remainder of the population. In the aftermath of 1970, the government was able to regain its balance as a result of the apathy of the intelligentsia. They stood aside, perhaps as Kołakowski suggested, because 'they had been persuaded to believe in the complete inflexibility of the system under which they lived'.[33] In the summer of 1976, however, a small part of the intelligentsia began to consider ways of breaking out of this impasse. Rejecting the traditional pattern of protest, romantic insurrection, which Piłsudski had recommended for each generation,[34] and determined to overcome the vicious cycle of post-Stalin Poland – long periods of apparent acquiescence, punctuated by sudden, short-lived and ineffectual explosions – they came forward with the notion of social self-defence. This was defined by Kuroń as 'a form of joint action' through which continuous pressure 'from below' would wrest concessions from the authorities.[35] In place of revolution it promised evolution.[36] Its first practical expression was the founding of a Workers' Defence Committee (KOR) in September 1976.

KOR had no structure or organisation: it was simply an informal association of like-minded individuals. The members all had outstanding records of resistance to one or other form of authoritarian repression: five were veterans of the Russian war of 1920; thirteen took part in underground resistance to Nazi occupation; many others were victims of the show trials in the Stalin and post-Stalin era.[37] Their initial aims were to provide material, medical and legal assistance for workers arrested after the June events. Trials were attended, families supported and protests made against physical ill-treatment. Although their appeal for an independent investigation into the brutalities by a special commission of the *Sejm* went unanswered (as it had in December 1970), a call for the release of those imprisoned –

including members of KOR – proved surprisingly successful. All workers were amnestied in July 1977 and reinstated, though often to inferior positions. This was the first great success for the political opposition. Additionally, in the course of its legal interventions, KOR was approached by numerous other people unlawfully persecuted. Rather than disband, therefore – as the authorities had perhaps hoped – KOR decided to expand its activities to the defence of the whole society (KSS), retaining the label KOR to show continuity. A new programme of September 1977 called for 'social initiatives' from all sections of society and promised to support them against lawlessness.[38] Its subsequent 'Appeal to Society' noted that 'a number of social initiatives have now been taken'.[39]

Foremost amongst these was the defence of workers' interests through the uncensored journal *Robotnik*, compiled in Warsaw from materials sent in by worker-correspondents. Its first aim was informational: to end the isolation of workplaces in different parts of the country through a nationwide distribution network, covering major steel mills, shipyards and industrial enterprises, which reached 100 000 to 200 000 workers. A community of interest and experience soon became apparent. Reporting on the strike wave of late 1978, the editors found that 'All cases of workers' protests known to us had the same character: workers have been defending themselves against unjust wage reductions or exploitation.' Strikes had been successful, but only in the short run. Concessions granted – such as a bonus payment or improved food supplies – proved temporary, and, once protests subsided, were withdrawn. *Robotnik*'s conclusion echoed KOR's: lasting improvements would result only from constant pressure on the authorities. They urged workers to organise themselves into 'more permanent bodies such as Strike Committees or Free Trade Unions'.[40] The lesson had already been learned by workers themselves.

The first Free Trade Union had been founded in Silesia, in February 1978. It declared that

Faced by the centralised and all-powerful apparatus of the state, and complete dependence of factory directors and trade unions upon it, we ordinary workers are isolated and weak. We are exploited because ever greater efforts are demanded from us, while our standard of living and that of our families deteriorates rather than improves. We believe this state of affairs will be perpetuated for as long as we fail to organise ourselves into independent trade unions.[41]

This was followed, on the eve of May Day 1978, by the formation in Gdańsk of Free Trade Unions of the Coast, whose stated purposes were 'to organise the defence of the economic, legal and humanitarian interests of employees' and 'to assist and protect all employees, regardless of their beliefs or qualifications'. The statement was signed by three persons, including Andrzej Gwiazda.[42] They issued an uncensored journal *Robotnik Wybrzeża*. Educational courses were organised with the help of Dr Leszek Kaczyński, a specialist on labour law. An attempt was made to defend those dismissed for Free Trade Union activity at 'Elektromontaż', where Wałęsa worked. The effort failed. Gwiazda concluded: 'We were not strong enough. There are seven million industrial workers in Poland and only 25 000 copies of *Robotnik* are published. The truth is that very few people knew of us.'[43]

The final years of Gierek's rule, from the massive use of the workers' veto in 1976 to their strike movement of 1980 which pushed him from the stage, present a puzzle. Warnings of a coming crisis were issued time and again: in 'Open Letters' to Gierek from Edward Lipiński[44] and from a group of senior communists, headed by Ochab;[45] and in discussion documents, such as *Uwagi* by economists[46] and reports of the 'DiP' colloquium of Party and non-Party intellectuals.[47] All indicated an imminent explosion, yet were ignored. Instead, censorship was tightened and the media saturated with a 'propaganda of success', informing an increasingly incredulous public that all was well. Two alibis were offered later. The Party attributed much of the 'drift' at the top to Gierek personally, to the conspicuous 'high life' enjoyed by himself and his entourage.[48] Yet this is not a satisfactory answer, spectacular though some instances of corruption were. Nor is the second – liberalism – entirely convincing. While it is true that the first free union movements in the USSR (also founded in February 1978) and in Romania, were dealt with even more harshly,[49] it is not the case that the Polish handling was 'liberal'. Resistance to repression was the Free Unions' principal activity. In explaining how they developed from obscurity into a mass movement we must describe two precipitating factors.

The first was spiritual. In the late 1970s, the Polish Party made a serious attempt to improve Church–state relationships. This was signalled in autumn 1977 by a meeting of the Party Secretary with Cardinal Wyszyński – the first since 1963 – and by his visit to the Vatican at the end of the war. Relations were metamorphosed by the election of Jan Paweł II the following October. The secular authorities put on a brave face and welcomed the accession of a Pole to the Papacy, which occurred, they mentioned, 'for the first time under socialist Poland'. Arrangements for a papal visit, however, were a different matter. An Episcopal proposal that this should coincide with the feast of St Stanisław (a bishop martyred by the king) was vetoed. The suggested itinerary was restricted to exclude the mining regions of Silesia. There were to be no days off or organised trips to see the pontiff; a special tax of $350 was to be imposed on foreign correspondents. Despite these precautions, the papal visit (2–10 June 1979) became a massive festival in which the nation experienced itself as a community.[50] Ten million Poles saw the Pope in person and heard his cycle of sermons. Although tactful towards the Soviet Union, the message was clear. He called for dialogue between Church and state while recognising their 'diametrically opposed concept of the world'. At Auschwitz he preached transformation of Poland through peace and love. In Kraków, his home diocese, he made 'non-conformism' a theme: 'the future of Poland will depend upon how many people are mature enough to be non-conformists'.[51] Some two million people watched his departure from the Kraków meadows. The authorities had left stewarding of these vast gatherings to the Church itself. There had been a momentary displacement of the communist state.

A second precipitant was economic. By the late 1970s, Poland entered the period aptly entitled 'After the Great Leap'.[52] Her international indebtedness rose sharply from $8000 million in 1975 to $20 000 million in 1979.[53] Debt servicing amounted to 92 per cent of hard currency earnings by this point. One consequence was that Western imports had to be drastically cut back, including cement, metallurgical products, plastics, pharmaceuticals, fertilisers and foodstuffs. Shortages of inputs reduced production and bottlenecks occurred, sending the economy into a downward spiral of late completion dates, impossibility of completion and wasted investment. This dramatic downturn could not be blamed entirely on ill-luck with international interest rates and the business cycle. The investment strategy was itself questionable. As Portes comments: 'To expand heavily into steel, motor vehicles, shipbuilding and petro-chemicals in the mid-1970's was clearly unwise.'[54] Disparities between industrial and social investment were particularly apparent on the coast, where housing shortages contrasted markedly with a harbour investment programme, including the Gdańsk Shipyard, held up to foreign visitors as a miracle of modernisation. National income fell 1.8 per cent in 1979 – according to official statistics – and the outlook for 1980 was even more alarming, as Gierek admitted to the Eighth Party Congress in February. The Prime Minister was sacked, but this did not solve the problem. There was a further economic 'manoeuvre' but no reform. As in 1970 and 1976, the authorities embarked on price increases. The procedure they adopted was more sophisticated, but its rejection by society was equally emphatic.

On 1 July, local Party secretaries appear to have received a circular telling them to put basic food prices up: if and when they could. Next day, the increases were mentioned on television. The 'Ursus' tractor plant near Warsaw had already come to a halt. On 3 July, several dozen stopped work at the Gdańsk Shipyard, but a strike did not develop. Stoppages also occurred at the Cegielski Works in Poznań and at numerous smaller enterprises. These responses were sporadic and local, reflecting the manner of the price increase.[55] Managers were under instructions to pay compensating wage increases. A group of them was flown to Warsaw and told to buy 'social peace' through material concessions.[56] An important new stage in the strike movement started in Lublin on 11 July when a 'stoppage committee' was formed and called for negotiations with the central authorities. Urban transport came to a halt, and railway workers threatened to strike. Free unions were now mentioned as an explicit demand. The Politburo met in emergency session and dispatched Deputy Premier Jagielski to settle the strike, which he achieved within two days.[57] After Lublin, the authorities relaxed, and Gierek left for three weeks in the Crimea. The Central Committee's propaganda secretary, Łukaszewicz, told foreign journalists on 12 August that the strike wave was over.[58] Two days later, a strike took place in the Gdańsk Shipyard.

As Anna Walentynowicz recalls, there had been animated discussion of the Lublin events amongst the Free Trade Unions of the Coast but 'even we thought there was little prospect of doing the same. Shipyard workers were still too frightened. We anticipated at least two more years of persecution before society at large would be ready to act.'[59] An issue was presented, however: her dismissal on 9 August. Colleagues in the Free Trade Unions decided to protest. Three workers on the early shifts put up posters demanding her reinstatement and a wage increase of 1000 złotys. Leaflets and *Robotnik* were handed out as the first workers came in. Jerzy Borowczak told them: 'Lublin rose up, now it's our turn to fight.'[60] Groups gathered round the posters and discussion began. The temperature rose when an official attempted to pull the posters down. Then Borowczak led a small group to the large ships' hull department. Somewhat later, the yard's Party Secretary drew up at the gates in his Fiat 1300 and explained that Walentynowicz had been sacked for 'disciplinary reasons'. After reminding him that she had worked there for 30 years and gained three service medals, the crowd, now numbering 1000, moved on. A minute's silence for the victims of December 1970 was observed beneath Gate Two. The national anthem was sung. Borowczak declared 'We must defend Walentynowicz. If they can sack people like her, what will they do to us? We have nothing to lose.' A Strike Committee was created, with a special appeal to older and trusted workers to come forward.[61] As Borowczak explained later: 'I wanted no repeat of 1970 and 1976, when two department heads were on the Strike Committee and simply sold us out.' The Director climbed up on a bulldozer and appealed for a return to work. Nobody listened. Wałęsa, who had got into the yard over the fence, scrambled up alongside him and took charge of the strike.

The broadcast of negotiations and the reinstatement of Walentynowicz were set as preconditions for holding talks. Technicians rigged up loudspeakers in the health and safety building and two delegates from each department assembled there for talks with management. On one side of the table sat Wałęsa, Borowczak and Bogdan Felski, on the other Director Wójcik, his assistant, the Socialist Youth Union (ZSMP) leader and the cadres chief. The latter made an involved and ideological speech to which the strikers responded: 'Why don't you use our language? Whom are you addressing? Speak simply and clearly.' They called for discussion of their demands and suggested that the Prime Minister, Edward Babiuch, came to hold talks 'because he has the authority to do so'. The Director announced that he would receive authorisation 'on the hot line' at any moment. It was nearing 4.00 p.m. (the end of office hours) and nobody believed him. Wałęsa announced: 'We are staying the night.'[62]

Negotiations began shortly afterwards. The provincial Party Secretary, Tadeusz Fiszbach gave written acceptance of several demands: Walentynowicz and Wałęsa were reinstated; strikers were guaranteed their personal safety and freedom from victimisation; a monument would be constructed in memory of those shot in front of Gate Two in December 1970. In return, the Director proposed that the strike be ended, leaving other matters to be settled by agreement later on. The strikers reiterated their unfulfilled demands: free elections to trade unions, a 2000 złotys wage increase, and unexpectedly added a further point: the freeing of political prisoners.[63] The meeting adjourned. When talks resumed at 8.00 p.m. the Director confirmed a wage increase of 1200 złotys for all employees and promised that family allowances would be increased to equal those received by the militia and security services. The remaining proposals would be dealt with during the next few weeks, with the exception of the two 'political' matters: the questions of trade union elections and of political prisoners, which would be referred to the central authorities. The strikers replied by restating their demand for 2000 złotys and adding two important new proposals: reinstatement of all those dismissed from work after the December 1970 and June 1976 demonstrations (it was thought there were 80–100 of them) and dissolution of the Central Trade Union Federation. They suggested the Strike Committee could become a permanent institution to represent them. The idea was rapidly emerging that existing unions – 'neither authentic nor representative' – should be replaced by newly-elected and free trade unions. Both sides were hardening. Following a fruitless third meeting with the Director, talks were adjourned until the morning. He failed to turn up.[64] At noon, Gdańsk was cut off from the outside world. The Soviet News Agency (TASS) announced 'routine manoeuvres' of the Warsaw Pact in East Germany and the Baltic.[65]

By the third day (16 August), the authorities had narrowed negotiations down to the wage question.[66] The Director repeated his offer of 1200 złotys, while mandated departmental delegates all insisted on 1500. When the Director withdrew to consult with higher authorities, the trade union issue reemerged and a list of 'founder members' was circulated, but what they were founding was extremely unclear as no free trade union statute yet existed, nor any programme other than its name. Then the Director returned to announce acceptance of the 1500 złotys on two conditions: immediate evacuation of the shipyard 'for security reasons' and a return to normal work on Monday (18 August). Debate amongst strike delegates ensued. Wałęsa tried to terminate discussion: 'Let's not be provocative. This is enough.' Others reminded him this was a matter for collective decision. The remaining issue concerned guarantees for what had been agreed. Strike delegates were adamant that oral promises would not do: 'Kociołek appealed to us to return to work next day (15 December 1970) and machine guns were waiting for us.' The Director offered his word of honour and asked 'Why are you afraid?' The answer came 'December. So many corpses.'[67] It was agreed that guarantees would be given by Party Secretary Fiszbach.

In the early afternoon, when negotiations had ended and the written guarantees had been given, Wałęsa asked the shipyard workers over the loudspeaker whether they confirmed the delegates' decision to end the strike.[68] They did so and he asked – in accordance with the agreement – that the shipyard be vacated by 6 p.m. As delegates filed out of the hall, they encountered members of the strike committees at other enterprises: the Repair and Northern Shipyards, Urban Transport (WPK) and various factories, who accused them of accepting 'worthless guarantees' and abandoning the smaller workplaces which would now be 'crushed like flies'.[69] Pandemonium ensued. Wałęsa changed his mind on the instant and tried to countermand the evacuation order but the loudspeaker system was already disconnected. Walentynowicz rushed to Gate Three and tried to explain the need for a strike in solidarity with smaller enterprises. No one listened.

Someone shouted 'You want to strike – go ahead.' I burst into tears, but Alinka [Alina Pieńkowska] jumped onto a barrel and began to speak about the need to show solidarity with those who supported us. Someone in the crowd called out 'She's right. They're not going to forgive us these three days either.' The gate was closed. The scene was repeated at Gates 1 and 2. When the last one was shut about 2000 [of 16,000] employees remained in the Shipyard.[70]

Later that day an Interfactory Strike Committee was elected[71] and a fresh list of demands drawn up. A second stage of the strike had begun.

Events in the Gdańsk Shipyard were an acute embarrassment to the authorities. Gierek flew back from the Crimea a week early, but was no longer in charge. 'From 16 August, Central Party activity was coordinated by comrade Stanisław Kania.'[72] From the same Party journal we learn that 'grave weaknesses' had appeared in the functioning of the Politburo and Central Committee Secretariat. As for the apparatus: 'The Chairman of the Council of Ministers had resigned and the government virtually ceased to function.' The response to the strike was correspondingly disorganised. A first stage was denial or euphemism by official spokesmen. Every effort was made to keep the strike local, to push the strikers towards economic issues and to resolve them by rapid concessions: the time-honoured technique in the Soviet Union. It almost succeeded. Once the Strike Committee had called a 'solidarity strike' however, a second stage of government policy went into operation. Attempts were now made to isolate the movement. A Deputy Premier, Pyka, was sent to Gdańsk as Chairman of a commission 'to investigate grievances of workers on the Coast', with orders to divide the strikers. He was joined on 18 August by Kania, Jabłoński (the Head of State) and various chiefs of staff, for a 'widened session' of the Gdańsk Party Committee. It heard a first-hand account of the strike from Fiszbach, who emphasised its 'genuinely working-class character' and stressed the need to find a 'political solution'. Kania then argued that the strike raised fundamental problems of state and proved the necessity for 'agreement between the authorities and the nation, the Party and its class'. We are told that this conciliatory line was echoed by Admiral Janczyszyn who stated that the armed forces could not do anything 'to loosen their connections with society.' We have no record of which way President Jabłoński spoke. The meeting concluded that 'political methods' were the 'only possible means'.[73]

While this session was in progress, Gierek spoke on national television – his first public comments on the crisis. His tone was broadly conciliatory: there would be a revision of economic priorities (of both the annual and quinquennial plans); improved food supplies; a reform of wage and pricing policies on which experts would – yet again – be consulted. The message was that dialogue could be countenanced on economic issues, but new institutions could not. Trade unions were cumbersome and should be streamlined, perhaps at their November Congress.[74] The speech was relayed in the Gdańsk Shipyard, while mass was being celebrated in front of Gate Two. Workers talked it over. One commented: 'In 1970, I was optimistic about Gierek's nomination, now I only trust ourselves.' Others recalled the famous appeal of 1970-1: 'Let him talk to Party members. Let them help him.' Wałęsa, as usual, caught the mood: 'Nothing to do with us. We have our demands. We'll talk to a government team. We stay on strike until they turn up.'[75]

Pyka's Commission, however, ignored the Interfactory Strike Committee which now represented 200 enterprises at the Gdańsk Shipyard and instead sought separate settlements with individual workplaces.[76] He let it be known that he had the 'personal authorisation' of Edward Gierek to sign an agreement. On the afternoon of 19 August, he was approached by small groups from the Gdańsk Port Authority and Repair Yard which somewhat diffidently presented the Twenty-one Demands (discussed in detail below). To their astonishment, the Deputy Premier led them to believe that all were acceptable. His promises were repeated to representatives of sixteen enterprises that evening and a formal ending of the strike was agreed. The strikers pointed out that they could not get to work while all public transport remained at a standstill. A team sent to negotiate with them returned at midnight to report that transport workers would not hold talks outside the Interfactory Strike Committee. Further magical promises then issued from Pyka: on meat imports, free Saturdays and censorship. A small team stayed behind to edit the final agreement. This done, Pyka abruptly declared the document would have to be submitted to the Council of Ministers for approval. An answer soon came: of the twelve-point agreement, they accepted only three, minor ones at that. Pyka was recalled to Warsaw and replaced by Jagielski as head of the Government Commission. The Interfactory Strike Committee drew its own conclusion: 'Individual Strike Committees should not negotiate any of our common demands with the state authorities.'[77]

The state's propaganda sections now moved into action. The shipyard was showered with copies of a leaflet signed by Director Gniech, promising a 1500 złotys rise for everyone and calling for a return to work.[78] The Secretariat of the Central Committee in

Warsaw dispatched a circular of 19 August to all Party members stating that 'national survival' was endangered by a group of 'political enemies', terrorising and intimidating anyone who was not with them. Their disturbances 'have already encouraged West German revisionists, who openly admit that recent events in Gdańsk and on the Coast are very welcome to them'.[79] Senior Party officials began to adopt a menacing tone, exemplified by that of the Chairman of the Trade Union Federation, Jan Szydlak, in Gdańsk the same day. He stated: 'We will not give up power, nor will we share it with anyone.'[80] 'Prophylactic' measures were put in hand to isolate workers from their intellectual supporters. *Robotnik*'s editor Jan Lityński was arrested and beaten up on 19 August. Jacek Kuroń's home was raided – and many KOR members detained – the following day. The Interfactory Strike Committee noted: 'Workers are not surprised by the vile methods of psychological warfare conducted by the authorities . . . Everybody knows that they are deliberately deferring negotiations.'[81]

Pressure on the Party to negotiate came from a new quarter. Church leaders,[82] meeting on 22 August, declared that present tensions were the consequence of 'accumulated errors' over many years and could only be corrected 'in an atmosphere of calm and internal peace'. An honest dialogue should take place between the Strike Committees and government representatives. 'Poles must know how to talk to each other, resolve their problems themselves and put their own house in order.' The statement ended with a comprehensive catalogue of human rights including 'the right to assemble, to elect independent representatives and autonomous committees'.[83]

Practically the whole Baltic region from Szczecin to Elbląg was now on strike. The Strike Committee in the Gdańsk Shipyard had been joined by over 400 workplaces. Faced with a deteriorating situation, Deputy Premier Jagielski finally agreed to receive its delegation.[84] This tried to reassure him that those on strike were not inspired by any 'political' or 'anti-socialist' aims. Jagielski did propose the expulsion of three 'militants' – Gwiazda, Wałęsa and Walentynowicz – from the Presidium, as a precondition for talks. It was eventually agreed that there would be a preparatory meeting at the Shipyard next day (23 August).[85] This paved the way for negotiations.

*   *   *

Negotiations were based upon the Twenty-one Demands which the Strike Presidium selected from the hundreds put forward by its constituent committees. A number had been formulated at the 'Elmor' enterprise, where a distinction had been made between 'political' demands addressed to the central authorities and others directed towards the local management.[86] During editorial work at the Gdańsk Shipyard, a member of KOR, Bogdan Borusewicz, argued for exclusion of demands for the abolition of censorship and for free elections, citing the fate of the Czechoslovak reform movement.[87] They were duly omitted. Those included may be summarised as follows:

(1) *Free Trade Unions.* Before the strike Polish trade unions were organised in twenty-three branches, according to particular industries, and federated in a Central Council, to which 95 per cent of the labour force compulsorily belonged. The apparent right to form other unions granted by the Labour Code was qualified, if not removed, by the 1949 Trade Union statute which laid down that 'every new trade union must join the Federation'. Failure to do so would result in dissolution. Szydlak's speech of 19 August was followed by a mass withdrawal from his Federation, though what could replace it under Polish legislation remained unclear. In arguing their right to form unions of their own, the strikers relied heavily on Conventions of the International Labour Organisation,[88] and adduced further arguments from natural justice, of which the international conventions were held to be an expression. They were assisted in this by the Episcopal communiqué of 22 August which declared that 'amongst elementary human rights is the right of workers to free association in unions which genuinely represent them'.[89]

Free unions in communist Poland had a short and unpromising history. Their founding father, Kazimierz Świtoń, was arrested on numerous occasions,[90] while his colleague in Silesia, Władysław Sulecki had been demoted, persecuted and driven into exile.[91] Activists in the Gdańsk region were treated almost as harshly. The authorities were willing, however, to allow considerable reform of the old unions. Strikers were offered new rules for union elections under which the state would forgo its right to nominate 85 per cent of candidates. Candidature of Strike Committee members was even welcomed. This promise had helped to end the strike in Lublin a month earlier, but was not acceptable in Gdańsk. Workers on the Coast insisted that new unions, independent of the Party and state, should be created. Tadeusz Kowalik records: 'In the course of a week's negotiations, I did not meet a single striker or delegate who was willing to compromise on this issue.'[92] Yet the whole history of communism suggested this demand was unrealistic.

(2) *The Right to Strike.* Soviet theory treats the strike as a weapon for securing the liberation of the working class from capitalist exploitation. The need to strike is thus removed by the abolition of capitalism. All Soviet officials met by an International Labour Organisation delegation in 1960 declared that remaining differences could be resolved through the various organisations in which workers were represented – unions, production conferences and so on – by 'social pressures' on management. 'It was therefore felt that the need for strike action was non-existent.'[93] Admittedly, passages in Lenin do seem to recognise the need for a workers' organisation to protect them from 'bureaucratic' features of the communist state. These are extensively quoted in the one communist country where strikes are legalised: Yugoslavia.[94] But when strikes do take place in the Soviet Union, notably at Novocherkassk in 1962, they are suppressed and evidence for them is concealed.[95]

The Polish Constitution makes no provision for a right to strike but does not preclude it. However, Article 52 of the Labour Code, introduced in 1975, entitles management to dissolve a work contract 'without notice' – a so-called disciplinary dismissal – where an employee is found guilty of a 'serious breach of basic duties of an employee, in particular by causing a serious breach of the peace or good order at the workplace; or of unjustified absence from work.' This clause was widely used to dismiss workers after the strikes of June 1976.[96] Its repeal was regularly canvassed in *Robotnik*, whose 'Charter of Workers' Rights' called it an 'anti-strike statute' and urged that the right to strike be legally guaranteed.[97]

At issue here are two separate notions of strikes, stemming from radically different views of society. The 'Soviet' view sees society as a unity with common interests and values in which strikes are 'dysfunctional, destructive of the social fabric, nonrational responses to the work situation, indicative of ignorance, prejudice and the presence of alien influences and values'.[98] The second view, a pluralist one, regards strikes as a rational and legitimate means of putting pressures upon an employer to put right a grievance or to meet a demand when all other remedies have failed. The difficulty arises, of course, when the employer is also the state. The distinction between an 'economic' grievance against an employer and a 'political' demand of the state is thus narrowed, if not obliterated. The Government Commission therefore sought to circumscribe its 'political' implications, while the strikers sought *de jure* status for an activity that did *de facto* exist.

(3) *Freedom of Expression.* Free unions, if granted, could not function without freedom of expression. At the least, they would need their own newspapers and the right to print what they wished in them 'whether or not this suits the authorities'.[99] Thus censorship, sometimes thought to be simply an 'intellectual' concern, became a major issue for the striking workers. They demanded a clear statute on censorship, to explain and delineate its purposes. The intention was to bring it within legal jurisdiction and to institute a right of appeal. They also attempted to protect 'independent publishing': the production and distribution of books and journals outside the censorship.[100] The need for this alternative channel to the state's monopoly was amply demonstrated during the strike itself.[101] While the world's press was present in the shipyard and relayed events fully, the Polish media remained silent. It was also stated that published works and broadcasts should present a variety of ideas, opinions and evaluations, with access to both for spokesmen of 'all denominations'.

(4) *Release of Political Prisoners.* The official attitude, repeated by Deputy Premier Jagielski, was that Poland had no political prisoners. The strikers, however, gave three specific examples of 'social activists' who had been sentenced on trumped-up criminal charges.[102] Their release was requested. They also repeated the demand from the first stage of the strike for reinstatement of those dismissed from the shipyard for participation in the 1970 and 1976 demonstrations, together with students expelled from their studies in 1968 for the same reason. Finally, there were the numerous strike supporters detained on the Coast and inland. A

list of those arrested in Warsaw was brought to the shipyard with a request that the Strike Presidium press for their release.[103] It became a major issue in the last hours of the strike.

Quite apart from altruism, there was the justifiable fear that the strikers themselves, and especially their leaders, might become the next victims. Gwiazda was not just being rhetorical when he asked the Deputy Premier: 'What guarantee is there that false witnesses will not be found to prove that the entire Interfactory Strike Committee is a gang of criminals?'[104]

(5) *Economic Reform*. While the strikers were far from presenting a fully-fledged economic programme, they did demand that 'definite steps be taken to lead the country out of its present crisis'. The key was thought to be a more democratic means of decision-taking based upon 'giving the public full information about the social and economic situation and enabling all social groups to participate in discussion of a reform programme'. Yet even 'participation' was regarded with some diffidence: workers had no wish simply to ratify decisions that management had already taken, still less share the stigma of support for unpopular measures. It was eventually agreed that the trade unions should 'have a real chance to express their opinion in public on the major decisions which determine the living standards of working people'.[105]

Short of reform, however, the strikers put forward proposals on prices. In theory, the population was still paying 1960s prices for basic goods in 1980, although wages had more than doubled during the interim. While some of this was eroded by inflation – estimated unofficially at around 10 per cent per annum – state food subsidies, especially for meat, had risen steeply.[106] In an effort to reduce them, the government had introduced a two-(and later three-)tier system of pricing through the institution of 'commercial' (and later 'super-commercial') shops, selling superior cuts of meat at much higher prices. The strikers demanded the abolition of such shops and reduction of meat prices to an 'average' level. They proposed that meat shortages be overcome by rationing and by termination of exports, unless they were surplus to the domestic market. They further insisted that dollar shops (PEWEX) should not stock Polish goods unavailable elsewhere. There was a strongly egalitarian flavour to these demands, as also for wage increases that would be across-the-board[107] and for removal of privileges from certain groups.

(6) *'Positive Selection'.* Point Twelve proposed that 'people in leading positions should be chosen on the basis of qualifications rather than Party membership'. The Government Commission blandly accepted this, stating that it had been Party policy for years that those appointed to responsible positions should possess the appropriate qualifications. The strikers then formulated the point more sharply. They demanded abolition of the *nomenklatura*: the process by which all key appointments in a Soviet-type system are vetted by the political authorities.[108] Jagielski told them this was non-negotiable. On a second proposal, 'abolition of privileges of the militia, security service and Party apparatus, by equalising family allowances and closing special shops, etc.' he was more forthcoming. He saw no reason why supplementary payments to the militia and security service should not be assimilated into basic pay. He could not comment on the apparatus as he was 'not a Party worker'. Central Committee Secretary Zbigniew Zieliński, however, stated that: 'The Party apparatus have no privileges.'[109]

(7) *Welfare.* The remaining points were concerned with social policies. Point Fourteen, which called for lower retirement ages (fifty-five for men and fifty for women) at least for those in the most strenuous occupations, was rejected as too costly. Point Fifteen, equalisation of pensions under the old scheme with that more recently introduced, was accepted. Point Sixteen sought improved working conditions in the health service, on which some thirty specific proposals had been drawn up by Alina Pieńkowska. The final demands were undisputed and were accepted either for early implementation or 'when economic circumstances permit'. Points Seventeen and Eighteen sought improved crèche and nursery facilities, and extension of paid maternity leave to three years. Nineteen demanded a shorter waiting-list for housing; Twenty improved travelling allowances for those on official business and Twenty-one a reduction of the working week. Though politically less salient than earlier proposals, these issues were important none the less. In articulating them, the strikers present a most revealing account of everyday

life in a communist state. Their voices 'from the chorus' which tell of 'real life: life as it is experienced by an ordinary person'[110] provide some of the most telling moments of the negotiations.

Throughout the eighteen-day strike, city life went on. Anna Walentynowicz recalls:

> We issued permits for food shops to reopen. Delivery lorries still operated, so too did the bakeries. The canning factory stayed at work so that the fish would not be wasted. The factory making tins had to work as well, as did the transport. Drivers wore red and white arm-bands and flags were flown outside the shops. As Joanna Duda-Gwiazda put it; 'We have taken power in this town, we had better get things organised.' We had a wealth of experience from 1970 and knew that success would depend on our calmness and prudence. We used our influence to stop the sale of alcohol, in order to prevent provocations. Even the sale of beer was prohibited. All this was directed by the eighteen-member Strike Committee, consisting principally of workers. Only one of us, Andrzej Gwiazda, was an engineer and Gruszecki had a doctorate in chemistry.[111]

But the Strike Presidium was assisted in its presentation of demands by a team of intellectual advisers, headed by Tadeusz Mazowiecki. While not altering their content in any way, these 'experts' did help 'to express the proposals in the language of negotiations'.[112] Their role in drawing up the final text, pre-liminary drafting of which took place in a joint 'working group' between the plenary sessions, together with many details about the intense discussions amongst the Strike Presidium behind the scenes, are fully described by the distinguished Polish economist, Dr Tadeusz Kowalik.[113] He reveals that it was Mazowiecki who contributed the important notion of reciprocity on which the entire Agreement is based. Thus, the government undertook to ensure the independence and self-government of the new trade unions, and to provide conditions both for their legal registration outside the existing Central Trade Union Council and for the fulfilment of their functions. In return, the Interfactory Strike Committee guaranteed that the new unions would observe the Constitution, accept the 'social ownership of the means of production', not play the role of a political party and not challenge Poland's 'international alliances'.

Where did the name Solidarity come from? Since Deputy Premier Jagielski could not let the phrase 'Free Trade Unions' pass his lips, we consulted the experts. This was a 'solidarity' strike and our bulletin was called 'Solidarity': so the name chose itself.[114]

The signing of the Gdańsk Agreement on 31 August 1980 was greeted by general euphoria. As Anna Walentynowicz puts it: 'I thought this was a real break-through, that a new life would begin. I had no idea what difficulties were to follow, how much bitterness and disappointment.' Yet she ends her mémoire, written a year later, on a prophetic note: 'If we had to start again from the beginning, I would do the same without a moment's hesitation. Perhaps with more experience.'[115]

NOTES

Works are cited in translation where available.
1. Adam Michnik, 'What We Want and What We can Do', *Telos* (St Louis, Missouri), no. 47 (Spring 1981) p. 67. This is the text of a lecture delivered at the 'flying university' in Warsaw on 14 November 1980.
2. Zygmunt Bauman, 'On the Maturation of Socialism', *Telos*, no. 47 p. 51.
3. As Jadwiga Staniszkis observes: 'It is very difficult to formulate your own claims when you do not have an autonomous political language and, at the same time, do not believe it is possible to express yourself in the official façade language.' 'Contradictions of Socialist Society', *Soviet Studies* (Glasgow) (April 1979) p. 179.
4. No scholarly work on Polish Stalinism yet exists. There are valuable mémoires: Stanisław Mikołajczyk, *The Pattern of Soviet Domination* (London: Low, 1948); Czesław Miłosz, *The Captive Mind* (London: Secker & Warburg, 1953).
5. The standard work on the Party is M. K. Dziewanowski, *The Communist Party of Poland* (Harvard University Press, 1959).
6. See George Kolankiewicz in David Lane and Kolankiewicz (eds), *Social Groups in Polish Society* (London: Macmillan, 1973) ch. 3.
7. Sheila Fitzpatrick, *Education and Social Mobility in the Soviet Union, 1921–1934* (Cambridge University Press, 1979) p. 17.
8. Officially named after Stalin: Zakłady im.Stalina Poznań (ZISPO), during this period.

30　　　　　　　*The Birth of Solidarity*

9. The following account is based on the archival study by Andrzej Choniawko, 'Przebieg Wydarzeń Czerwcowych w Poznaniu' in Edmund Makowski (ed.), *Wydarzenia Czerwcowe w Poznaniu, 1956* (Poznań, 1981).
10. Paul E. Zinner (ed.), *National Communism and Popular Revolt in Eastern Europe* (New York: Columbia University Press, 1956) p. 135.
11. *The Anti-Stalin Campaign and International Communism* (New York: Columbia University Press, 1956) p. 305.
12. Zinner (ed.), *National Communism*, p. 166.
13. Ibid., pp. 197–238.
14. This episode is summarised by George Kolankiewicz in Lane and Kolankiewicz, *Social Groups in Polish Society*, pp. 104–40.
15. J. F. Brown, *The New Eastern Europe* (London: Pall Mall, 1966) p. 51.
16. Adam Bromke, *Poland's Politics: Idealism vs. Realism* (Harvard University Press, 1967) ch. 12; Andrzej Micewski, *Współrządzić czy nie kłamać?: Pax i Znak w Polsce, 1945–1976* (Paris: Libella, 1978) Part Two.
17. One need only recall the writings of Leszek Kołakowski, Oskar Lange, Edward Lipiński, Włodzimierz Brus, Władysław Bieńkowski and many others.
18. Their reflections may be found in 'W 10 lat po Wydarzeniach Marcowych', *Krytyka*, no. 1 (Warsaw and London, 1978) pp. 5–66 and in Stefan Amsterdamski (ed.), *Marzec 1968* (Warsaw, 1981).
19. The chronology is based on *Głos Wybrzeża* (Gdańsk) 28 December 1970.
20. Zbigniew A. Pełczyński, 'The Downfall of Gomułka' in Adam Bromke and John W. Strong (eds), *Gierek's Poland* (New York: Praeger, 1973) p. 4.
21. For many years all mention of this incident was taboo. The first published account by an eye-witness was Małgorzata Niezabitowska, 'Sztandar i drzwi', *Tygodnik Solidarność*, no. 37 (11 Dec 1981).
22. Interview with Stanisław Wądołowski, *Tygodnik Solidarność*, no. 21 (21 Aug 1981).
23. Ewa Wacowska (compiler), *Rewolta Szczecińska i jej znaczenie* (Paris, 1971) p. 37.
24. Ibid., p. 32.
25. Although no transcript is available, the main speeches by Gierek and Jaroszewicz were broadcast by Warsaw Radio on 27 January 1971.
26. This has been described as a 'New Social Contract'. See: Antonin J. Liehm, 'Intellectuals and the New Social Contract', *Telos*, no. 23 (Spring 1975) pp. 156–64.
27. Edmund Bałuka, 'Myths and Realities of the Workers' Movement', *Labour Focus on Eastern Europe* (London), no. 2 (May–June 1977) pp. 6–8.
28. Michnik, 'What We Want', p. 71.
29. *Raport o stanie oświaty w PRL* (Warsaw, 1973). See Janusz Tomiak, 'Educational Policy and Educational Reform in the 1970s' in Jean Woodall (ed.), *Policy and Politics in Contemporary Poland* (London: Frances Pinter, 1982) ch. 8.
30. Peter Raina, *Political Opposition in Poland, 1954–1977* (London: Poets and Painters Press, 1978) pp. 210–28.
31. *Polityka*, 18 Oct 1980.
32. Joseph Kay, 'The Polish Opposition', in *Survey* (London) (Autumn 1979).

33. Leszek Kołakowski, 'Hope and Hopelessness', *Survey* (Summer 1971) p. 51.

34. Bromke, *Poland's Politics*, p. 26.

35. Jacek Kuroń, 'Reflections on a Program of Action', *The Polish Review*, no. 3 (1977) pp. 51–69.

36. Adam Michnik, 'The New Evolutionism', *Survey* (Summer 1976) pp. 267–77.

37. Jacek Kuron, 'List otwarty', *Bratniak* (Gdańsk), no. 16 (Spring 1979).

38. Raina, *Political Opposition in Poland*, pp. 342–4.

39. Peter Raina, *Independent Social Movements in Poland* (London: LSE/Orbis Books, 1981) pp. 219–30.

40. *Robotnik*, no. 27 (4 Jan 1979).

41. Adrian Karatnycky et al. (eds), *Workers' Rights, East and West* (London: Transaction Books, 1980) p. 119.

42. *Robotnik*, no. 15 (16 May 1978).

43. Jean-Yves Potel, *The Summer Before the Frost: Solidarity in Poland* (London: Pluto Press, 1982) p. 31.

44. *Robotnik* (London), no. 4 (May 1976).

45. Raina, *Political Opposition*, pp. 444–5.

46. *Aneks* (Uppsala), no. 20 (1979) pp. 7–40 (Preface by Lipiński).

47. *Poland: The State of the Republic, Reports by the 'Experience and Future' Discussion Group (DiP) Warsaw* (London: Pluto Press, 1981).

48. *Nowe Drogi*, nos 10/11 (Oct–Nov 1980) *passim*.

49. Viktor Haynes and Olga Semyonova, *Syndicalism et liberté en Union Sovietique* (Paris: Maspero, 1979) and *Labour Focus*, nos 2 and 5 (1977).

50. Andrzej Szczypiorski, 'The Limits of Political Realism', *Survey* (Autumn 1979) pp. 28–30.

51. Alexander Tomsky, 'John Paul II in Poland', *Religion in Communist Lands* (Keston College, Kent) (Autumn 1979) pp. 160–5. Also: Neal Ascherson, *The Polish August* (Harmondsworth: Penguin, 1981) pp. 141–4.

52. Waldemar Kuczyński, *Po wielkim skoku* (Warsaw, 1979).

53. Richard Portes, *The Polish Crisis: Western Economic Policy Options* (London: Royal Institute of International Affairs, 1981) Table 1, p. 46.

54. Ibid., pp. 7–8.

55. *Robotnik*, no. 57 (12 July 1980).

56. Daniel Singer, *The Road to Gdańsk* (London: Monthly Review Press, 1981) p. 213.

57. *Robotnik*, no. 58 (22 July 1980); Singer, *The Road to Gdańsk*, pp. 213–16.

58. Kevin Ruane, *The Polish Challenge* (London: BBC, 1982) p. 10.

59. 'Opowiada Anna Walentynowicz', *Gdańsk–Sierpień 1980* (Warsaw, 1981) p. 5.

60. The following is based on Borowczak's own account, related to Krzysztof Wyszkowski, in *Tygodnik Solidarność*, no. 20 (14 Aug 1981).

61. Those elected were: Borowczak, Bogdan Felski, Ludwik Prądzyński, Kunikowski, Bobrowski, Marek Mikołajczak, Jan Koziatek and Zbigniew Lis.

62. Borowczak, *Tygodnik Solidarność*, no. 20, p. 10.

63. *Strajki w Polsce–Sierpień 1980: Dokumenty* (Studium Spraw Polskich, London) 29 August 1980.

64. Ibid.
65. *August 1980: The Strikes in Poland* (Munich, 1980) p. 11.
66. Negotiations had resumed on the second afternoon (15 August). Point One of the demands, safety for strikers, was confirmed. Point Two, reinstatement of Walentynowicz to her previous position, was accepted, under extreme pressure from the strikers. Discussion then moved on to Point Three:

> **Wałęsa:** We demand a 2000 złotys increase for all employees. This was not accepted yesterday, so we are putting it again today.
> **Director:** Please understand me: I cannot afford it. The enterprise cannot afford it . . . I must consult further.
> **Wałęsa:** How much can you give us?
> **Director:** On average, perhaps 1200 złotys.
> **Wałęsa:** We defer this until tomorrow. Maybe you will think again. The meeting is adjourned until tomorrow [*loud applause*].
> **Director:** I appeal for your understanding. The country is in such a situation. [**Voice:** We didn't bring this situation about.] I cannot pay you from thin air.
> **Wałęsa:** We have been swindled for years. We know where the money is.
> **Director:** Why do you blame me? Is it my fault there is nothing?

This and other fragments are recorded by Tadeusz Strumff, 'Początki', *Meritum*, no. 1 (Sept 1981) pp. 139–49.
67. Ibid., p. 147.
68. W. Giełżyński, Lech Stefański, *Gdańsk – Sierpień 80* (Warsaw, 1981) p. 44.
69. Ibid., pp. 44–5; Strumff, 'Początki', p. 149.
70. Walentynowicz, 'Opowiada', p. 8.
71. It consisted of:

1. Lech Wałęsa, electrician
2. Joanna Duda-Gwiazda (Ceto), shipbuilding engineer
3. Bogdan Lis (Elmor), machine setter
4. Anna Walentynowicz (Gdańsk Shipyard), welder
5. Florian Wiśniewski (Elektromontaż), electrician
6. Lech Jędruszewski (Gdynia Shipyard), fitter
7. Stefan Izdebski (Gdynia Port Authority), docker
8. Henryka Krzywonos (Urban Transport: WPK), tram driver
9. Tadeusz Stanny (Refinery), chemical technician
10. Stefan Lewandowski (Gdańsk Port Authority), crane operator
11. Lech Sobieszek (Siarkopol), metalworker
12. Józef Przybylski (Budimor), metalworker
13. Zdzisław Kobyliński (State Transport: PKS), storeman
14. Andrzej Gwiazda (Elmor), engineer
15. Jerzy Sikorski (Repair Yard), fitter
16. Jerzy Kmiecik (Northern Shipyard), shipbuilder
17. Wojciech Gruszecki (Gdańsk Technical University), research chemist
18. Lech Bądkowski, writer (coopted later).

72. *Nowe Drogi*, nos 10/11 (Oct–Nov 1980) p. 46.
73. Giełżyński and Stefański, *Gdańsk – Sierpień*, pp. 66–7.
74. *August 1980*, pp. 109–13.
75. Walentynowicz, 'Opowiada', p. 10.
76. The fullest account is by Giełżyński and Stefański, *Gdańsk – Sierpień*, pp. 74–8.
77. Statement No. 1, 20 August 1980.
78. Giełżyński and Stefański, *Gdańsk – Sierpień*, p. 61.
79. *Solidarność*, no. 2 (24 Aug 1980).
80. Giełżyński and Stefański, *Gdańsk – Sierpień*, p. 87.
81. Statement No. 2, 21 August 1980.
82. The Bishop of Gdańsk, Kaczmarek, was also active in making contacts between the two sides. See Raina, *Independent Social Movements*, p. 481.
83. *Solidarność*, no. 9 (29 Aug 1980). A papal message to Cardinal Wyszyński added the pontiff's prayers for the nation 'in its struggle for daily bread, social justice and the natural right to its own way of life'. *Solidarność*, no. 2 (24 Aug 1980).
84. The delegation comprised: Florian Wiśniewski, Józef Przybylski and Wojciech Gruszecki.
85. The meeting is described on pp. 181–2 (below).
86. *Strajki w Polsce* (Studium Spraw Polskich, London) p. 8.
87. *Le Monde*, 19 August 1980.
88. In particular, they quoted No. 87, 'The Freedom of Association and Protection of the Right to Organise Convention, 1948' which had been ratified by Poland in December 1956:

> Workers and employers, without distinction whatsoever, shall have the right to establish and, subject only to the rules of the organisation concerned, to join organisations of their own choosing without previous authorisation.
> Workers' and employers' organisations shall have the right to draw up their constitutions and rules, to elect their representatives in full freedom, to organise their administration and activities and to formulate their programmes. The public authorities shall refrain from any interference which would restrict this right or impede the lawful exercise thereof.
> Workers' and employers' organisations shall not be liable to be dissolved or suspended by administrative authority.

They further referred to No. 98, 'The Right to Organise and Collective Bargaining Convention, 1949', also ratified by Poland, which provides *inter alia*:

> Workers shall enjoy adequate protection against acts of anti-union discrimination in respect of their employment, in particular to acts calculated to . . . cause dismissal of, or otherwise prejudice a worker by reason of union membership or because of participation in union activities.

89. *Solidarność*, no. 9 (29 Aug 1980).
90. *Robotnik*, no. 28 (24 Jan 1979).
91. *Robotnik*, no. 21/22 (25 Sept 1978).
92. See: 'Experts and the Working Group', p. 145 below.
93. *The Trade Union Situation in the USSR* (Geneva: ILO, 1960) p. 66.
94. Neca Jovanov, *Radnički štrajkovi u SFRJ od 1958 do 1969 godine* (Belgrade, 1979) pp. 13–20.
95. Blair A. Ruble, *Soviet Trade Unions* (Cambridge University Press, 1981) pp. 100–3.
96. H. Wujec, 'Prawo pracy w socjalizmie', *Głos* (Warsaw) no. 9.
97. Particularly in Nos 1–12. The Charter, many of whose points anticipate the Twenty-one Demands, first appeared in *Robotnik*, no. 35 (18 July 1979).
98. It is a view also found in Western sociology. See the very interesting analysis by Leslie MacFarlane, *The Right to Strike* (Harmondsworth: Penguin, 1981) p. 62.
99. Gwiazda during the negotiations.
100. The earliest to appear was the KOR bimonthly *Biuletyn Informacyjny*. It was followed by the literary quarterly *Zapis* (the first publication of NOWA, the Independent Publishing House). NOWA soon built up an impressive list of *belles-lettres* by Polish authors (Andrzejewski and Konwicki) or from abroad (Grass, Mandel'stam, Orwell and Solzhenitsyn) and of discussion documents edited by KOR, the 'flying university' and 'Experience and the Future' (DiP). A number of other publishers appeared subsequently.
101. The strikers were assisted by Konrad Bieliński and Mariusz Wilk who produced the strike bulletin *Solidarność*. Dissemination of strike news was undertaken by KOR (see their statement of 8 August 1980 in Raina, *Independent Social Movements*, pp. 457–60) and by the Church. As Anna Walentynowicz wrote: 'To protect ourselves from lies and slander, such as that spread during the occupation strike of 1970 – "the Germans have attacked Gdańsk again" – we decided to let the truth about the situation within the Shipyard be known through the Bishop's Curia in Gdańsk. The news reached the Polish Episcopate and the Pope, which gave us added confidence.' 'Opowiada', p. 6.
102. Biographical details of all three appear in Notes, pp. 183–4.
103. Ewa Milewicz, 'Ja, happening, Stocznia', *Biuletyn Informacyjny*, no. 6 (40) (Aug–Sept 1980) pp. 42–56.
104. From the negotiations.
105. These were defined as 'the division of the national product between consumption and accumulation; the allocation of the social fund amongst various sectors (health, education and culture); the basic principles for calculation and determination of wages, including that of automatic increases to compensate for inflation; long-term economic planning; the directions of investment and price changes' (from the Agreement).
106. Their cost was put at 260 billion złotys by 1980.
107. It was Strike Committee policy to demand increases across-the-board: 'How to Strike', *Solidarność*, no. 1 (23 Aug 1980).

108. The system is supposed to be secret, but two lists have become available: the Central Committee *nomenklatura* for 1972 (reprinted in Denis MacShane, *Solidarity: Poland's Independent Trade Union* (Nottingham: Spokesman, 1981) pp. 165–9) and that of the Gdańsk Shipyard for 1977 (*Solidarność*, no. 9 (29 Aug 1980)).

109. The interventions of Zbigniew Zieliński are in a class of their own. Even his colleagues seemed embarrassed by his constant mendacity.

110. Andrzej Gwiazda, during the negotiations.

111. 'Opowiada', pp. 11–12.

112. Tadeusz Mazowiecki, interview with *Tygodnik Powszechny*, 12 October 1980.

113. See: 'Experts and the Working Group', below.

114. 'Opowiada', p. 14.

115. Ibid., p. 14.

Negotiations

PROLOGUE[1]

Lech Bądkowski: We have an announcement: 'The Prefect of the Gdańsk Region, Jerzy Kołodziejski, has proposed a "working contact" to prepare for talks between the Interfactory Strike Committee and the Government Commission. The Strike Presidium selected a four-man commission and asked the Prefect to meet it in the Gdańsk Shipyard at 2 p.m. Our invitation was accepted.' [*lengthy applause*]

Lech Wałęsa: Ladies and gentlemen. Our Presidium decided we must appoint a team of experts to help us do well. You all know we have to act wisely. This will be a good start. Did we do the right thing? [*applause*]. One of them will speak now.

Tadeusz Mazowiecki: Two of us have come here, Professor Geremek[2] and myself, Mazowiecki. We are signatories of the 'Appeal of Sixty-four' Warsaw intellectuals[3] which has, I think, already reached you. It declares our solidarity with your struggle, one concerned not only with your interests but with those of the country as a whole. Since our arrival, we have been impressed by your great prudence. We hope you will manage to maintain it and preserve the greatest strength you have: your solidarity [*applause*]. As to the position of experts: we shall do our best to help you. But our role is purely advisory. All decisions will remain in the hands of your Presidium. [*applause*]

Wałęsa: Ladies and gentlemen, some people have doubts about this four-man commission. It's only preparatory. It just has to sort out when, where and what we talk about. Someone has to talk to them. If we all talk at once, we'll get nowhere.

Those selected are: Lech Bądkowski, Andrzej Gwiazda [*applause*], Zdzisław Kobyliński and Bogdan Lis. Nothing's going to be decided without our voting on it. It's just a technical business.

Wojciech Gruszecki: A colleague has arrived from Silesia. [*applause*]

Delegate: I don't know how to make a speech. I was sent here as a factory delegate from Tarnowskie Góry, bringing a resolution of solidarity with strikers on the Coast. So I will read it out:

'In the present economic situation of the country, workers of the "Fazos" factory have decided to speak out on matters of concern to us and to the whole nation. We held a strike on 21–22 August 1980, to support the demands regarding the economic situation and food shortages made by employees striking on the Baltic Coast. We also support the demand for setting up free trade unions for all employees. [*applause*] In view of the difficult situation in the country, a general meeting of all our employees decided to return to work, to prevent further losses to the economy that will hurt us in the end. At the same time, the factory made several demands which must be met within the next few days. If the workers' chief demands are not met, the factory will stop again on 1 September 1980.' [*applause*]

Gruszecki: The colleague tells me his factory has 6000 employees. [*applause*] He had great difficulty in getting here through the blockade[4] and only managed it with our help. [*applause*]

Delegate: I would like to describe the situation in Silesia, as perhaps you don't know what it is really like. Silesia is completely disorientated. Radio and television tell us nothing. We have been cut off from the rest of the country. I was sent here specially, by my factory, to find out what is really going on. Someone tells you that fifteen factories are on strike, then the radio news says that a similar number have gone back to work. So I am here to observe at first hand what is happening on the Coast. And I believe that Silesia will join in. [*applause*]

Zdzisław Kobyliński: 'To Professor Jerzy Kołodziejski, Prefect of the Gdańsk Region:

Demands

We categorically demand that all repression of Interfactory Strike Committee helpers cease and that any further repression be prohibited.

In the last few days, the militia and security service have repeatedly picked up, interrogated and detained people distributing Strike Committee publications: For instance:

1. The Interfactory Strike Committee delegation was held up by the militia on its way to see Deputy Premier Jagielski, on 22 August. Although they explained where they were going, they had to produce documents, which made them late for the meeting.
2. Daniel Matyja was detained on 17 August for distributing Strike Committee leaflets.
3. On 19 August, Sylwester Niezgoda was held for five hours and Mirosław Chojecki for forty-eight hours.
4. On 20 August, Andrzej Słomiński, Piotr Szczudłowski, Maciej Budkiewicz and Andrzej Madejski were held in Wrzeszcz for forty-eight hours for distributing Strike Committee leaflets. Słomiński and Szczudłowski were brutally beaten while in custody.
5. On the same day, Sylwester Niezgoda, Kazimierz Żabczyński and Lech Borowski were held in Starogard Gdański for forty-eight hours, for distributing Strike Committee leaflets. A fifteen-year old, Michał Wojciechowski, detained by the security service for some hours for distributing leaflets, was brutally beaten at the militia headquarters in Starogard Gdański.
6. On 27 August, Jordan Cezary, held by militia and security service in Gdynia, for many hours for distributing Strike Committee leaflets, was brutally beaten.

Faced with such acts of violence by the militia and security service, and the tolerant attitude of the state and administrative authorities towards such practices, working people represented by the Interfactory Strike Committee unequivocally declare such provocative and criminal actions to be in total contravention of the Constitution of the Polish People's Republic and Poland's obligations under the International Conventions on Human Rights. Signed: the Interfactory Strike Committee. 23 August 1980.'

Wałęsa: Ladies and gentlemen, we are not quite ready yet. A communiqué is still being written. But I expect you have heard. The preparatory talks ended successfully.[5] A government delegation is coming to us at 8.00 p.m. We will hammer it all out, point by point. [*Lengthy applause. Shouts of 'Bravo'; 'Long Live Wałęsa'.*]

FIRST MEETING (23 AUGUST)

Wałęsa: We welcome the government delegation. [*applause*]
Mieczysław Jagielski: May I shake hands with the Presidium?
Wałęsa: Please do. As we agreed, the delegation will pass through to the smaller room for the discussions.[1] Please make way. [*applause and cheering*] Can you hear me in the hall? Good. Since time is short, I propose we begin.

Deputy Premier!

We welcome you on behalf of the Interfactory Strike Committee representing about 370 enterprises of the Gdańsk Region and some from Elbląg and Słupsk. The fact that we represent hundreds of thousands of people makes us feel sure that the cause we are fighting for is just. Coming here may bring home to you what a shipyard is like when the workers are governing themselves. You can see for yourself how orderly it all is. The serious matters we must settle require us to act prudently and without haste. We have been waiting patiently for nine days and we have plenty of patience left. So I suggest we end today's negotiations by 10 p.m. I also suggest that by then you present the government's general position on our proposals, and then on each one in particular. We hope today's meeting will be the first step towards a speedy ending of the strike.

Jagielski: Thank you, Mr Chairman. I, too, on behalf of our Commission, whose direction the Party and government leadership has entrusted to me, would like to greet all members of, as I understand it, the Presidium of the Interfactory Strike Committee. I would also like to state at the outset that it is my intention, as well as my duty and responsibility, to conduct these talks in a most straightforward and constructive manner. We wish to resolve fundamental and important problems of the greatest concern to workers on the Coast, together, mutually, to the best of our ability. That is my firm intention. I need not introduce members of my Commission, since it seems that you know them already.[2] It is only necessary to mention two not able to be present. We expected that Minister Kopeć would be here, but he was called away on urgent business: Vice-Minister Kuczyński is deputising for him. The other absent member of our Commission, Central Committee secretary comrade Lewandowski, is occupied by urgent Party business, as a session of the Party leadership has just been held.

How are we to conduct these talks? Perhaps it would be helpful, Mr Chairman, if I set out in a short and summary form, as it were outline our point of view, on the issues as I see them so far? You said that this has gone on so long already that there is no need for haste now. I would like to mention that this is only my second day here. We have already held talks with the strike committees of various workplaces. I am familiar with the problems. So, in accordance with yesterday's agreement, we decided – in this case I refer to our Commission – that now is the time to sit down at the table and talk. What do you think, Mr Chairman?

Wałęsa: Of course, only as we said, it would be good if you made your position on all these proposals clear, because they were handed to you some time ago. Going through them, one by one, so we will know if we have the same views, or if there are great differences.

Jagielski: If I understand rightly, you will permit me to present our general point of view on these matters, with supporting arguments. I proceed from the assumption that our talks should be based on the understanding that if one side has set out its proposals, then I would like to present our point of view on certain matters. I do not know whether I should take them strictly in the order in which they were presented, or as I choose, in some other way. Perhaps I will begin with Point One. If I am mistaken in my reading of the propositions then please correct me. I have here the document containing the strikers' proposals.

The first refers to acceptance of free trade unions, independent of the Party and employers, based on ratification by the Polish People's Republic of ILO Convention No. 87 concerning freedom of unions. I would like to state quite frankly and honestly, speaking as I do on behalf of the Commission, how I view this matter. Both I and other members of the Commission have been thinking over the question of free trade union activity, thinking it over seriously. The question was also raised during talks with the strike committees and is now a matter of great interest to workers at many factories across the country. It is simply a question of great importance for working people, for the country, today, tomorrow and for the future. Please allow me to say how I read the formulation of this proposal. As I personally understand it, I repeat, I am speaking quite sincerely, the underlying purpose of this proposal is that trade unions should be the real, authentic and effective representative of the interests of all employees. I must point out here that I am speaking as a representative of the government on a question which does not lie within its competence. This matter concerns the trade union organisation. We cannot dictate its statute nor any of its functions. I would, however, like to express an opinion.

Looked at in this way, I think the question is how to change the position of trade unions in the state, in accordance with contemporary requirements and demands of the workforce. The practical first step in this direction will be the drafting of a new law on trade unions. The present one, setting out the existing legal framework for trade union activity, dates, so I discover, from July 1949. It is more than thirty years old. Working conditions have changed and so, evidently, have demands. A law must be drawn up which will meet the present requirements of working people. It is an established fact that the existing trade union structure fails to meet the current requirements and aspirations of working people. I didn't know much about it beforehand, but I have done some arithmetic. We have at present: twenty-three branch trade unions, forty-nine provincial council trade unions and over 30 000 factory councils. If we add to full-time employees of the unions, the number of those active on factory councils, we reach a total of a million and a half people. So if the public feels that the unions do not fulfil their function satisfactorily, and that this overgrown structure has become outmoded, then it must be changed. Another must be sought, or alternatively, we can use what already exists, by replenishing it with new people without delay. This is something to think over and discuss. If they see the need, the workforce can use their existing rights to change the factory council. I refer to the present moment, about what may be done today, because I want us to find a constructive solution.

What did I mean when I said that workers could choose 'their own people'? 'Their own people' in the sense that they will represent the workforce reliably and effectively, and strive to resolve its problems in the light of recent events both here on the Gdańsk Coast and in Lublin, where I was for some days, and for which I am a *Sejm*[3] deputy. I notice on the strike committees with whom I am negotiating a great number of, so to speak, new people, with genuine authority and real talent: natural activists. Why shouldn't such people join factory councils or unions at some level? But it's up to you, to your opinion on this matter. So, I express my sincere conviction – I don't know whether we agree on this, but I express my own profound personal conviction – that trade unions should represent the interests of employees and defend their rights more effectively. That is the first point.

A second is that we must find ways to contain social conflicts and conflict situations and resolve them properly at the work-place. A third is that trade unions should have greater influence over the shaping of our social policy as a whole. By social policy, I mean wages policy, social security benefits, pensions, annuities and other allowances. And this is connected to the problem of the shaping of living and working conditions. Talks between trade unions and the authorities on these matters should take place on a regular basis. In my view, such discussions should be permanent and continuous: a dialogue between partners.

The first precondition for this is to change the law on trade unions according to the new draft shortly to be published. Before the *Sejm* vote, there will be wide public discussion of this draft in which factory workforces will participate. I don't want to flatter you – on the contrary, I want to speak the plain truth as I feel it – but I must say that so far as I could tell from the way problems have been presented here on the Coast over the past two days, a good law will be passed with your participation. Its central theme should be increasing the union's rights but also increasing the workforces' responsibility. I consider a second precondition to be that trade unions should analyse, independently of the government, what the living costs for different groups and employees will be and on that basis determine the wage increases or other forms of compensation they need. I will return to this later. A third precondition is a change in the law on workers' self-management. A draft is in the final stage of preparation and will shortly be brought forward for discussion at the workplace.

What I have said does not foreclose but rather opens the door to further changes in the way trade unions function. But this needs to be thoroughly considered and discussed. That, Mr Chairman, is what I wanted to say about the first point.

Wałęsa: This is not what we expected but, well, it is a matter for discussion. So I propose you go straight on to Point Two.

Jagielski: Point Two, so far as I understand it, is to guarantee the right to strike and the safety of strikers and their helpers. I feel that the point of issue in the present discussion is the right to strike. But can we take a decision on this today? No one could deny that we are living through days of great emotion and excitement, in which often-justified resentment and grievances are being expressed. Can we decide this in such an atmosphere? Would it not be sensible to seek society's views on the question? I don't deny there is a problem here: on the contrary it is an important one and needs discussion. Perhaps it should be considered alongside the draft law on trade unions. That would throw open this problem for debate.

As to the safety of strikers and their helpers, I want to state that those participating in the strike and their helpers will not suffer any consequences. The only exception may be those whose actions contravene the law: theft, destruction of property or the like. This is a legal matter, and I am not a lawyer, but even so, I state, with a full sense of responsibility, that the safety of strike participants and helpers is guaranteed and that they will not suffer any consequences.

Mr Chairman, may I go on to the third question?

Wałęsa: We don't see it quite like this. Plenty of people are sitting in prison, and plenty more are beaten up. These are the facts. Since we were to speak frankly, I think this matter should be made known. We'll give you the names if you like.

Member of the Government Commission: Do you have a list?

Wałęsa: Yes, there is a list of those beaten up, with medical reports. Some of those beaten up were rearrested. So, it is not true there are no consequences.

Jagielski: May I have the list?

Gruszecki: A new case has just been reported to us. The mother of Andrzej Słomiński, a doctor from Tczew – whom we have already mentioned because he was arrested on 20 August – came here in tears because he has been rearrested and beaten, together with four others, including his brother Wiesław. I tried to telephone the Prefect, Mr Kołodziejski but unfortunately did not get through. I request that this matter be cleared up straight away. It is worth adding that his mother, who came to us, is a pensioner and invalid living on an allowance of 1300 złotys a month.

Jagielski: I only received this document a moment ago. Will you let me deal with these problems at the end? I will clear them up, together with the case just mentioned. [**Wałęsa:** Of course. I agree.] Thank you.

Florian Wiśniewski: Prime Minister, the problem is not so simple. It looks different from your position. We work on the shopfloor. I have worked in trade unions for many years and know that the problem is really serious. At the moment, it looks difficult from the legal angle because the Labour Code is presently so formulated that anyone who goes on strike can get the sack. People come to us from Southern Poland – one brought a paper to show he lost his job for going on strike. That would be impossible in the present atmosphere on the Coast. Things have gone further here. My own view is that this part of the Labour Code should be changed, I think it is Article Twelve. This must be put right if people are to be satisfied. We know how strongly people feel on this. We have representatives here from 382 factories whose workforces are on strike. I think we should decide this on the spot. We are fully representative.

Prime Minister, this is not the first time such events have taken place on the Coast. We simply want to make sure they don't happen again, for no one needs them. Such events must be examined thoroughly. To prevent them happening again, the government must send its own people to negotiate with those on strike. In the past, the strikers tried hard to make contact, often reaching out directly to the government, but there was no response. Instead, lies were circulated about us and various incidents staged. They let it be known that such activity is purely political, which is completely untrue. We are social activists concerned with social and economic questions. I trust we can reach agreement on them.

Wałęsa: May I ask . . .

Jagielski: Let me say something. I fully appreciate the importance of what you said. I quite agree that when such problems arise, an essential element, as you rightly said, is to resolve them promptly by participation of the organisations concerned and the administration. I agree that this is the proper course. Perhaps your proposal is really just a change in the Labour Code. That would certainly be one solution. But, gentlemen, how can I make such an alteration today? You must remember that the Labour Code is a document emanating from the *Sejm* – a *Sejm* statute. What you propose may be put forward as a draft amendment to the Labour Code. That is my view of this matter.

Wałęsa: I suggest we move on. This is a large subject and we won't exhaust it now. Everyone will express their views and then we'll tie them all together.

Jagielski: As to Point Three, 'To uphold freedom of expression and publication as guaranteed by the Constitution, not to suppress independent publishing and to grant access to the mass media for representatives of the clergy', what do I want to say about this? I have no reservations about the point of principle: freedom of expression and publication are constitutionally guaranteed. The difficulties arise in the sphere of practice. We must, therefore, consider the workings of the censorship – I gather this is what concerns you most – in the wider context of the operation of all the institutions of our socialist democracy. I think it is the functioning of one of these bodies, that controlling the mass media, which must be dealt with. We are all concerned – I speak on behalf of the Government Commission – that information should be complete, true and reliable. However, censorship must serve such essential interests of the state and socio-political life as protection of state and military secrets, and perhaps even in some cases – as is universally practised – economic ones. It also covers dissemination, or rather preventing the dissemination, of material hostile to our system, protection of the feelings both of believers and of atheists and preventing dissemination of morally damaging or even, I would say, pornographic material.

The principles on which censorship operates must be defined clearly and precisely. A similar proposal is being canvassed in literary and scientific circles. So we must draw up an appropriate document. We must decide how it should be prepared: which organs of state will do the drafting and final editing. Such practical questions need to be resolved straight away. As to the proposal in Point Three about non-suppression of so-called independent publishing, some clarification is required. Such publishing has so far been extremely diverse, ranging in content from those that are critical, while still accepting the constitutional bases of our system, to some that are, frankly speaking, anti-socialist, sometimes even demanding a change of our state system. Are we to publish those? They are the real problem.

'Access to the mass media for representatives of all denominations.' This proposal can be considered. We have some experience in this field both of press and broadcasting. An essential problem is the degree and range of access granted to all denominations. These are matters for discussion by the interested parties. The ever-improving relations between the state and the Catholic Church hierarchy, and the atmosphere of complete religious freedom, seem to me to guarantee that all such problems can be resolved in the spirit of your proposal. May I have two more minutes to elaborate on this? [**Wałęsa:** Certainly.]

So, I would like to present some facts on this subject. I am not directly responsible for these questions, but they do interest me. May I point out that the size of circulation and editions of religious publications in this country is the largest of all socialist states. There are 115 denominational journals, appearing in a total of 816 580 copies. They are put out by sixty-two publishers, by churches (seventy titles, almost fifty of them by the Catholic Church), by church institutions, denominational unions and social bodies. We can single out here: twenty-five official church magazines, nine pastoral journals, twenty-seven scientific titles (I read them), sixteen social and cultural journals, ten liturgical and pastoral titles and a further sixteen of an informational character. I don't want to take up more time, but I could add *Gość Niedzielny*, a weekly in 90 000 copies, *Słowo Powszechne*, 95 000 on weekdays, and 150 000–200 000 for the weekend issue. I think that such journals have ample opportunity to put forward the Church's views and those of denominational unions and social bodies, on matters connected with belief and also on social problems. The circulation of such journals is not restricted to this country, but extends abroad to the Polonia.[4] May I proceed to Point Four?

Wałęsa: Certainly. But staying with [Point] Three for a moment, there were numerous suggestions. Thousands of people asked for radio broadcasts of mass for the bed-ridden.[5] This demand has not been met. I think it should be. After all, the mass media are ours. If this is what people want, I don't see why they should not have it.

Gruszecki: I would also like to dwell on this for a moment, if the Prime Minister will permit. The figures he quoted do not accord with reality. As a research worker, I don't have much time for reading the newspapers, but I would like to see *Tygodnik Powszechny* occasionally. However, this standard Catholic paper is unobtainable here on the Coast. On average there is one copy for sale per kiosk: larger distribution points sometimes have more, but many minor outlets have not a single copy of this excellent and popular weekly. By contrast, I can almost always get *Głos Wybrzeża*, *Dziennik Bałtycki*, *Życie Warszawy*, *Trybuna Ludu* or any other official daily. I don't think the question is one of size of circulation – I mean of the total circulation of the Catholic press – but rather one of demand. It seems to me the true proportions are reversed: *Polityka*[6] 200 000, *Tygodnik Powszechny* 40 000. Does the Prime Minister think this ratio appropriate for a Catholic country, in which the Church has such a mass following?

Jagielski: You started by saying that my figures do not accord with reality. I don't know why you make such an accusation. The figures I gave you were true. I said at the beginning: I will not lie to anyone at this meeting. Not to anyone. I will speak the whole truth. I can quote my sources. As to the question you raised – whether the circulation is sufficient or not – I would reply, in the light of your statement, that it is not. I, too, could quote examples of papers unobtainable in Warsaw: the same ones that you mentioned. There is a need to increase their circulation. Mr Chairman, may I continue?

Alina Pieńkowska: Another section of Point Three was also omitted: 'not to suppress independent publishing'. I am concerned about this. Will the Prime Minister, please, say something about it?

Jagielski: I have answered very precisely. You can read it out, I understand there is a record of the proceedings. My reply was precise and unambiguous.

Wałęsa: I suggest we move on.

Jagielski: As to Point Four: (a) reinstatement of those dismissed for breaching the Labour Code, in particular participants in the strikes of 1970 and 1976; students expelled for their beliefs or opinions; (b) release of all political prisoners including Edmund Zadrożyński,[7] Jan Kozłowski[8] and Marek Kozłowski;[9] and (c) cessation of repression for beliefs or opinions', I think it would be better to treat these matters in concrete terms. We should define what the particular problems are, name those concerned, reopen the investigation in each case, and where mistakes were made, correct them. The principle of no persecution for strike activity will be applied. Sub-point (b) proposes the release of all political prisoners, naming three persons convicted of criminal offences: theft and assault. These are sentences imposed by independent courts, after due process of law. If, however, these matters are not sufficiently known to the general public, perhaps because those convicted are not from the

Gdańsk Region, and you want to know the facts, then we can deal with this straight away by publishing a suitable article or by some other means. So, I replied positively.

As to the final point: on the basis of information given me before my departure, there are no political prisoners in Poland. That is, persons convicted for their political opinions. I received this statement from the Minister of Justice.

Wałęsa: Prime Minister, these three cases are known to us and to the public. We know what kind of trials they were. And so, if we are to be honest, I propose that these people should be released while their cases are reexamined. For the truth is we attended these trials. I was there, and others too. I can say straight out because I am a worker and don't mince words that they were rigged. [*applause*]

Wiśniewski: Prime Minister, you presented the whole matter as the relevant department put it to you. We look at it quite differently: that no one should be persecuted for acting in accordance with their convictions.

Let me illustrate. Here I am in the shipyard. My block of flats is ringed by the militia, who tried to catch me in the car park. I go home when my family situation gets difficult, after all I have four children. Obviously, a man with such responsibilities would not take risks stupidly. The Chairman of our meeting has seven children. I know him because he also worked at 'Elektro-montaż'.[10] I realise these matters are difficult, but they must be seen in their social context and not just according to the letter of the law. People can be done for anything. I know such cases. I know life. I know how careful you must be. They can easily set a trap for you.

When the Americans were fighting for independence, their slogan was 'Man is born free and lives free'. I consider this 'born free' is a great help to us. I think, Prime Minister, you understand me.

Jagielski: I do understand you. I do.

Andrzej Gwiazda: Prime Minister, until recently the press said all was well in our industry and our economy. The obligatory official line was that, despite some minor difficulties, everything was running smoothly. Now it transpires that great deficiences were being deliberately concealed or glossed over. Don't you think, Prime Minister, that something similar may be happening in the administration of justice? Why should it be any different? I think that the cases which give rise to the most widespread public doubts – well-founded or not – should be reexamined thoroughly and impartially, if only to clear the name of the judicial apparatus. [*applause*]

Jagielski: So, I understand that the cases of these three should be reviewed or – because I would like to note this down – or . . .

Wałęsa: We don't know every case. There may well be more. But these were followed by the public, who know what they were like. And so it would be good if they were let out at once. Then, perhaps, they could be reviewed. After all, people are suffering.

Wiśniewski: The proposal here – it is one of many, Prime Minister – comes down simply to asking the public, carrying out a survey of public opinion. That would improve some matters. It would certainly restore trust in the authorities. I'm certain some local authorities abuse their powers and lie to the central state organs.

Jagielski: As I understand it, your concern is not only with specific cases, but also very general. There are two points: we can take a position as regards these three cases only after an appeal to the Supreme Court. That is the way to proceed in the three particular cases to which the Chairman referred. Then there is the general matter which was just mentioned . . . [*sentence indistinct*]

As to Point Five, 'to put information in the mass media about the formation of the Interfactory Strike Committee and to publish its demands', I have the following suggestion. People know that we are talking. They know from the news that talks have begun, that we are working with the Interfactory Committee . . . [*indistinct*]

Wałęsa: What about the publication of demands?

Jagielski: Pardon? As to the other matter, I propose that as we have begun talks, we should not publish the demands, but should prepare a communiqué on the mutual agreement which – I am sure, Mr Chairman – we shall reach. I think that what interests us most is the outcome of our talks. That is my suggestion. Let us take this course. After all, it is now well known that we are talking, and, therefore, with whom: the Interfactory Strike Committee. Should we publish the demands? Let us publish the outcome, agreed in our talks. Won't that be far more useful and far more constructive? I am acting in a constructive manner. I want to find a joint, constructive solution.

Gruszecki: I read our local press. So far, I haven't seen a single item from which I could learn that an Interfactory Strike Committee exists. This name was nowhere to be found. If I haven't found it, then it doesn't exist for the readers.

A second point. People come to us from all over Poland, and are often deeply moved by what they see happening here. They frequently beg, with tears in their eyes: 'give us some printed materials, we know nothing of all this at home'. All that is happening here is kept secret: the local press says nothing and telephone links with other towns are cut. Workers come from very large enterprises. Delegates arrived recently from Świdnica and from Tarnowskie Góry, from factories with thousands of workers. Tourists come; others return from their holidays. They state unanimously that they knew nothing of what was going on in Gdańsk. They are astonished. How, then, can one speak of reliable information?

Jagielski: I can answer you quite truthfully. I look at it like this: at 7.00 p.m. the radio news stated that a Jagielski commission is going for talks with the Interfactory Strike Committee. A communiqué will be broadcast tomorrow. Perhaps there wasn't one today – nor in the press – but there certainly will be, and television will probably report in tonight's late news that talks have begun. It may be in the press tomorrow.

Gwiazda: Prime Minister, I second your proposal that we speak the truth. But the truth must be the whole truth. So let's speak the whole truth: what we are demanding, why we are on strike, what you and the Government Commission propose. We can report later what we have agreed.

Jagielski: But let us first start talks. After all, you say you want to talk with me, with us. So, let us proceed with the talks.

Wiśniewski: I realise that the presence of the Prime Minister here is an act of good will. Yesterday. I was able to ascertain that he is a man of great standing. I understand and appreciate the words of a diplomat. This alone, however, cannot satisfy us. I will explain why not. Take yesterday's *Trybuna Ludu*:[11] did the Prime Minister see what they say about us? [**Jagielski:** I didn't manage to.] Well, I had much to do, but I did manage it. It turns out that we sat down to discussions before a conciliatory approach towards the Strike Committee had materialised. The moral aspect is that they slandered us. Were we not so deeply convinced of our moral rightness, we could not withstand it. Some people here have gone to hospital with nervous breakdowns, even from the Strike

Presidium,[12] such was the moral pressure. After yesterday's discussion with you, Prime Minister, I went back to my family at last. I thought I could trust your word and an officially-signed statement of immunity.

I fully understand how difficult these matters are, but I consider a man of great standing and broad outlook capable of taking great steps. This means releasing a communiqué in the usual fashion, through the national press and television. Making our demands known in this way will restore our reputation after all the slanders that were heaped upon us. It seems to me that this would satisfy all of us and greatly help the Polish Government, because other provincial authorities will not dare conceal the truth any longer. Please remember: they are the guilty people. What did Szydlak say when he came to Gdańsk?[13] God in heaven, that was a scandal! These are the people most to blame. That's how we regarded it, and how we put it in our bulletins. Maybe the Prime Minister would agree with us?

The moral aspect requires redress after all this evasiveness and avoidance of the truth. Let's remember that truth brings us progress in our economic life. We won't tolerate prevarications. Truth cannot be concealed. The workforce will make sure of that. The great barrier here is censorship. It is enough to call something 'political' and it won't be published. But these are not political matters. They really aren't. That's simply what this apparatus of ours got used to calling them. They take the easy way out. They say it's 'political' and the matter is closed. So, Prime Minister, I entreat you to allow publication. That would be moral redress for our nation. [*applause*]

Wałęsa: I have a question for the Prefect. We agreed at the outset, that a precondition for our starting talks would be restoration of telephone links with other cities. But it turns out that the telephones are still not working. There's something wrong here. May we know what the blockade is for?

Bądkowski: If I recall correctly, the Prefect stated that from the morning lines with Szczecin were restored, but as to the reconnection with Warsaw which we wanted, he said he would let us know by telephone before talks started, or, if that was not possible, at the latest in the course of the talks. Wasn't that so? [**Reply:** Yes.] Thank you.

Jagielski: I can't answer now. I must look into it. I can't answer now.

Wałęsa: But it was a precondition . . .

Jagielski: You told me about it yesterday. I made enquiries and it was established, technically, that telecommunication links between Gdańsk and Szczecin are open.

Wałęsa: We didn't ask for reconnection with the whole of Poland, but only with Warsaw. That was it. Yes. So you really didn't keep the agreed conditions.

Jerzy Kołodziejski: My answer to the question is that this is probably a central decision. It is not one for a Prefect to make. I cannot answer your question.

Gruszecki: May I ask, then, if we are talking to a Government Commission or to a local one?

Jagielski: I think I have explained unambiguously whom I represent. I can make enquiries and tell you later, but I am not in a position to do so now.

Gruszecki: Does this mean that what the Prefect Kołodziejski said cannot be taken as the explanation?

Jagielski: I don't see why not. It is up to you.

Kołodziejski: I think the problem can be resolved in the course of our talks. That was the agreement: at the latest in the course of our talks. I repeat: this is a matter for central decision. It does not lie within my authority. So it requires an explanation from . . .

Jagielski: May we move on, Mr Chairman?

Kobyliński: I would like to dwell on this point. I sent my child to a summer camp near Warsaw. He was due back on 18 August. When he didn't come, I tried to phone to find out what has happened. I could not do so. I am not alone in this predicament. Many people on the Coast have children away at summer camps or other family concerns. Prime Minister, this should be treated as an important problem, really upsetting to us as a society, as working people. It cannot be like this.

Jagielski: May I reply, Mr Chairman? I can look into this, but not now, because I would like to go through all the points, as you requested, and then clear up this matter with the central authorities. I shall get in touch with them and pass on this information.

Lech Sobieszek: Let me read out the agreed conditions. One of the first conditions for starting the talks is 'restoration of all telephone links'. In my view, this has not been fulfilled. I propose we suspend our meeting. That is my opinion.

Wałęsa: There should simply be a decision to reconnect.

Gwiazda: Prime Minister, we regarded reconnection as a gesture of goodwill. We cannot comprehend the purpose of the telephone blockade. We find the explanation offered by the Prefect, well, completely unconvincing. Our view is precisely the opposite. But I think that once talks have begun, or are about to, then even the Prefect's reasons lose their relevance. Reconnection would be an act of goodwill and greatly simplify things for us. I am genuinely surprised that you, Prime Minister – head of a Government Commission, for talks with us – should have done nothing about it. This was a demand clearly stated as a precondition for talks. It didn't just crop up today. Thank you.

Jagielski: I suggest you give me an opportunity to clarify this matter. I came to the meeting because I wanted to talk, to explain our point of view. That is how I understood our conversation of yesterday. So – let's clear it up. Perhaps what cannot be settled today will be done tomorrow. After all, I am not in a position to clarify everything straight away.

Wałęsa: What time limit do you propose?

Jagielski: I think I will manage to clear it up sometime tomorrow.

Wałęsa: No, no, no. However, despite everything, I propose we go on. So that we will know your attitude to the remaining points. But you will have to speed up the ending of the blockade. It surely can't be so difficult. Of course it isn't.

Member of Government Commission: It cannot be done in the next few days.

Zbigniew Zieliński: A hurricane passed through Warsaw last night, destroying buildings in large areas of the city. I was in Warsaw at the time, to be exact just after the hurricane. You can see whole streets – such as the avenue from the airport – where huge trees, huge limes, beautiful limes are completely demolished along half the route. The central telephone exchange was completely demolished. So I don't think telephone links with Warsaw will be restored today – even though I haven't been in Warsaw today – and I don't know how advanced the repair work is, or whether it can be finished tomorrow.

Secondly, from what the Prefect told us of the discussions with you, the problems of telephonic disconnections with the rest of the country were explained and from what he said, you accepted this. There was the proposal of reference to Warsaw. Everything cannot be sorted out in so short a time – it was by then the afternoon, and today is a non-working Saturday. And that is the first matter, or rather the second, to have been cleared up.

And thirdly [*protests from the hall*], excuse me, but there are many serious matters among the points you raised, deserving discussion. It is worth-while for the several hundred sitting in the hall to listen to them and think them over quietly. Time should not now be wasted on inessential matters. I do not want to leave you with the impression that your side is not interested in these talks. Our side has come with the sincere intention to continue them.

Pieńkowska: May I point out that telephone links with Warsaw were cut off last Friday, a week ago. Nothing was said then of any hurricane.

Zbigniew Lis: I would like to ask the Deputy Premier why today's press and television made no mention of this hurricane. We have heard nothing about it. The other thing is; we had to wait nine days. Why must we now rush through all the proposals so urgently?

Gwiazda: I would like to inform the Minister that in modern telephone exchanges there is no need to push a block into the socket of every subscriber. Disconnection is done simply by transmitting appropriate information to the register from the centre, or by removing it. It really just amounts to issuing an instruction.

Jagielski: I consider all problems raised by these Twenty-one Points to be of great importance. Accordingly, I propose we give a thorough examination to those regarded as most significant by workers on the Coast, instead of giving so much time and attention to this one. We will sort this one out after the meeting. There may be technical or other reasons, or perhaps the reason that the Prefect gave. I will find out and let you know. Gentlemen, these matters are sufficiently fundamental to warrant our full attention. Are our talks to be suspended over such an issue? We have come here with goodwill to hold discussions.

Andrzej Kołodziej: Since a telephone connection is not possible, but we want to let the public know what is going on here, I propose that the next meeting – it is too late for today – should be broadcast on radio or television. [*applause*]

Jagielski: Let's think it over. It's possible: I am open to all constructive proposals.

Wałęsa: We have got into difficulties here. Maybe we should stop the general discussion. Let's just hear your views on the remaining points without discussion. Just to find out what the Prime Minister and government think about these matters.

Sobieszek: May I enquire why we were not told about the non-fulfilment, or impossibility of fulfilment, of our demand that telephone links be restored?

Jagielski: All I can say is: if someone sets a precondition of that sort, then I want to know their reasons. No one has told me the reasons for this precondition. Why is it being put to me? I set no preconditions whatever. I simply told the three gentlemen who came to see me yesterday, that I was speaking not as head of the commission but as a citizen and a Pole. I did not set any preconditions for talks, nor did I know that this one was so basic that we cannot talk without it. I share the Chairman's view that the significance of these problems is so great that they should be discussed thoroughly.

Henryka Krzywonos: I would like to emphasise that we tried to see the Prefect long before this, but were not admitted to his office, nor were we treated seriously. We did not wait so many days just to have our conditions rejected. We want, in fact, we demand that, the whole of Poland knows what is happening here. We are fighting on behalf of the whole population – workers, employees, peasants – because all of them are here, even peasants have taken work in the shipyard or nearby. From the very beginning, when we showed our willingness to talk, there hasn't been a single word here for us about the opening of talks. We have waited a very long time. Now we are in no hurry. [*applause*]

Wiśniewski: Discussion of all the points is our central concern. We set the precondition deliberately, as a test of whether this government would show goodwill. Perhaps the Prime Minister didn't pay much attention to it, in view of all these major issues. We did bring it up yesterday when we were speaking seriously. Surely, it is a straightforward matter which should now be settled. But what can I do about it? If I were Prime Minister, I would order my Minister of Communications to set about restoring automatic connections with all regions, and if there are technical difficulties to sort out in Warsaw, to get on with it. If we had such a verbal assurance from the Prime Minister himself, I think we could continue the meeting. That's how I feel.

Wałęsa: Ladies and gentlemen. Of course we could do one thing or another. But I think it would be best if before the end of today's session, we hear what the Prime Minister has to say. Just to see how he looks at these things. So we'll know his views. I propose we hear him on the remaining points without discussion.

Jagielski: I have a constructive proposal. We can agree that we will have a radio transmission of our next meeting, as suggested, to let local residents know about our talks and their progress. Yes, I am in favour of this. We must work out the technical details. I am not myself a technician, but we must work out how it is to be done.

Let me explain another point. I have concentrated on what are called here, 'Demands of the workforces on strike, represented by the Interfactory Strike Committee'. This one was not included. Well, maybe it was an oversight. We all make mistakes. So I propose . . . [*interruptions*] Must today's talks be suspended on this one issue? So I propose that, if you like, I can present my point of view on the remaining matters.

Kołodziej: Perhaps, as our colleague Wałęsa proposed, we should simply listen to the opinions of the Government Commission, without discussing any of them today. And tomorrow, if we are to broadcast, it should not just be locally, but to the whole country. Because we are not talking about communications on the Coast, but with Warsaw and the whole of Poland. [*applause*]

Jagielski: I have made my proposal.

As to Point Six, 'To take definite steps to lead the country out of its present crisis by (a) giving the public full information about the social and economic situation and (b) enabling all social groups to participate in discussion of a reform programme', I think this proposal is justified and can be met. We also agree with both sub-points. I wish to state that we too, as a Government Commission, consider that only an aware society is able to initiate and effect a programme for putting our economy in order. I see from the talks and proposals that society was insufficiently informed. I can state frankly from my own experience that it is not ready for further, difficult conditions of development. For this reason the matter expressed here: 'enabling all social groups to participate in discussion of a reform programme' is of utmost importance. And so, permanent, deep and authentic consultation, real social dialogue, is an essential element in resolving the basic problems of national development. Our position on this is unambiguously positive – identical to yours.

On Point Seven, 'To pay all employees taking part in the strike, wages equivalent to vacation pay for the duration of the strike out of Central Trade Union Council funds', please don't blame me. I have no right to dispose of any trade union funds. No such right. The matter may be settled as follows: strike pay may be given on the understanding that lost production will be made up. Ways of doing so, and a deadline, will be determined by the workforce. I haven't managed to find out yet whether the Central Trade Union Council has the means to finance this or not. In our view, it should come from the employees' wage fund. But the problem of how to increase production, which is the source of what we have to share out, will depend on mutual trust.

I would like to proceed to Point Eight, 'To raise the basic pay of every employee by 2000 złotys, to compensate for current cost of living increases'. Let us consider for a moment whether this proposed increase across the board is realistic or just. We have twelve million employees in the state sector. Are 2000 złotys needed as much by someone earning, say, 8000–10 000 złotys as by someone on 3000? Surely not? Those paid least feel the cost of living increase most: it is less painful for the better-off. Why, then, should everybody get the same amount? Superficially, this proposal seems fair, but I will tell you frankly – you assured me yesterday I could speak openly and frankly – I, personally, consider it to be profoundly unjust. That's my first point.

Secondly, what would 2000 złotys per head amount to? It would come to 240 000 million złotys a year, more than a quarter of the present wage fund. Even the richest state in the world could not afford to increase the total sum of money wages by such a huge amount at the stroke of a pen. This year's increase in the supply of goods by value comes to approximately 60 000 million złotys. But you are talking about 240 000 million złotys. I think this is impossible, unjust and would simply lead to profiteering, to galloping inflation and to the emergence of a black market. This proposal, as presently formulated, is completely unrealistic.

I don't want to cause offence by comparing different groups: food industry employees with construction workers or construction workers with shipbuilders. I mention them only as examples. Let me simply pass on the information that since 1 July, three million people have so far received wage increases, averaging 8 per cent. Of course, compared to the rise in cost of living this is not much. It is, however, some compensation for many of these three million, whose increases ranged from 300 to 1000 złotys. In addition, I have instructed each member of my Commission to examine the social and wage policies in their particular industry. Minister Jedynak is here: he can speak on problems of shipbuilding. Comrade Kopeć has left, but Deputy Minister Kuczyński can speak on problems of the machine industry. Appropriate working groups can discuss the problems of food industry, construction and others including health care – because there was even a proposal on that. I told a representative of the Ministry of Health to come. Deputy Minister Grenda could not come but Deputy Minister – what's his name? – Marcinkowski did come. That, my dears, is how I view this matter.

Point Nine comes next: 'to guarantee automatic wage increases that keep up with price rises and a fall in the value of money'. A serious one, but there is a problem here, namely how to achieve genuine wage increases equivalent to the increase in prices and fall in the value of money. May I digress a little and tell you how I see it? About 105 countries in the world – I may be wrong, perhaps 104 or 106 – use a so-called 'cost of living basket'. This consists of items whose cost is recorded four times a year. The same procedure is employed in Poland. The Central Statistical Office takes 1360 items to be representative. However, the range of goods included in the basket is too broad. We need to select those goods and services which cater for the basic needs of a worker on average pay. When their price increases, hence the cost of living, we must offer some form of compensation. It comes down to this: determining which items should be on the list, and subject to control by the State Price Commission. Three bodies should be involved: an official body, the state's Central Statistical Office; another parallel, independent, the trade unions; and a third, possibly, research institutes. We could then see whether their methodology differs or not. If it does, we will have to determine what the real increase amounts to, and on that basis, decide whom to compensate. We must hold consultations and grant the right to express opinions, especially to trade union organisations. Should we compensate the lowest paid, working women, or women with large families, or – some will ask – should there be equal shares for all? I, personally, do not think the increase should be across the board. I was looking into this subject before coming here, but then I was told to leave for Gdańsk; another team continues the work in my absence. So, that is my general view on this matter and how it can be settled fairly. It seems to me fully in accordance with your proposal.

We are in general agreement with Point Ten: 'to supply sufficient food for the domestic market exporting only and exclusively the surpluses', but it does need some clarification. As to meat, should we export 'only surpluses', as you put it? I ask the meeting, how can there be surpluses when we have such a huge meat shortage? We have no surpluses. [*interruptions*] You are becoming impatient, but I will explain in full, to the best of my ability.

We have decided to improve the market situation by meat imports. I can't tell you the exact amount. So far as I know, it is 50 000–60 000 tons. This does not mean there are no meat exports. We do export. Total meat exports this year, including meat products, are 150 000 tons. Someone may ask: why do we export? Meat has been a traditional export for fifty or sixty years. It consists primarily of ham sold to the American Polonia, and exports of bacon which grew ten years ago to 60 000, 50 000, 45 000 tons, depending on the country: England, Belgium, Holland. It is a lot. I may be wrong – I don't keep all the figures in my head – but I think exports of meat products amount to 5000– 8000 tons. Competition for such products is so strong that we can never regain a market. Once you withdraw, you lose it permanently.

But there is another side to this. It is vitally important to increase domestic meat output by all possible means. I can tell you that this year we will have to import six million tons of corn and 1 400 000 tons of fodder at a cost of 2 500 000 dollars. It is extremely difficult to increase and intensify livestock production from our own resources. A further problem is price structure which must, unavoidably, be regulated. Finally, when we have the meat we need, there will be the problem of distributing it fairly, both within regions and amongst them. I think there is great scope for regional initiative in raising output and that when this brings results, meat supplies should be improved within that region.

'To introduce ration cards for meat and meat products – food coupons – until the market is stabilised.' I gather this is a specific proposal. It would be exceptionally difficult from the technical point of view. Meat is not like sugar, which could be rationed fairly easily. Consequently, meat rationing would be very expensive to administer. And further questions would arise. Could one devise a system of rationing that would be acceptable to all sections of society? What attitude would we adopt towards meat distribution to private peasants? How would they purchase it? Should workers in heavy industry receive larger rations and, if so, how much larger? I think we need to put forward a specific set of proposals or alternatives in the near future so that the public can make its views known. We have had coupons before and I must say they led to abuses. To restate my position, therefore, I regard increased output as the best way to improve the supply of basic articles – in this case meat – to the domestic market.

'To abolish commercial prices and sales for hard currency in shops for *Internal-Export.*' This proposal is expressed in very categorical terms. 'To abolish commercial prices': the question is more complex than it at first seems. Let us consider for a moment what abolition of commercial prices for meat would mean, given the existing situation. Broadly speaking, the present national food shortages arise from the fact that agricultural output grew much more slowly in the 1970s, and particularly from 1976–80, than the purchasing power on the market. I can give the meeting some data on this. Meat supplies to the domestic market this year, including imports, amount to approximately 2 090 000 tons. The figure for 1971 was 1 004 000 tons. Total wages trebled over this period. If we were to accept the proposed increases of wages and of family allowances, even allowing for the additional meat imports, the disproportion between supply and demand would become still greater. The basic problem, I repeat, is price structure – the cost differential between foodstuffs and industrial goods. We need not go into this whole question now, but I would like to point out that all extra revenue from sales of commercial shops will be used as promised: to raise the lowest wages, pensions or annuities and family allowances.

By 'Internal-Export' shops, you mean the dollar shops 'PEWEX' don't you? It so happens that a number of people in this country receive hard currency from their relatives abroad. We also have thousands, perhaps nowadays tens of thousands, who are employed abroad: on construction projects under contract from the Ministry of Foreign Trade, in diplomatic or trade missions, as sailors or fishermen. They have dollar accounts. If they had nowhere in Poland to spend this money I am sure it would all be used abroad. If we had to close the duty-free shops, dollar shops and shops selling cars for foreign currency, wouldn't those people lose on their foreign currency? They would have to pay much higher prices abroad than in 'PEWEX'. There is a profit on sales and that would go abroad. Under existing regulations, we allocate the entire profit made in these shops – I speak here with full responsibility, we can produce the documents – to the purchase of foodstuffs. This year we bought 7500 tons of butter. We bought additional meat with it, and want to buy more. Your proposal that goods made in Poland should be withdrawn from 'PEWEX' is justified. We shall speed up the decision to withdraw them, where this occurs. It is an open question whether also to exclude alcohol, of which there is no shortage on the domestic market.

As to Point Twelve, 'To introduce the principle that people in leading positions are chosen on the basis of qualifications rather than Party membership. To abolish privileges of the militia, security service and Party apparatus by equalising family allowances and closing special shops, etc.', what can I say about this? I entirely agree with the first proposal: selection of high officials according to qualifications rather than Party membership. This is justified. A party resolution, of the Sixth Congress [1971] I think, states that the basic criteria which candidates for high office must meet are professional qualifications, active support for the principles of our system, and moral standing. It should be a requirement that those in responsible positions display great responsibility as well as good professional and social discipline. This is essential for proper organisation of work, for leadership and simply for establishing good interpersonal relationships. So we fully agree with this proposal. The specific evaluation of a particular person's work is, of course, another matter. There are cases of careerists holding on to their positions, motivated mainly by self-interest, unable to cooperate with their closest colleagues. Such people should be brought to account. We must constantly perfect our work in this field.

As to the proposed abolition of privileges of militia, security service and Party apparatus employees, this, I think, refers to family allowances. If I am rightly informed, functionaries of the militia and security service really do receive such allowances. I am told it is 1000 złotys for non-working wives and 105 złotys for one child. Should this remain a supplementary benefit? There is no reason why it should not be incorporated into basic salaries. But here I have a request, simply a request. Let us look at this dispassionately and objectively. There are no fixed hours of work in this profession, they must be available at any time. [*laughter*] They have to change their place of residence and move to places where wife cannot always find work and where the child cannot easily get to school. [*renewed laughter*] Does this happen in all jobs? No, the specific nature of such work must, of course, be taken into account. Even so, it is a general principle of our social policy to raise family allowances as frequently and systematically as funds permit. That is our general principle and I am certain it will be followed. I cannot comment on special pay and conditions for Party apparatus employees, as I am not a Party worker.

Zieliński: Maybe Comrade Fiszbach or I could answer this one?

Jagielski: Go on then.

Zieliński: I can tell you that less than 40 per cent of meat produce is sold at commercial prices. The latest exact figure is 38 per cent or thereabouts. Long ago, when commercial prices were first introduced, all goods in Party restaurants and special shops, including those in the Central Committee building, were sold at commercial prices. So the Party apparatus has paid commercial prices for longer than any other group of citizens. I direct a department in which high-class specialists are employed. Quite a number of them have doctorates. A person entering the Party apparatus from administration, no matter whether he had been director of a large association or big enterprise, from the rank of senior inspector to that of a deputy head of department, loses no less than a third of his salary. So much for the privileges of the Party apparatus! And they work really hard, as you can see from the Party secretaries at factory level. Of course, even here, a negligent worker can sometimes be found. But it is very hard work, requiring great responsibility and sacrifices. Comrade workers! there is really nothing to envy. I used to be a worker myself. These people do not deserve such reputations.

Jagielski: I would like to take Points Fourteen and Fifteen together. One concerns lowering the retirement age for women to fifty and for men to fifty-five; the other proposes raising pensions and annuities of the old portfolio to present levels. I don't know whether the first was carefully thought through. I perceive a certain contradiction in it. I wonder how widely this was discussed with people of the required age or approaching it. One has difficulty imagining many women or men who are nearing fifty-five accepting it. Life expectancy is increasing nowadays, and so is people's physical and psychological capacity for work. No country in the world has such a retirement age. There are even statements by scientists and various groups who consider it should be raised. Several research institutes in Hungary, for instance, are working on a plan to reemploy pensioners so that they do not feel that they have been discarded by fellow-workers and cut off from society.

I asked the research institute of the Ministry of Labour, Wages and Social Security whether the proposal is realistic. They say it would reduce employment in the state sector by about 15 per cent. That means a reduction in national income of 200 000 million złotys per annum, while increasing the cost of pensions by about 90 000 million złotys per annum. Given the present labour shortage and supply situation, this proposal cannot possibly be fulfilled. However, the adjustment of pensions and annuities proposed is justified. This is already under consideration. In any case, it does not say the change must be immediate. From the beginning of 1981, there will be an increase in pensions and annuities of the old portfolio as well as improved pension regulations, aimed both at systematic improvement for those living in the worst conditions, and at reducing excessively high payments.

With regard to Point Sixteen, 'To improve working conditions in the health service, so that full medical care can be provided for all employees', this point is justified, we agree with it. We take it to refer to improved supply of medicines and medical equipment, construction and extension of buildings, to make the health service more effective and accessible to all. I take a personal interest in these matters as someone who suffered a number of ordeals in his life. Let me digress.

I was beaten and tortured in prison for a year. The rest of my family were murdered: father and two brothers. My mother went out of her mind for three years because she was tortured inhumanely. They beat me day and night, three times daily with a whip and a loaded stick. I can show you all my scars. I was imprisoned by the Gestapo in Płock for a year. I had one foot in the other world then and subsequently when faced with the murderous bandits of those days. And a few years ago I was also half dead, not from high living, but after a very serious heart attack. Although not a doctor, medicine does interest me. I dabble a little, so far as time allows.

Certain decisions have already been taken. We are short of pharmaceuticals. We cannot produce all we need, so we cooperate with other socialist countries, particularly the most advanced – Hungary. We have too few pharmaceuticals of our own production or synthesis. Moreover, we lack appropriate concentrates for all medicines, particularly for such illnesses as heart disease, the great new social disease, and cancer.[14] We have decided to build our first Institute of Cardiology. A Cancer Institute exists already. As to imports: we bought some licences. I don't know which exactly: the Vice-Minister was brought here to tell you. A recent decree has also allocated sixty million dollars for the purchase of special medical equipment: X-rays, cardiological and gastroscopic apparatus and the like. So I regard this proposal as justified. This sphere of our social life must be better provided for.

I will take the related Points Seventeen and Eighteen together: 'To provide sufficient crèche and nursery places for the children of working mothers' and 'To grant three years' paid maternity leave, so that a mother can bring up her child.' I think these proposals are justified and can be implemented. The only question is: how quickly can we do so? I was given some figures showing that Gdańsk, for instance, is at present short of 7000 nursery places and 11 000 in kindergartens. Construction of nurseries and kindergartens must be speeded up by every possible means. With regard to paid maternity leave and its duration, I can reply on behalf of the Commission that this proposal is justified and that with the increase of funds it will be implemented. But this will take some time.

Point Nineteen, 'To shorten the waiting-time for flats', is justified. Perhaps the Prefect would like to say a few words on this. Just before coming here, I heard of a proposal thrown up during these events, for construction of two housing factories. I raised the matter at a session of the Politburo then in progress. It was decided to build two housing factories as a matter of urgency and so help resolve this extensive and socially important problem.

Tadeusz Fiszbach: I would like to intervene here, since living problems of people in this region are unusually important, linked as they are with what we have done so far in the sphere of material production. I refer to modernisation of the shipyards and harbours. As you know, I said publicly before these difficult days that the disproportion in investment between the two spheres appeared more sharply and sooner in the Gdańsk Region than anywhere else. I presented this fact, frankly, to a session of the Politburo of the Central Committee on 3 June. The Politburo accepted my view on this and other problems and recommended that the government and Planning Commission take them into account when drawing up the programme for socioeconomic development of the Gdańsk Region for 1981–5. The further decisions just mentioned by the Premier confirm our intention to resolve these important and serious problems.

Jagielski: Point Twenty: 'to increase travelling allowances from 40 to 100 złotys plus compensation for separation from family'. The total cost of this must be calculated. I cannot do it now. This is a matter, a decision, concerning the whole country and we must work out exactly what it would cost. I can say that we accept the point in the sense that it will be considered when the budget for next year is being worked out.

The same applies to Point Twenty-one, 'to make all Saturdays work-free. Employees on a three-shift and four-brigade system,[15] will be compensated for the loss of free Saturdays by extension of annual leave or other paid days off.' That is, we will consider it. Reduction of working hours in Poland began within the context of improved organisation of work; the introduction of a four-brigade system within a forty-three hour week, which we started in 1972. There is a recommendation that a programme be worked out and brought before the *Sejm* as to what the next steps should be concerning free Saturdays. I think the proposal made here should be taken into account, together with problems of unifying the wage system for piecework on free Saturdays and other elements, such as compensation for arduous work and so on. Looking at other socialist countries, we can see various systems of payment for the number of hours worked. By the end of this year – the recommendation is to do so even sooner – a programme for the introduction of free Saturdays will be drawn up and brought before the *Sejm*.

Mr Chairman, members of the audience. I have tried to summarise my views on the points presented. I stress, yet again, that I spoke with a full sense of responsibility for the interests of workers and of the country. I want to say, in conclusion, I spoke in such a way that no one could make the accusation – irrespective of who I am today or tomorrow – that what I said could not be implemented. I want to be honest and able to look everyone straight in the face here in Gdańsk and beyond. I want to be able to come again – and maybe my children – so I spoke with a full sense of responsibility for actual conditions, in order that what we undertake can later be implemented. If I undertook what could not be done, that would simply mean that we were dishonest. Thank you for your attention.

Wałęsa: Thank you. Mr Premier, we have listened to you very carefully. It seems, though, you did not explain why we keep returning the same place. This time it took ten years. I expect that in another ten we will be back again where we are now. We must prevent this. But to prevent it and to draw conclusions, we must know the causes. We have not found out from what you said why we keep going round in circles and returning to the same spot. What guarantees do we have, as workers and employees who want to work and not to have to strike and make demands like this, of what is our due? In my view, something is wrong with the steering, managing and controlling. I am only a worker, but that is how I see it. We will never correct mistakes unless we know what causes them. Though we said we were only to get to know your views, I think, Mr Premier, you should explain to us what the government proposes to do so that we don't go back onto this bad road we have just left.

Jagielski: Amongst other things – I did not manage to note them all down – you said that the causes of events taking place, which we are discussing, are related to there being something wrong with steering and managing. I agree. Something is wrong. I propose you accept the following. Let it be settled – you have to trust me – by what is said about it at the next Central Committee plenum.

Wałęsa: We can tell you what one answer is from our own experience. You can find it in our first proposal: free trade unions, strong and active, as working people desire. This is not a political matter. It is a real counter-balance and control. We will do the controlling ourselves, spot the mistakes, propose solutions. There will never be such methods as are used today: making things difficult for those who want to say or do something by arrests, detention and strengthening the apparatus of power – the militia. That is why things should be controlled. If we are in order, if the authorities and government are in order, they will not have to surround themselves so much with the militia and security service. [*applause*]

Jagielski: I have suggested – and I propose we return later to the subject you have mentioned – I have told you that I agreed with you. Something is wrong with the system of information, managing, steering and planning. So we must make a full survey of all the causes, both those independent of us and those dependent on our activity. Simply to bring all causes to light. This will be discussed in the near future by the plenum of the Central Committee of our Party. It will make a full survey of the causes and present an action programme.

Wałęsa: I propose we finish now. We should fix the date for the next, more detailed discussion, providing that the two conditions set earlier have been met. That is: reconnection of telephones and also our concern that there should not be detentions or arrests. And then we can really talk seriously because we want to help, and we shall help. And our actions will astound the world. We will show how one really does it, but only, exclusively, in the way we understand, the way we wish, our way: through free unions, through our sensible and considered proposals. That is how we will overcome our present troubles. I suggest we end here, fixing a date for our next meeting.

One last thing. I want the communiqué to be drawn up jointly, with agreement of both sides, so that we won't find any more surprises in it. I propose the communiqué be agreed jointly before issuing it. Perhaps not with everybody present, but by representatives of both sides. To see it is all right. We want fair play. And I propose we fix the day and time of our next meeting. We shall wait, because next time we should settle matters like men, not dragging them out but really getting down to work. Because it doesn't look as if we could have a meeting like this again.

Jagielski: We have mentioned reconnection of telephones and agreed to discuss it further after our meeting. I will clear it up. As to the safety of strikers and their helpers, that is guaranteed as we established. The third matter you raised is the communiqué. I am in favour of a joint communiqué, discussed by both sides. No one can write a communiqué at a meeting like this. You should select some people on your side. I know from experience that such a large company cannot write anything. I can tell you what may be done.

Wałęsa: Well, we have draft amendments ready . . .

Jagielski: So I propose to delegate from our side . . .

Wałęsa: And we also request radio transmission, even just in Gdańsk.

Jagielski: I beg your pardon?

Wałęsa: We agreed earlier that the next meeting should be broadcast. Someone may think we want to spread this business. It's not that. But we do want our agreement, if we reach it – and we must – to be understood. So that people who count on us, believe in it and go straight back to work. But only and exclusively when our conditions have been agreed and fulfilled.

Jagielski: So I gather that a fourth matter has been added: broadcast of our talks. Is this so?

Wałęsa: We agreed earlier, at the beginning, that it is possible. After all, there are no problems.

Kołodziejski: Excuse me, but how do you see this, how do you envisage it?

Wałęsa: But you, yourself, told us there was no problem. So I am only keeping you to your word.

Kołodziejski: When did I say so? There is a problem: Gdańsk Television has only limited viewing time of five hours. The same goes for Gdańsk Radio. It is hard to envisage. Today's discussion lasted for two hours didn't it, and this was mainly a preliminary clarification of views. I hope the others are got through so effectively. We could all do with some rest couldn't we? The form in which the relay is to be done must be thought out. I propose that specialists are consulted on this question. I am no specialist on broadcasting. But it would perhaps be a problem if all the radio and television programmes – I am talking of those for Gdańsk – were entirely taken up by our meeting. That would not be in the public interest, nor in ours.

Wałęsa: I propose a solution: longer communiqués, agreed ones.

Jagielski: Yes, that may be the solution. Good. Would the First Secretary – the Chairman of the Regional People's Council – like to speak.

Fiszbach: I do want to address the Presidium of the Strike Committee and Shipyard Workers, as we have been presented with enlarged and additional proposals. We are responding to some of these with definite decisions, others will be considered, beside those so kindly expounded by the Premier under the Twenty-one Points, the basis of our discussion. I want to state very briefly what I feel – and I know this view is shared by those living on the Coast – in addition to what has already been expressed.

A wave of pain and regret is passing through the region, but also one of hope which can I trust be fulfilled with our help. You have put your requests to us, may I make one of my own? It will be a token of what we are hoping for. Tomorrow, communications will be restored. This will be a sign that we began in a spirit of goodwill and that a part of our daily life can be restored. It will signify that we are dealing with matters properly.

Wałęsa: These matters are already agreed. That is why we ask you to deal with them promptly. For, however difficult and unpleasant things are, no factory can break ranks. [*applause*] I suggest we do not prolong this meeting. The Premier certainly has other business to attend to. We should prepare to settle these matters quickly.

Jagielski: I don't have anything more to discuss. I propose . . .

Wałęsa: A date and time?

Jagielski: I propose that the communiqué is prepared by the Prefect, for our side, and someone here will help him. Regarding the time of tomorrow's meeting, I suggest we use the same method as before. That is, we will pass it on through the Prefect, because we must also be in Warsaw tomorrow.

Wałęsa: We shall wait. Let us all sing 'So that Poland should be Polish'. [*They sing.*] We shall wait here patiently for your return. Ladies and gentlemen, I would like us to say a polite farewell to the government delegation. It is certain we shall reach agreement. Everything will be settled as it should be.[16]

SECOND MEETING (26 AUGUST)

Wałęsa: I welcome the Prime Minister and Government Commission to the Gdańsk Shipyard for the second meeting with the Interfactory Strike Committee. We all hope this meeting will be fruitful for our country. In a moment, we shall discuss those demands of workers striking on the Coast which the Strike Committee included in its list. Three important days have passed since we last met.[1] I hope that the new situation which emerged during this interval will make discussion easier. Matters raised by the strike demands are very important. For us, the most important is that concerning trade unions. We want free, independent and really self-governing unions. The economic position of the country is difficult and in crisis. This came about because working people did not have their own, authentic, union representation.

You can see from talking to us, Prime Minister, that we are not fighting against the socialist system. We are fighting for our own trade unions, a right due to us amongst others put forward on our list of demands. We do not want to disturb the basis of the social ownership of the means of production. We regard our workplaces as the property of the Polish nation. We demand proper management both of factories and of the country as a whole. This has been promised to us time and again. Now we have decided to back our demand with a strike. The question of unions will be explained in greater detail by my colleagues Gwiazda, Lis and others. Our talks will not be easy. We must all have great patience and goodwill. [*applause*]

Perhaps, Prime Minister, you would like to put forward something new, in the situation which has now arisen? If not, then we will start to present our position on Point One in more detail.
Jagielski: Mr Chairman, this is the first time I have had the pleasure of being filmed continuously by a television camera. Can the lights be switched off? They are no help to us, simply unnecessary, a technical thing. As I told you, my eyesight was damaged by the period in prison.

[*Short, indistinct, dialogue.*]

Mr Chairman, until the arrival of our experts who will hear your point of view on the subject of free trade unions, I will attempt to summarise what was said at the last meeting, supplying any new information that has been transmitted to us and our further thoughts on certain issues. I want to begin by expressing my personal satisfaction in the fact that we are meeting again and are able to discuss questions which we regarded and do still regard as of essential importance for the working people of the Gdańsk Region. At the last meeting, I presented and elaborated the views of the Commission on the Twenty-one Points. I want to add only one observation – which is on my conscience. I received information that some figures were circulated, casting doubt on the sincerity of my pronouncements and will to conduct negotiations, on account of the circulation of some leaflet.[2] I want, therefore, to state that I know of no such leaflet. I affirm that it is simply untrue. I did not know anything about it then and I still know nothing now. I started work on Friday. That evening I met representatives of the Strike Committee Presidium and on Saturday we began talks. I came with the Commission, again, as I said, on Saturday evening, so that we could together resolve outstanding problems in a straightforward and constructive manner. And now I would like to sum up what and how, in concrete terms, the Commission of which I am head proposes to settle.

I expressed myself positively and unambiguously towards the majority of proposals which directly concern the interests of the workforce on the Coast – those that are most vital for employees, which interest them the most, those relating to their living conditions, work, their families and friends. I can say sincerely, speaking with full sense of responsibility, that I assumed what is just and realistic must be settled quickly – that is, dealt with – and the decisions passed on to those concerned. A communiqué has already been issued on the opening of talks with the Interfactory Strike Committee. Publication of my speech will acquaint the public with the full proposals of the Interfactory Strike Committee.

We agreed with you that it is appropriate to publish full information about the social and economic position of the country and to enable all groups to participate in discussion of a reform programme. We confirm that as government representatives we have no right to dispose of Central Trade Union Council funds. Strike pay may be awarded but lost production must be made up by agreement between the workforce and management. It will be financed from the wage fund. Concerning, for instance, Points Eight and Nine, I gave an extensive explanation and proposed that a good starting-point will be the holding of talks with the Ministers and Deputy Ministers here from various sectors of industry, on matters of wage increases, improved working conditions, social and other problems of concern to the workforce. Wage rises have been awarded to shipyard and harbour workers, machine-industry workers, for light industry, food industry and – I want to emphasise this – to public transport employees. For these groups, matters are settled: those which, as I understand it, were the cause of strikes. Point Ten, for instance, is justified. We are concerned to improve market supplies. There are no export surpluses, but we retain traditional exports. I mentioned on Saturday that we are importing 50 000–60 000 tons of meat: following a decision of the Government Presidium yesterday, it will be 60,000 tons. We are exploring further ways to increase meat supplies. We regard Point Eleven as a just proposal: it is right to apportion meat justly. Introduction of ration cards would give rise to a number of difficulties. We do not rule it out. Why don't you propose a way of doing it? I presented arguments and explanations pertaining to Point Twelve. Point Thirteen – justified – we accept and undertake to draw up a programme for raising family allowances by the end of November. Point Fifteen likewise. We cannot equalise all pensions at once. Pensions under the old scheme will be increased, beginning next year. I wish to state that what I told you is true. Some people rang up to question whether I was right about family allowances for non-working wives of militiamen. In fact the allowance is 300–400 złotys if they bring up children, but there is a differential family allowance depending upon the point on the wage scale. I will give you details when we find the document. Points Sixteen, Seventeen and Eighteen – improving the working conditions for those in the health service and improving medical care; increasing the number of crèche and nursery places for children of working women; shortening the waiting time for flats – are all justified and will be implemented.

Kołodziejski: We confirm the decision to construct two new housing factories for the Gdańsk Region.

Jagielski: Mr Chairman, I said at the outset I would fulfil all obligations I undertake on behalf of the Commission to the best of my ability. I promised there would be telephone links between Gdańsk and Szczecin. That was the first undertaking. When I got back to Warsaw I went straight to a plenum of the Politburo. Afterwards, that same night, I clarified matters, and, following a session of the Government Presidium, came back to Gdańsk. The purpose was to restore telephone links between Gdańsk and Warsaw. You told me there was no connection but I discovered there is a semi-automatic one. I am not myself a specialist, so I have asked Deputy Minister Wyłupek, who is, to explain everything so that there would be an automatic connection between Gdańsk and Warsaw.

Bądkowski: I rang Warsaw direct and did get a connection immediately.

Another Voice: There is a connection.

Gwiazda: Prime Minister, there is a special code one dials from the exchange in Gdańsk to have the blockade lifted. I managed to get an automatic connection, probably through such a code.

Jagielski: Please explain from where you are.

Stanisław Wyłupek: Esteemed Comrade Prime Minister, members of the audience. In accordance with my instructions from Comrade Prime Minister Jagielski, I would like to explain the situation which arose during the last, so to speak, burning days through which we are living in Gdańsk. I want to state categorically and responsibly that telecommunications between Warsaw and the whole of Poland have been maintained throughout this period. [*Noise in the Hall.*] In the first phase, the accumulation of demands for telephone connections was so tremendous that the central exchange made mistakes, registers began to overheat and fuses blew up in flames. Automatic connections were therefore switched off, but operator connections kept going all the time. Yesterday, for instance, we received more than 4000 bookings and made 3840 connections to various locations. [**Question:** From these 4000 bookings?] Yes, of more than 4000 calls booked, only 300 were not connected, mostly to Warsaw. Following instructions given me by the Comrade Prime Minister, automatic connections were yesterday switched back on.

Members of the audience: exactly the same happened as on the first day. I spoke today to the manager of the Central Exchange who told me that the rush was so horrendous during the night that the same phenomena occurred. Moreover, there are various dialling codes from Gdańsk for different cities. I quote here: Bydgoszcz 15, Łódź 14, Katowice 13, Koszalin 194, Olsztyn 18, Słupsk 195, Szczecin 191, Toruń 10, Wrocław 17. Here we are dealing with the phenomenon that everyone trying to get a connection with these codes immediately receives the engaged tone, so horrendously has our equipment got overloaded by the traffic that wants to generate out from here. Naturally, we maintained operator connections with all parts of the country. We are able to accept all calls which get through to us. As the example of yesterday showed, the majority were connected. We could not connect every one because the excessive overburdening of our equipment made it impossible to deal with them all simultaneously.

Gruszecki: It seems somewhat strange that in this age of electronics and high technology in telecommunication, when something is happening here and only here on the Coast, a blockade should suddenly occur. You tell us that the blockade is purely technical, but the whole audience of Strike Committee delegates, and ordinary people, are convinced that it is neither a pure accident, nor a technical failure, but deliberate. To prove it is not deliberate, I think the government should meet us half way, by making accessible some means of communicating with the rest of Poland, whose fuses do not blow, whose electronic equipment does not get overburdened. Namely: radio and television.

There would not have been such a stampede in the telephone exchanges if the press had written about us properly – properly in the sense of truthfully: if the press had come here and listened to ordinary working people like me. I am a working man, even though my job is at the Gdańsk Technical University. We have here a cross-section of all occupations: farmers, health service employees and people with no affiliation whatever. As we mentioned, many private individuals came to us for information. The Prime Minister must be well-informed about the information famine not just here on the coast but nationwide. It was mentioned in the Prime Minister's speech, as published in *Dziennik Bałtycki*. I fail to understand why it was not mentioned in the press release nor in *Trybuna Ludu*.

Gwiazda: Minister, according to my information – it did not come from experts – last night's blockade included: Katowice, Łódź, Poznań, Bydgoszcz, Wrocław, Olsztyn, Lublin and Toruń. I don't know about other cities. It was possible to phone Warsaw.

Wiśniewski: At issue here are public feelings and everything that the Interfactory Strike Committee stands for. There were various attempts to provoke us. They wanted to drag us into politics, pure politics. That's the real problem, as you surely know. We had great difficulty getting our truth out. We had to resort to leafletting and other means because we were isolated. We had to pass on information. The rest of the world was informed, all the foreign news agencies were here. Only ours were missing. People came from our broadcasting stations, serious reporters, and said privately 'Well, I want to relay this, but I can't guarantee that it will be. You know what it's like.'[3] It was just plain censorship. So we had to take action ourselves. They simply slandered us.

Reasons for our gathering here are plain for all to see. Our action is completely apolitical. It is basically social and economic. We want to bring the truth out by reasoned argument and popular pressure. We know that those Poles who brought the economy to its present state, who made the mistakes and bear the responsibility, are still there hindering us. They are frightened of the truth and base their arguments on their lofty positions. They are scared of losing their jobs. But these matters are important to the whole nation. We want to get out of this crisis. We can argue our case and know what has to be done. We are genuine people, whom the public trusts. That is why it is so important for us to reach the outside. There is no question of anything 'against the government' and so on. I ask you to pass this on.

Wałęsa: We are together on this issue. No one wants to come back every ten years to the same point. Something must be done about it. The fact is we don't want political games of any sort. We want straight dealings like those of peasants or workers. We will show you how. Do understand us: we don't want power. We don't want more stoppages, more strikes. This is a last resort, a necessity. But we must have this point. We really won't give it up. Even if we get the twenty points but not this one there will be no agreement. [*Arrival of government experts.*]

Jagielski: I must repeat one sentence of my opening remarks, which perhaps you did not hear. I want to express my great satisfaction in the fact that we are meeting again, and are together – as you yourself just said – able to discuss questions which we regarded and do still regard as of essential importance for working people of the Gdańsk Region. I expressed my attitude last Saturday towards all the specific matters outstanding and will, therefore, not repeat myself now. I tried to resolve then what can be resolved, and specified the date and method of implementation. I agreed with the great majority of issues relating to the interests of the workforce: wage increases, pay adjustments, working conditions, job safety, improved food supplies and an improved health service. I accepted them in a positive way, defining the size of wage increases for shipyard workers, dockers, workers in machine tools, construction, public transport and others. I thought this was what the demands were about and that it was my duty to deal with them. Had I not done so, you would have said 'What have you come here for, if you do not want to deal with these things?' I did deal with them.

Mr Chairman, I would like to say, well, I would like to come to the point which may be expressed thus: I think we are in a position to settle all matters included in your Twenty-one Points. I reply, with full sense of responsibility, that we shall sit down after the meeting and write them out: Point One – settled, how and when. Point Two – settled, and so on. There are three points outstand-

ing, starting from Point One which you, Mr Chairman, treat as the most vital.

Wałęsa: Not only me – everyone! [*applause*]

Jagielski: I understand that you are the Chairman and so speak on behalf of the whole meeting. I think you said you have three people who are to speak on this, didn't you? [**Answer:** Yes.] So, perhaps I shall give you my opinion once again. As to the most vital matter, this is Point One, isn't it? I reply: you know my views on this from Saturday's meeting, don't you? [**From the Hall:** Yes.]

So now I will come to the nub of the problem. It was said that renewal of trade union activity is an important and urgent task. I believe there is a Central Trade Union Council Plenum today. I say 'I believe' because I am fully occupied with this work. It is essential that steps be taken which open the way to a radical improvement of the situation and allow the trade union movement to strengthen its class character and regain its position amongst the masses. It is planned to hold trade union leadership elections without delay, in every factory where the workforce wishes them. I propose that such elections be conducted throughout the Gdańsk region within the next few days or weeks, as you prefer. Such elections must be democratic,[5] by secret ballot.

The Central Committee Plenum just held, proposed that 'if – and democratic elections will show this – the authority of representatives who emerged so recently in certain factories proves lasting, then such people will find themselves in the new union leadership'.[6] Our Party – for in this sphere I speak for the Party since trade unions are not subordinate to the government – our Party, considers that the primary and overriding function of trade unions is to defend the interests of employees. Genuine fulfilment of this trade union function is an essential element in preventing deformation of the state's economic policy and in shaping proper relationships between management and the labour force. I said this on Saturday and it was later confirmed by the Plenum. I spoke here feeling the atmosphere, the climate of opinion, which your representatives mentioned to me during our brief Friday meeting. I conveyed the atmosphere of our Saturday meeting to the Plenum, saying that it would be sensible to pass a new law on trade unions. Experience shows it would be advantageous to include regulations within the law which, so to speak, lay down the conditions and procedures for work stoppages as a form of pressing workers' claims when all other remedies, more expedient and appropriate from the social point of view, have been exhausted.

One of you suggested we might change the Labour Code. Mr Chairman, you said yourself: 'A strike is not the best solution.' I share your view. We think it should be included in the law but realistic conditions should be attached, as they are the world over. After all, strikes do take place. That much I can say. I spoke throughout in all sincerity. I consider my position to be well-founded. Is it essentially – essentially, not nominally – so different from your aspirations?

Gwiazda: Prime Minister, High Commission!

We meet amidst a social and economic crisis whose origins we should ponder and define clearly. For many years, the Polish economy, its regional authorities and different branches of industry, have all been run on the basis of the quantity of coal, the amount of steel, the metres of cable and so on, to be produced. No thought was given to what life is like for ordinary people: workers, teachers, engineers and clerks in offices. There were trade unions whose declared purpose was to defend the interests of working people. They did not do so, quite the contrary. Dominated by the factory administration, making life easy for directors, terrified by whispers of dissatisfaction at union meetings, and ever ready to come out hand in glove with the factory administration which blindly followed directives from above, these unions acted against the interests of the workforce.

We should recall the Marxist theory of crises, formulated in conditions of early capitalism. Then enterprises, factory owners, pursued profit at any price, neglecting the living conditions and wages of employees – the real producers. Under our system, this was converted into blind implementation of directives, plan fulfilment and overfulfilment. The absurdities that were reached are best illustrated by the fact that although a central plan can only be implemented when it is precisely detailed and all-embracing with precise calculation of the needs of each factory, our press and publications simultaneously propagate plan overfulfilment. Prime Minister, if a plan is overfulfilled in one factory, that disturbs the flow between branches and bottlenecks must occur somewhere. We were told recently, I think by the Minister of Communications, why the railways cannot function properly:

industry overfulfils its plan but railways had only prepared to transport the planned amount.

We know that the stability of market economies is ensured by trade unions. Our system is completely different, but crises happen here time and again: 1956, 1970, 1976 and 1980. They recur after shorter intervals. These were not just political crises, they were also economic. All were caused by the fact that working people had no influence over what was happening. Despite paper democracy, the worker had no influence over what was done even in his own union and factory, let alone in the state. We were forced to abstain from work for so long, sleeping on the floor, not because of whimsicality but by necessity and by our realisation that economic concessions, hasty increases of wages or allowances, are worthless in themselves. They can only cause inflation and deepen the crisis. Our concern is with the future: so that we won't have to go back on strike after a fortnight or a month. The electoral system of the existing unions makes it practically impossible for employees to exercise any influence over what goes on within the factory, let alone over what the state is doing. These unions have lost all trust and authenticity. Trust will not be restored by means of a new law because the public has also lost faith in laws. Nor will the shipyard, whose employees are in this hall, now have faith in any law. Our aim is to create a genuine organisation for employees, in which people can have confidence.

Ladies and gentlemen, Poland ratified ILO Conventions 87 and 98 through the *Sejm* on 14 December 1956. They not only guarantee trade union freedoms but also provide for the creation of new unions. Yet guarantees of an existing organisation, even legal ones, cannot be depended on. Every organisation may degenerate. It may be manipulated from outside or from within. History provides countless instances of such degeneration. Numerous institutions and organisations which had all the capacities for fulfilling their appointed tasks instead became deformed monsters. Trade unions, even new ones, can go the same way. The only means of counteracting it is to have the right to keep creating new ones. I admit this could lead to a degree of disorder. Unions may be established with only a few hundred members. Radical unions may appear which go on strike every few days. But I think agreement can always be reached in such cases. Polish society, as seen here on the Coast, has demonstrated its rationality, calmness and maturity. The applause we hear from the hall every time the words 'free unions' are mentioned is evidence that people have already matured. People don't believe in ephemeral improvements. They realise that economic concessions alone – wage rises – cannot solve the problem.

Prime Minister, not so long ago a 50 groszy roll was bigger than a fist, now you can hold a 90 groszy roll in it. Suppose we do get these extra 2000 złotys. It may turn out in no time at all that our wages, even with these additional 2000, are worth half what they are at the moment. Take my own case. I could buy more basic products as a student than now after twenty years of work. To gain the confidence of employees and of the working class, new unions should be created. New ones – we are not concerned about the name. [*applause*] I am personally opposed to disbanding the old ones. That would be a breach of the *Sejm* statute, since Article 4 of Convention No. 87 states that no employees' organisation can be suspended or dissolved by administrative fiat. This seems obvious to us. Many legal and regulatory problems remain to be discussed, such as cooperation between these unions – two or more – if we are to restore the real meaning of the ILO Convention, as ratified and binding in Poland.

It is precisely this social maturity seen here on the Coast, and the calmness which accompanied the Pope's visit, that prove agreement can be reached. No doubt the problems are multi-layered and complex. Under the terms of the ILO Convention, we will have to modify the 1949 law on trade unions, Articles 52, 64 and 65 of the Labour Code, and a great many other instructions and decrees regulating union activity. In general, however, interunion agreement will have to be a process of mutual adjustment, without drastic legal changes.

Trade unions cannot function without access to their members. Mass organisations cannot operate simply by private conversations. They must be provided with publications of their own to convey information from the top down, and from the bottom up. They must have their own press and be able to write the truth in it, regardless of whether this suits the authorities. [*applause*] Our press would then cease its efforts to manipulate society. Such manipulation tends to work. It does bring results, but they are, regrettably, short-lived. Society realises in the end. Indignation flares up, ferment spreads and the next explosion occurs. I think Poles have heard quite enough about 'mistakes' and 'distortions' which recur with every cycle. [*applause*]

We want to uncover mistakes before they grow to such proportions that it is almost necessary to make a revolution in the country.

Were public opinion to be listened to now, immediately and without restriction, then I think we could together avoid mistakes. But for its voice to be heard, the public must have an organisation of its own which no one dominates. Employees must have freedom of expression, enabling them to speak out both when they are right and when they are not. Discussion is only possible when speakers are heard who cannot be assumed to have had the authorities' approval beforehand. [*applause*] Of course the question arises: who is to decide which of the speeches is correct? Thus far, it was only up to the authorities. I reemphasise, therefore, the popular will here on the Coast is to create new unions, independent and self-governing.

We are aware of the difficulties that will arise in creating such unions. If they really are to come into existence, there will have to be special regulations and guarantees concerning their scope and organisation, formation and drafting of statutes. We are waiting for a government declaration promising that the future unions will not encounter any obstacles to legal registration.[7] [*applause*] We shall start working out the statute as soon as the union is formed[8] and the statute will also be registered. I consider that the new union must have a say in the division of national income between investment and consumption. According to our figures, Prime Minister, only one quarter of the national product is earmarked for society: the rest is ploughed back into production for production. Such a policy is impossible in the long run. We have been developing, investing, investing and investing for thirty-five years, but so far society has little to show for it. Finally, trade unions must do research of their own into the living conditions of employees. They must be able to influence them, by making statutory proposals in draft form. Depriving trade unions of this ability has meant that our laws lost touch with the interests of ordinary people. [*applause*] [*Commotion. Voice indistinct.*]

Jagielski: Perhaps it would be best if all those down to speak should do so. After they have spoken on free trade unions, we will have a short interval and then open the discussion.

Wałęsa: Next to speak is our colleague, Lis.

Bogdan Lis: Prime Minister, we don't see why the government is trying so hard to reorganise the old trade unions rather than agreeing to form new ones. The old trade unions are so discredited that even our joining the leadership would not restore them. We don't want an infusion of new blood, we want a completely new organism. The new unions need more than a right to be formed. We want legal guarantees that they will be able to act effectively in the interests of all employees at every level, starting from the enterprise. We . . .

Jagielski: I didn't hear your last point.

Lis: We want legal guarantees that they will be able to act effectively in the interest of all employees at all levels, starting from the enterprise. We demand the creation of such conditions. We are ready to transform the present factory strike committees into founding committees of new trade unions, and the Interfactory Strike Committee into the Interfactory Founding Committee. [*applause*] As my colleague Gwiazda has already said, we are guaranteed this by ILO Convention No. 87. We want the government to guarantee the freedom of activity of the new union. That is what I had to say at the moment. Thank you.

Wiśniewski: As I am the only person on the Strike Presidium from the building industry, my colleagues have delegated me to express our problems. Although construction workers are dispersed all over Poland, we have interests in common. Our problems should be heard here, since the ones presented in the media are marginal and do not reflect the truth.

I feel that we are meeting here because we have confidence in each other as people of goodwill. We have gathered here in the Interfactory Strike Committee, which represents those on strike in more than 400 workplaces in the region, to resolve these problems. We are bound together by common views. The basic cause of the economic crisis which brought us here is lack of representation of the interests of working people in economic decision-taking. This is so particularly over the division of the national and social product. At present only 26 per cent of what Poland produces is consumer goods. This is the latest figure, given in *Trybuna Ludu* on 23 August. Almost all the rest is devoured by heavy industry, defence and so on. In the absence of social control industry produces for itself. Such control, at all levels, can only be ensured by independent, self-governing, free trade unions. [*applause*]

A second cause of the crisis is economic anarchy. Unrealistically high plans are imposed from above and then revised downwards in the middle of each five-year period. Uncompleted investment projects stand idly in fields. A great proportion of foreign borrowing is wasted in this way. The plans neglect energy and transport. Stoppages in the last six months due to lack of energy and transport grew 56 per cent, according to a Central Statistical Office report, and we know it is really worse than that, particularly in construction. These aren't called stoppages, officially they are 'underutilisation of working time'. I am a senior foreman with a diploma. I took a course for foremen. I met many colleagues with whom I discussed such magnificent subjects as ergonomics, the psychology of work and sociology. Things that give an absolute guarantee of good work. But to do that we must have properly supplied workshops and building sites. That's the real problem.

The views of those of us who deal with these things every day must be taken seriously because we are in effect experts on construction. Take the two housing factories proposed: there are plenty of people here who know about this. It would be good if they could put forward their opinions, though this need not be discussed in such a large gathering. More housing is needed, but not necessarily more investment.[9] Existing housing factories are not used to full capacity. When you put up such a colossus, such a moloch, you have to transport what you build long distances, and transport is very costly. Factories which don't require such transportation are preferable. Bad management costs more than strikes.

Economic reform is imperative. [*applause*] We know that when such reform is first introduced, it can be painful for the workforce. The powers that be and the existing unions have no authority amongst workers. [*applause*] Economic reform can only be carried out with the support and participation of independent, self-governing, free trade unions. Working people simply must have confidence. We have to unite if we are to rise from the depths of this crisis. Only the formation of independent trade unions across the whole country, without the manipulation that has happened so far, can guarantee a way out of the present crisis and economic chaos. I speak here on behalf of building workers. We are employed all over the country and know what it is like there. Believe me, we really do care about it. [*applause*]

It is essential that there should be control over the authorities' decisions in the social and economic spheres. Reforms of management and planning are imperative. Here again, only free, independent and self-governing unions can bring them about. There are people here with genuine authority, who could take the initiative in these difficult circumstances and show us the way forward. We are determined to find it. After all, why did we assemble here, why did we go on strike? Just for its own sake? No, we want to find a way to settle everything and we think the government has understood this by now. Do, please, have confidence in us, so that we can really put this right, for Poland.

On hearing what the Chairman of the Central Trade Union Council, Szydlak, had said, these 400 or so workforces took a considered decision to withdraw from the existing trade unions. We don't want to break the law, and are not dissolving the old unions. We don't have that right. We are just leaving them. We want to create these free, independent trade unions in order to rescue our nation. This is our fundamental duty. We are all Poles. We simply want to settle economic matters, internal to our country. Working people have that right. [*applause*]

Sobieszek: May I express my hope that the incident with the telephones will not recur? Had today's session not gone ahead, I feel sure we would all have been talking in the big hall, watched by everyone to see how we were responding and what our general behaviour was. I also want to express my anxiety over the Prime Minister's statement to the effect that the new trade unions apply only in the Gdańsk Region. [*applause*] I appeal to your hearts, gentlemen: you are Poles too. Statements like these can bring the whole country out on strike.[10] [*applause*] We should issue a national appeal, explaining our proposals and what the issues are, so that society as a whole can express its opinions on them, in order to avert a tragedy. This is not a matter of the private welfare of you government representatives, but concerns the whole of society, which is ours and not to be trifled with. [*applause*]

May I add, to avoid any misunderstanding, that no Pole really cares whether one gentlemen or another occupies this high position or that. My friends, that honestly does not concern us. We are concerned that these gentlemen should function as a healthy organism, permitting themselves to be criticised from time to time, whether rightly or wrongly, so that the flow of information is truthful and honest. [*applause*]

Jagielski: I gather you have all made the point about trade unions the major one. None of you has mentioned any other. In a moment, I shall have a proposal to make. But first I must mention that I was hurt by what you said. I have feelings too. I came as chairman of a commission on problems of the Coast. It is not within my competence to deal with problems of the country as a whole. I have concentrated on my mission; to come and discuss problems of the Coast. I had no intention of causing anxiety. On the contrary, I sought a constructive solution from the start.

My proposal, Mr Chairman, is for a ten-minute interval while we consider our position on matters as you have presented them. We will use it to determine our attitude towards the point you say is the major one.

Wałęsa: Prime Minister, I may add . . . All right, we'll have the break.

Kobyliński: Prime Minister, Ladies and Gentlemen. Previous speakers have just about exhausted matters relating to the existing union. I would like to add one small example from here on the Coast, of how little say it had on behalf of the workforce. We have two housing factories here, one at Gdynia and one at Kokoszki. The Gdynia factory is at present operating at one third of capacity and the other at half capacity. The machinery at the Kokoszki factory needs cement of only two types, but is supplied from twenty-one separate mills. This fouls up the works, as pointed out time and again by employees, engineers, technicians and economists. Nobody takes any notice. Even engineers from Gdynia, whom I can name, have pointed this out, but no one listened to them either. The fact is that our present trade unions do absolutely nothing and never have done anything – or if they did it was utterly insignificant.

May I go back to what the Prime Minister said about these two new housing factories planned for the Coast? The design office here should be consulted because their view is that new factories are unnecessary. Full utilisation of existing ones would be sufficient to meet the demand for flats from people working on the Coast.

Jagielski: Your opinion on the housing factories is justified and acceptable. You know, in this situation, no decision should be taken without specialists.

Wałęsa: I suggest we have the break.

[*Interval*]

Wałęsa: I have a request. Since some people don't know that we have started talks, it would be good to issue a short, joint communiqué saying that talks have begun.

Jagielski: Can I be heard? I propose we follow the procedure agreed last Saturday. A short communiqué should be prepared and issued after our meeting as we did then.

Wałęsa: But it would be good to have a short announcement that talks have begun.

Jagielski: We can have both: talks began, talks continued and so on. The text will be agreed in the same way as before.

I noticed that your speeches, to which we listened with all due respect, were all sharply critical of the conduct of trade unions. You provided various instances, both of a general character and from your own particular experiences, which indicated shortcomings in trade union activity. I can say, on behalf of the Commission, that we are in full agreement with such criticisms. Our views on this are identical. From what you said, I feel that we share a similar determination to renew the trade unions, to make them fulfil the function that unions, in the nature of things, should fulfil. I will not repeat myself: you heard my position. We listened to yours, most attentively I would say. You emphasised that this subject is very difficult to resolve in detail. Mr Gwiazda, I recall, even used the world 'multilayered': requiring detailed elaborations. This is what I propose: let us, without interrupting the work of our committee, choose a group of three people from our number who will work out the particular problems in more detail. Once Prefect Kołodziejski has consulted briefly by telephone, we will be able to announce, without troubling you further, who is selected on our side. To save time, these people could start work after a short break.

Wałęsa: This is tricky, because you are still talking about curing or correcting. We are not talking about cures or corrections. We are talking about creating new unions. So we don't quite understand each other. [*applause*]

Jagielski: I do understand, Mr Chairman, I do. Let's follow our usual procedure: we put our point of view and you yours. While they work out some of the details, we shall discuss these problems further. Now let us set a time for the next meeting.

Bądkowski: Excuse me, are you talking about a group of three?

Jagielski: Yes. Do you think it should be larger?

Bądkowski: No, I think a group of three.

Jagielski: No, no, three on each side.

Lis: I hope experts could take part?

Jagielski: I expect so.

Lis: Does that mean our meeting is now closed?

Jagielski: I would not say it is finished for the day, but rather is suspended for a while. The working group will commence, with experts as you wished,[11] and then we shall arrange the time of our next meeting.

Wałęsa: Prime Minister, I still demand a clear answer: free trade unions or patching up these ones? We really must come to an agreement on this, man to man, because I still don't understand. We must have a clear answer: free unions or the old ones, corrected and patched up? Our starting-point is still not clear.

Jagielski: Mr Chairman, I repeat that I am not prejudging any issue. I would like us to discuss this in a smaller group. Let us examine it more closely. Our side will listen to the views you have expressed here, in more detail, and you will hear what we have said, again in greater detail. It seems to me that is the only way to negotiate, to conduct talks.

Sobieszek: I would not like to ridicule anyone, but I think there is simply a misunderstanding here. Our demand for free trade unions is clear but the Prime Minister just sticks to his conditions about modernising the old ones. That's not what we are after. That's really not it at all. It's just fudging the issue. [*Noise in the hall.*]

Pardon the expression, but that is how I feel. We cannot agree to any troikas. We must discuss everything here in open session. With experts, if necessary, but without the troikas. These are our demands and we won't give them up.

Jagielski: I must tell you that I am not 'sticking' to any 'old unions'. I said there must be a renewal of trade union activity. You said yourselves they should be new, even using the word 'new' rather than 'free'. I proposed a working group because it is difficult to express an *ad hoc* view on some matters. The group may be larger if you like, but we should have to think about it.

Wałęsa: So, we on our side will have everything down on paper and wait quietly for your decision. We will simply accept it or discuss it all over again. Is this agreed?

Member of Government Commission: Your spokesmen

Mr Gwiazda and Mr Lis must themselves realise that some things need spelling out in greater detail. They were mentioned in very general terms.

Wałęsa: May we simply treat the troikas as unofficial and not binding?

Jagielski: Yes. What the experts say – well, not experts, not troikas, let's just call them a working group – will not be binding. They are only to define positions more precisely on the basis of the International Convention. You quote the Convention. So do we. Here we are in agreement. It won't be a position binding on anyone, we don't want to impose anything.

If need be, we shall come back with a further proposal. We must think it over. You said yourselves that the matter is very important.

Wałęsa: Of course, very important.

Gwiazda: Prime Minister, Esteemed Commission!

There seems some misunderstanding here on our part. We welcome changes or proposed changes to the existing unions. After all, we shall have to collaborate with them closely when we set up our own. I cannot imagine two union organisations, or more if need be, which would not cooperate because this would run counter to the interests of working people: their members. We really do welcome promises or attempts to modernise these unions, so that they represent the real interests of employees, because this will facilitate our cooperation with them.

'New' unions or 'old'? Well, we want to create unions which the public can trust. For this to come about we are convinced that the present unions will have to change. The coexistence of many unions will guarantee that none can detach themselves from society, since there will then be a free flow of members between them.

Wałęsa: I propose we end here, sending off the troikas and keeping in touch by telephone. We still have to prepare a communiqué and set the time of our next meeting. We would like to continue later today . . .

Member of Government Commission: When will we have your proposals in writing?

Wałęsa: We shall consider them in half an hour and in an hour's time put them to the delegates' plenum. The troika can be sent, but where?

Kołodziej: Everyone demands open sessions, not behind closed doors.

Wałęsa: It is not binding, nothing will be decided. It is simply to talk things over. The decision will be made in this forum.

Jagielski: I agree with what the Chairman has said.

Wałęsa: Thank you.

Jagielski: Thank you, gentlemen.

THIRD MEETING (28 AUGUST)

Wałęsa: Let's begin our meeting. On behalf of the Interfactory Strike Committee, I welcome the Prime Minister and government delegation. Has the government side determined its position on the first point?

Jagielski: First of all, I want to thank you for your welcome and mention that we are meeting for the third time. The number three is significant: it symbolises something. It would be good if this meeting were the last, in the sense of resolving the problems constructively.

Our experts worked with representatives of your commission on Point One.[1] Numerous questions were raised by both sides, and a good number of them were cleared up. May I suggest that we listen to your views on matters which we put forward and then try to make certain proposals of our own. We have also been thinking. We think all the time. We ponder on these matters.

Wałęsa: In that case, while we are having all this typed out, I propose we move on to Points Three and Four. When we have discussed them, we will return to Point One and state our position.

Jagielski: I accept.

Wałęsa: So, Point Three. Mr Bądkowski to speak.

Bądkowski: Point Three states: 'To uphold freedom of expression and publication as guaranteed by the Constitution, not to suppress independent publishing and to grant access to the mass media for representatives of all denominations.' The point is put briefly and we all know what it means, but some elaboration may be needed to make quite clear what the Strike Committee is demanding and what it seeks to achieve.

I want to quote, by way of illustration, from a somewhat surprising source. This is the speech of Władysław Gomułka at the Central Committee Plenum of October 1956.[2] It is only a section, but not out of context: 'There was much evil in those years. The legacy which this period left the Party, working class and nation in some spheres was more than disquieting.' Here is Gomułka again on one of the subjects we are discussing: 'At the cost of huge investment input, we have built a motor car factory in Warsaw. A new production enterprise has been created which provides, at disproportionately high production cost, a tiny number of old-fashioned motor vehicles, wasteful of fuel and of a type which no one else manufactures in the modern world.' We know many cases in which these words remain broadly relevant today.

Here is another highly characteristic quotation. 'We drew large credits for industrial development. When the first repayments became due, we found ourselves in the position of insolvent bankrupts. We had to ask our creditors for a moratorium. Those managing the economy were apparently unable to grasp the elementary fact that credit should be invested so that output itself will repay the creditors.' Or again: 'The balance of payments over the five-year plan is seriously in deficit.' Another example: 'The Party Central Committee could not bring itself to punish those responsible for this state of affairs.' From a different sphere, also typical of the present situation: 'It was great political naivety, a clumsy effort, to blame the painful Poznań tragedy on imperialist agents and provocateurs.'[3] We also encountered a clumsy effort of this kind when these events began. Unfortunately our history has a tendency to cyclicality and the worst parts of it repeat. Gomułka again: 'Elections will be held under a new law which gives people the chance to elect not merely to vote.' Now my final quotation: 'Truth is inescapable. If hidden, it will re-emerge as a menacing ghost which haunts and frightens, protests and enrages.' It is clear that words spoken so long ago remain highly relevant today.

At the outset of these events, attempts were made to steer the workers into making purely material demands. They responded by demanding their full rights as citizens. This led to the call for authentic and self-governing trade unions. There followed the demand for regulation of the Office for Control over Press and Publications – as the censorship is known – instead of the present, preventive censorship. The degree of maturity and responsibility now attained by workers freely associated in the Strike

Committee was indicated when they turned to eminent scholars with a request for assistance in defining their convictions more precisely. This was an expressive, and I would not hesitate to say beautiful, illustration of the genuine and vital links between workers and the intelligentsia – so often just an empty phrase. Let us rejoice that this fact has been demonstrated at such a difficult time. It offers a ray of hope that an agreement will be reached, not only one acceptable to the parties concerned, but one advantageous to the country as a whole.

Mr Chairman, Gentlemen. We fully realise that regulation of the controls over the press and publications – the censorship – must be carefully considered. It will be conducted within the framework of the Polish legal system in accordance with two basic principles: protection of the fundamental security of the state and observance of Poland's position in the international system. No doubt we will go into more detail during the discussion. Here I only underline emphatically that those of us associated in the Strike Committee do appreciate the security interests of Poland and the permanence of her alliance, the Warsaw Pact. The problem of independent publishing, outside the censorship, arises here. We are looking for a way to implement the constitutional right of Polish citizens to express their views in public and to produce books and journals. This includes the rights of believers – also mentioned in Point Three – who probably constitute an overwhelming majority of the population.

I will conclude with my earlier remark: workers associated in the Interfactory Strike Committee are entitled to full rights as citizens and are now demanding them vociferously. [*applause*]

Jagielski: We quite agree with the general line you take. You quoted the historic, or rather historical speech of former First Secretary Gomułka in 1956. As far as I recall, conclusions were drawn from the period 1950–6, not only economic conclusions but also political ones and those to blame were severely reprimanded by the Party and state.

As to the aspect of Point Three now under discussion, 'access to the mass media for representatives of all denominations', I may mention a case in which access was granted. The visit by the head of the Catholic Church, the Polish Pope, John Paul the Sixth – or is he the Second? – was broadcast in full. Moreover, the address by Cardinal Wyszyński to great crowds of the faithful at Częstochowa was also broadcast. Can all of you in the hall hear me? [*applause*] Cardinal Wyszyński, as head of the Catholic Church in Poland, expressed himself unambiguously.[4] I am not myself certain of the present attitude of the Cardinal and Bishop Kaczmarek[5] towards this question. I understand there is no mention here of access to television. We can enquire what the attitude of Cardinal Wyszyński is.

As to the Interfactory Strike Committee being slandered when these events began, I can only speak for what has happened since my arrival. At our preliminary meeting last Friday, I was told we were going to the Interfactory Strike Committee. My response was: 'As you wish. We must talk to them.' Whatever may be written about me afterwards, no one will be able to accuse me of not showing the Interfactory Strike Committee both respect and recognition from the outset. I underlined this yesterday, when I pointed out that we are holding joint discussions on matters of common concern.

On the basic question – censorship – well, fine. Its purpose must be to serve the most essential interests of the state and sociopolitical life. From what you said, we are in agreement. I don't see any difference between us. We are agreed that censorship should cover such interests as state and military secrets and some economic ones. In the West nowadays – I have my contacts, I deal with France, England, America, etc. – economic matters are sometimes even more secret than others. I agree that censorship should cover dissemination of material inimical to the Polish system and aimed at our alliance. It should protect religious feelings, and those of atheists, because, after all, we are a democratic country. It should, as Cardinal Wyszyński mentioned in his beautiful sermon at Jasna Góra, prevent the dissemination of morally damaging material. So where is the difference? Let us try to write a protocol, giving your attitude as an Interfactory Committee and mine as Chairman of the Commission. I propose to guarantee implementation of what was mutually established at the end.

Wałęsa: Prime Minister, you reminded us what it was like in the early days of our strike. But today's *Trybuna Ludu* has an article offensive to us. If something unfair happens here, we take responsibility for it. We try not to do it and anyway it happens rarely, but now we are abused. I suggest you check in *Trybuna Ludu*: there is something very unpleasant – accusing us of irresponsibility.[6] Texts should be checked because this is not how work should be done.

On the point about the Church, as a believer and a supporter of this proposal, I think the Church should have legal status. At present we don't know how things stand. That's something concrete. The other thing is that the Church should have at least one hour a week on the radio, to broadcast mass to the sick. This is a minimum which, as believers, we cannot give up. I think it can be accepted without any difficulty.

Jagielski: Since this is a matter of religious outlook and belief, I suggest it will be consistent with our legal order to resolve it between the state and the Catholic Church hierarchy.

Wałęsa: But the workforce here demand it.

Jagielski: We'll put it forward. I'll forward it later.

Wałęsa: Yes, but this hour is really needed by our society. Society won't want to give it up. It won't give up!

Fiszbach: I think this is a matter for discussion between the government and the Episcopate. Our commission will forward the proposal as you have expressed it.

I want to say a word or two on the issue Mr Bądkowski raised. As a Party member, I found it particularly disagreeable to hear such a negative account. I took it more to heart, perhaps, than most citizens. Our Party has already defined its attitude to the mistakes which occurred in recent social and economic policies. We did so at the Fourth Plenum and a further plenum has been announced which will evaluate what has happened more deeply, in a calm atmosphere and at greater length. Although we do not seek to defend or whitewash our mistakes, justified criticism must be balanced by an account of our achievements. I don't know whether those in this room or in the hall would agree, but I think that, despite all of this, we have developed Poland. In spite of what has happened here, Poland has a quite different position in the world than ever before. True, it can be asked if we needed to pay such a price. We must find our answer together. However, I think that total negation of these past thirty years of history would be a mistake. History itself is the best judge.

That was my first remark. My second refers to press freedom, access to the mass media and censorship. Of course, I am not a specialist in this field. I favour providing the public with the fullest possible information on social, economic and political affairs. Our attitude towards problems of the defence of state security, and which spheres it should concern, was presented by the Chairman of our Commission. I think we would all agree with it.

If you do have different opinions it would be worth spelling them out. Otherwise, that seems to exhaust this matter. There just remain the working out of legal technicalities and detailed regulations to prevent backsliding on the issue.

Gentlemen, I want you to look at these happenings in Gdańsk dispassionately. Forgive me, I did not want to cause offence, but we are speaking more calmly today than at the beginning. It was not always like this. I don't want to remind you of the graffiti, later painted over, which could have given the impression that people here were not thinking as they should. Of course, that was not my impression when I came here to start talks.

In conclusion, I appeal to everyone for good work and results. We must reach mutual agreement as soon as possible for the sake of all those living on the Coast and the whole country.

Jagielski: I propose we base our decision over Point Three on Article 182 of the Constitution, which will, I think, bring us to agreement. It states: 'The Polish People's Republic guarantees freedom of conscience and belief for its citizens. The Church and other denominational organisations may freely fulfil their religious functions. Citizens cannot be forced to abstain from religious practices or ceremonies, nor can anyone be obliged to take part in religious practices or ceremonies. The Church is separate from the state. The state's attitude towards the Church, as well as the legal and financial position of denominational organisations, are defined by statute.' I propose that after both sides have spoken and appointed representatives, we try to define our attitude, that is, discover what agreement we can reach on this matter.

Gruszecki: Prime Minister, the Constitution you just quoted has been in force a very long time. Perhaps you could tell us why, despite its wonderful provisions, an overgrown censorship regularly arises, an alien growth requiring periodic corrections. Would you gentlemen consider this for a moment and give us your opinion?

Jagielski: I have already exhausted the subject of our Commission's attitude to censorship and how it should be defined. If we broaden the discussion still further, it could take an hour. Our attitude to censorship is known. I suggest it be combined with yours to make a mutual agreement. That seems to me a constructive proposition.

Wałęsa: Yes, but if that fails the test, how can we appeal and where can we get redress? We have had a Constitution for years and things are still not right. How can we appeal against breaches of the Constitution and other laws?

Jagielski: So would you say that the existing censorship regulations should be changed to provide a procedure for complaints or appeals?

Wiśniewski: May I enter this discussion? We want the whole country to know the truth about us as the rest of the world does already. Foreign correspondents were here from the outset, while ours were absent like last time. They only come privately with statements of support. And Cardinal Wyszyński's sermon was cut. I understand that parts of it were omitted. May I raise a further point: the highly important pronouncement so beautifully made by Comrade First Secretary Fiszbach to the important session of the Politburo. Unfortunately, it was reported only here on the coast. There was no word about it in *Trybuna Ludu* while pronouncements by First Secretary Comrade Gierek were in all the newspapers. I think it would have been appropriate for the full text of Comrade Fiszbach's speech to be published throughout the country. It is generally accepted that the centre of events, which began in Lublin, has moved here to Gdańsk. [*applause*]

You can see from this that we have full confidence in the Party authorities, but the question remains whether all individual members should belong there. This is what the whole dialogue is about: proper representation. There have been so many difficulties. Deputy Premier Pyka did come here, it's true, but he wouldn't shake hands with us even though we were official delegates.[7] It seems that was a provocation. We were spat on and lies were spread all over Poland through this unfortunate censorship. Only the world's press helped us to get through.

Such things do matter at an historic moment like this when we are sincerely trying to find a way to improve our national economy. We don't want half-hearted improvement, in some sectors but not in others. If we are to make improvements, they must be everywhere. Imagine how things would stand if the resolutions of the Sixth Party Congress[8] had been implemented. Such splendid promises! I have a file of newspapers at home including reports of the textile-workers' strike in Łódź.[9] Splendid promises were made then but never honoured. We believed them all, but the trust was broken.

Our dialogue must be completely open. Here I would like to

appeal to the Government Commission and to its Chairman: let's try to talk like two intelligent brains. Let's cut out the formalities. I see here professors, university teachers and scientists, educated people with beliefs and opinions of their own. Let's try to talk like Pole with Pole, for the sake of our fatherland. This discussion has certain nuances of diplomacy . . .

Jagielski: Diplomacy? Where is the diplomacy? Well, I can guess what you mean: I have seen it written that I practise diplomacy. What diplomacy is there here? What sort of a diplomat am I? [*laughter*]

Voice from the Hall: It's always other people who play at diplomacy, Prime Minister. [*renewed laughter*]

Jagielski: I was never in my life employed in diplomacy.

Wałęsa: May we be brief. Time is short.

Gwiazda: Prime Minister, Esteemed Commission!

Our discussion has gone into minor details of what was written about the Strike Committee. I don't think this matters much because many positive phenomena in Poland were written about in even worse terms and we somehow survived it. The real problem is different. You gentlemen and some of the general public will know the rule-book on censorship. Some of these documents came to light.[10] I will quote two instructions from memory. One forbade publication of the information that this year's harvest was larger than last because price increases were imminent. A second stated that a critical article on the scouts' organisation was to appear somewhere, to be followed by a specified number of articles, before an authoritative article put an end to discussion. No further word would then be permitted. There are whole volumes of such instructions. They are what we should discuss because they give the real picture of the deception and ignorance in which Polish society is kept. They are the source of the greatest mistakes. [*applause*]

We should publish an account of everything that has happened so far and take steps to ensure such things cannot recur by adopting the practical measures the Prime Minister mentioned: instituting a right of appeal against decisions of the censorship and making a clear public statement of what is, and what is not permitted. Then it would be known what we may say and what we may not, and we could discuss it.

Wałęsa: It should not be thought, wrongly, that we want a big row in the country. We are quite capable of settling matters by agreement in this forum. We can even issue an appeal to other workforces not to stop. They can just declare their solidarity with us, and set the condition that if we don't manage to reach agreement, they may help us.

We must not bring the economy to a halt. We all agree we don't want to do that. That is why we should reach agreement, and I – or someone else who knows things better – will make the appeal. We don't want to paralyse the economy. We must settle these things for their sake and for ours.

Fiszbach: May I answer the question put to me? My speech to the Fourth Plenum was carefully considered and based, so far as time permitted, on the advice of senior officials. I realise it was incomplete and accept the point that it reflects the climate of opinion in the Gdańsk Region – one I think we all share. The speech will appear in *Polityka.* I gather it was not published earlier because the views it expressed require further elaboration. There was a large number of speeches: the session went on into the small hours. They will also be published in *Nowe Drogi,* putting this historic document on record.

My view on censorship is this. The institution of censorship, and the extent to which it intervenes, depend upon the prevailing sociopolitical system and style of government. It is extremely difficult, therefore, to consider the question in isolation. The readiness to democratise political life now declared, will lead to changes in the functioning of this institution. I see the need for change and share your view that it would benefit cultural, political and social life. The mass media can be made accessible to religious associations to the degree defined earlier by the Prime Minister, though you found this unsatisfactory for various essential, technical and organisational reasons. I want to mention that in addition to Article 82 of the Polish Constitution already quoted, legal relations between the state and the Church are regulated by international agreement, through the Concordats. The proposal made for control and enforcement is already being carried out. A statute on judicial control over the activity and operation of administration will become law on 1 September. So what you asked for had already been set in motion.

May I add that the first phase of the strike here on the Coast could not easily be defined or diagnosed. Various interpretations were offered of its origin and development but it would have been premature to lay one down authoritatively. We talk about democratisation and freedom of speech. They have their place in what is said by people 'on one side or the other'. But I would rather we avoided that expression. We have got to settle our differences. I want to state quite bluntly that I knew about the shortcomings and mistakes, even in decision-making, of a certain department, as shipyard workers in the Gdańsk Repair Yard, Gdańsk Northern and Gdańsk Harbour will tell you. I told the central authorities that the Chairman of the Government Commission needed to be changed. We can all see that things are going better in this second phase of the Government Commission. Thank you.

Bądkowski: Deputy Premier, Gentlemen!

I did not quote Gomułka for my own amusement but to illustrate the cyclicality of our history and to further my argument that we must break out of this fatal circle. It is obvious that issues raised here far exceed welfare. They are concerned with our life in its entirety. My speech emphasised that we seek full rights as citizens. I want to add that such rights cannot be restricted to the region covered by the Interfactory Strike Committee. We do not want to form a state within the state. Every peasant in every village has the same rights and duties as those mentioned here. As for the rights of religious practice, we realise we are not Church spokesmen but speak only as citizens, whether believers or not. There are some non-believers on our side of the table – which separates solely for the purpose of writing – but they too were brought up in Polish cultural traditions formed over the past thousand years. We simply reflect the view of one part of society, rather representative, I think, of the whole.

The Deputy Premier mentioned statutes, which are a natural continuation of the Constitution. A constitution cannot be all-embracing. It lays down principles which are subsequently elaborated or extended in particular statutes. What matters most in practice is the conformity of statutes with the constitution. If the constitution is simply a pious declaration and statutes enacted later do conflict with it, then it remains a dead letter.

Censorship is a prime example. The Polish Constitution guarantees freedom of expression, so far as this does not contravene the principles we mentioned. By contrast, the censorship decree of 1946 is brief and open to all sorts of interpretations. It contains no clause that clearly defines the limits of censorship. Some people say that this decree was essential, necessary or anyway justified in 1946. I disagree. In any case, it is absolutely unjustifiable in 1980. The Office of Control should be defined by law. Such a law must accord with the relevant articles of the Constitution. I gather we are to begin preparing such a document shortly.

Wałęsa: I suggest we go on to the next point. This one will be discussed in the working group and brought back here for completion.

Fiszbach: May I intervene once more? You expressed your readiness, Mr Wałęsa, to issue a joint communiqué to the country, exhorting people to continue work. I think that is a very important idea. Everyone would subscribe to it. Matters we are discussing today have very great significance and we know they have support far beyond this hall. They are a subject of profound deliberation by all citizens. This is one of the most essential joint decisions before us today.

Jagielski: It should be done as you proposed, not in any other way.

Wałęsa: I share the general feeling. It is important we don't sink into more chaos. That's my proposal. But let's not drag this out. The real problem is time. Let's go on now to discuss Point Four. Please proceed.

Gwiazda: Prime Minister, Esteemed Commission!

We now reach a point of vital concern to us at present: political prisoners, of whom we have given three names as examples. I have before me a summary of the charges on which they were convicted. All three were independent social activists, unaffiliated to any official structure or association, who acted on their own account. Each was convicted on criminal charges. The judicial process in each case gave rise to considerable misgivings: public opinion and commentary were more or less unanimous about that. I followed these trials. Lawyers considered the proceedings to be far removed from either the rule of law or elementary principles of justice.[12]

Edmund Zadrożyński, a former worker now invalided, had gained great popularity in Grudziądz, where he helped to organise the strike in 1976 and many later social activities. He was an editor of the journal *Robotnik*, published independently of the censorship. Following a trial on criminal charges in the district court, he is liable to serve a three-year prison sentence and pay a 70 000 złotys fine. His right of appeal is still pending. He faces a further trial on the charge of receiving stolen goods, under Article 215 of the penal code, which carries a minimum sentence of three years. The only prosecution witnesses at Zadrożyński's trial were prison inmates. One of the codefendants and chief prosecution witnesses was his own son, a notorious thief, a completely untrustworthy person, who is psychologically unbalanced: he successively withdrew his depositions and revoked what he had withdrawn. There were also signs at this trial – I don't recall the details at the moment – that physical violence had been used against witnesses following their arrest, to force them to sign statements.[13]

Next: Jan Kozłowski, sentenced to two years' imprisonment by the district court in Stalowa Wola, confirmed by the regional court in Sandomierz. Kozłowski was a peasant activist who came into conflict with the local authorities for defending the interests of the peasants in his neighbourhood. He was sentenced for allegedly assaulting a local hooligan. The evidence presented at this trial also gives rise to serious doubts. A further peasant activist, Tadeusz Kolano, was sentenced at the same trial to eighteen months' imprisonment. Last: Marek Kozłowski, a male nurse from Słupsk. After serving a prison term for offences whose sentences and procedures I have no intention of questioning he made public acts of lawlessness by prison warders and the militia. Two officers were convicted as a result. Then Kozłowski was charged with threatening a woman with assault or murder. The evidence presented in this case also gives rise to serious doubts.[14]

Prime Minister, Esteemed Commission! It is said we have no political prisoners but can we have complete confidence in the administration of justice in such cases? We are guaranteed personal safety for those taking strike action and their supporters and that they will not be repressed but can we be sure that false witnesses will not be found, and a rigged trial held, to reveal that the entire Interfactory Strike Committee is a gang of criminals? This causes us great anxiety. [*applause*]

Jagielski: I am not . . .

Gwiazda: Turning now to students, Prime Minister, I shall give you only one example. Jolanta Kozłowska, the daughter of Jan Kozłowski, was expelled from the teacher training college in Kielce. I will not read out the very detailed explanation given here, perhaps I can hand it to you. Doesn't this remind one of something? We all know there was a mass expulsion of students after the events of March [1968]. Those students came out for what the Prime Minister, on behalf of the government, has partially accepted. Their chief demand was the abolition of censorship. They demanded that the press should print the truth. For this, they were thrown out. Many did manage to graduate, by changing universities or enrolling in evening courses, though some will probably not return to their studies. Even so, it seems to me they still deserve some restitution.

Now: restoring the jobs of those sacked following the strikes of 1970 and 1976. I have here a list of eighty-eight workers from the Gdańsk Shipyard . . .

Jagielski: What list?

Gwiazda: A list of eighty-eight names of workers from the Gdańsk Shipyard sacked after 1976. Of course, I don't claim that the list is complete. It also includes a few people dismissed from other workplaces.

Prime Minister, Esteemed Commission! This is a matter of utmost importance. On it, depends whether our country can be described as a police state or a democracy. We live in a land where national unity is imposed by the police truncheon . . . [*applause*]

Jagielski: These statements are very far-reaching . . .

Gwiazda: Far-reaching and possibly demagogic. But forty-eight hour detentions of those holding opinions other than the official ones are an everyday occurrence. I have a second list here: naming people being held without charge, probably arrested because it is not known what views they hold or whether the ones they have accord with the required ones. I can give you this too. Finally, Prime Minister, we would like to know what guarantees there are, what solid guarantees, that such things won't recur. On paper, our laws are splendid, but practice is far removed from them. [*applause*]

Jagielski: It seems to me that you are taking matters very far. This is my personal impression, as Chairman of the Government Commission.

Gwiazda: Perhaps I am, Prime Minister. But if an old teacher has to go to church at the other end of Gdańsk, because she is frightened that her boss will find out, then the situation is extremely unhealthy.

Jagielski: You are giving a specific, particular example.

Gwiazda: So I am, Prime Minister . . .

Jagielski: Does one example make the rule? Do you think I favour the practice you describe? I condemn it as strongly as you do.

Gwiazda: Quite.

Jagielski: So what then?

Gwiazda: Prime Minister, if such cases do occur, it is evidence of a serious illness.

Jagielski: Consider what happens every Saturday and Sunday, every mass, every feast day. Hundreds of thousands, crowds of them, go to church freely. I may add that not only non-Party members but also Party members attend. [**Gwiazda:** I know.] Even those in senior positions.

Gwiazda: I know they do.

Jagielski: So you have given me one particular example. I do not deny there may be cases such as you describe. Something is wrong if there are. It means the director of the school has no political imagination.

Gwiazda: Prime Minister, I don't think the director would do anything to this old lady. But such fears do exist in our society. Fear of consequences and of repression.

Jagielski: For going to church?

Gwiazda: No, fear in general. Fear before a factory or union meeting. Fear of speaking out or making a bolder proposition. We must remove such fears. Thank you. [*applause*]

Wałęsa: I'm sure we all agree on one thing: law should be enforced. Take my own case. I have references and documents on me to show that I was dismissed illegally. We almost all have them. I tried to settle everything politely at the procuracy. They just refused or packed me off in the opposite direction.

There ought to be some body to supervise enforcement. On paper the laws are excellent, but who can enforce them if neither the courts nor procuracy will? I have now been taken back by three enterprises at once. Each had sacked me illegally. But I couldn't enforce the law myself. By myself! How could I?

Jagielski: Mr Gwiazda raised four matters. One related to those sentenced, mentioning various names. I have some information on these cases in front of me. You referred to the articles under which they were convicted. I could tell you who was sentenced, under which article, when and where the trial took place. I do not want to do this and I am not going to, but if there is new evidence in these cases, then I think the judicial process can be reviewed.

Gwiazda: Excellent!

Jagielski: That's one thing. I must tell you that your words stung me. How can you say there is no guarantee that the strikers here, and their Presidium, will not be revealed as – I don't even want to repeat your words – as 'criminals'. I must tell you that this stung me personally. After all, I am negotiating with you as respectable people, highly respectable. How could anyone treat the activists here like that?

Wałęsa: Prime Minister, I have received dozens of threats that when I come out this or that will happen. And not only to me.

Jagielski: Then I would have to be driven out as well . . .

Voice from the Hall: Let's not get carried away!

Jagielski: Surely, there's no such intention! There is a basic general intention to observe the law to the letter. Then you raised a third issue: the list of Gdańsk Shipyard workers sacked in 1976 or 1970. I propose to go through the whole list and settle the question.

Fiszbach: May I add something here? I want to tell the meeting that during the first days of the strike, a number of strike committees asked me for a written guarantee of their personal safety. I realised from the outset that this had to be given. Let it be a token of the trust we keep today. It promises as follows:

> With regard to the activity of citizen———within the limits of the Shipyard, I hereby testify that, in pursuance of the public welfare and interests of the Shipyard workforce, I guarantee that citizen———will not suffer any consequences on account of his activity. This immunity does not extend to perpetration of acts contrary to the laws of the Polish People's Republic.

We all know what acts are referred to. I think, therefore, Comrade Premier, that the matters to which the gentlemen refer under the headings of personal safety, order, and attaining a state of affairs that restores the normal course of events and everyday life are already taken care of.

Voice from the Hall: And this was signed by Comrade Fiszbach as Chairman of the Regional People's Council, so to speak, individually but for everyone.

Wiśniewski: One may add that everyone asked for it. I for one did not because I thought there is nothing to fear when one's cause is just. Many others thought likewise. In this way I think we proved our cause is just.

Anna Walentynowicz: Once the rule of law is mentioned, the question of guarantees can hardly be avoided. The principal guarantors will be the several organs of state charged with seeing that the law is observed and with prosecuting wrongdoers, whether they be private citizens, organs of state or other institutions. Existing institutions will certainly require numerous improvements if they are to serve this purpose. But that is a separate subject. I want to raise the more fundamental question of how the procuracy and courts themselves function.

Examples of elementary breaches of law by these legal bodies have proliferated in recent years. There are many instances of total passivity on the part of prosecuting organs when they had the duty to take the legal steps laid down: instituting proceedings or investigations. I know from my own experience that the state procuracy will, as a rule, take no action in response to information from citizens about a breach of law when the law-breakers were state functionaries, particularly the police. How can one have confidence in a state of affairs which renders the private citizen practically helpless? The law is not guaranteed. I believe the answer lies in our proposal that public opinion be enabled to exercise control over the organs of power. I refer, of course, to the abolition of censorship and to the formation of free trade unions.

Non-observance of the labour law is a whole subject in itself. Labour relations are the sphere in which the law is most often disregarded. Even legal judgements by organs which determine the basic norms of the Labour Code are sometimes disregarded. Article 42 paragraph 4, for instance, is regularly disobeyed: that specifying conditions under which an employee can be transferred to other work. Basic principles for wage-setting are also often ignored. The terms of contract for those on piece-rates often have little significance. All this gives rise to wholesale disregard of laws which regulate labour relations, thus greatly diminishing their role in resolving individual or even collective disputes. The legal judgement was not implemented in my case.

Consider for a moment the labour law in actual operation. The security service seize you on the street and lock you up for forty-eight hours before letting you out without a word of apology or preferring any charges. In the meantime, you miss two days' work. Much later, the militia forward a certificate to the employer. The section head forwards it, in turn, to the legal department, whose chief confirms that such a certificate entitles one to justified absence without pay. I have such written confirmation. The Labour Code, however, says something completely different. Moreover, when they seized me on the street and carried out a search, they took away diaries which I have kept since I was ten. They were not returned. I was beaten in detention and needed ten days' sick leave after my release. I sent a complaint to the procuracy but have never received a reply.

We, shipyard workers, addressed an open letter to the *Sejm*, requesting the creation of a Commission which would have the task of ensuring the observance of law in our country. We sent three such letters, with 178 signatures. To this day, we have had no reply. If the *Sejm* does not reply even in matters such as this, how can the labour law be respected at lower levels by directors and managers? The Constitution is a splendid document but is not observed. When I mentioned it at the militia station, the officer just laughed. That was my reply. [*applause*]

Jagielski: We entirely agree with what you said about the non-observance of legal regulations and the making of decisions that are contrary to law. I would like to add that a Supreme Administrative Court has been established for the purpose of reviewing all rules and regulations, to which appeals may be made within the time-limit laid down. Any institution which makes a decision contrary to the law will be required to give a prompt and unambiguous explanation. Those who make such decisions will be brought to account. I gather that its main purpose will be, as Mrs Walentynowicz mentioned, to strengthen the rule of law in our country. If I recall, she suggested that the *Sejm* might take some initiative in this matter. That has been noted and accepted. It is one of the most constructive proposals made during our talks.

Alojzy Szablewski: Prime Minister, High Commission!

I would like to take the question of relations between the authorities and believers a little further. Believers are discriminated against in our country. To attain high office, or any rank in the military or militia, people must conceal their religious convictions. If they give themselves away by accident, demotion or dismissal follows. This is widely known but may be illustrated by my own case and that of my family.

I used to be a career officer in the army, a profession I loved, but one in which my religious convictions were an obstacle to promotion. I was eventually discharged. Not wanting to be hypocritical, I did not hide my religious feelings and was therefore barred from practising my beloved profession. I might add that some of my fellow-graduates from the Officers' Artillery School in Toruń, who received a lower class of degree, were able to complete their military education and are now research workers or even lecturers at the General Staff Academy in Warsaw. I had to adjust to a new career. This was difficult because I had bad references from the army and had to overcome many obstacles and waste a number of years in order to complete my studies. My wife, a respected doctor at the local hospital of the Ministry of Interior, was continually harrassed on account of her religious views, and eventually dismissed in 1978 when my son entered a seminary. Though always an exemplary pupil, my son had to conceal this decision to enter the seminary: he would not have passed his school-leaving examinations otherwise. Indeed, the headmaster, who knew his attitude to religion, lowered his mark for behaviour, even though he was highly regarded by his school mates and teachers. All these facts are true.

Gentlemen, how can people be wronged like this? This is no way to gain the support of society. I would like to ask the Prime Minister why our state dignitaries so frequently address the nation with the phrase 'comrades and citizens, Party and non-Party workers, believers and non-believers'. Why do they divide society in this way? Wouldn't one word 'compatriots' do for all Poles? [*applause*] You propagate grand slogans about equality and justice while simultaneously dividing society into 'us' and 'them'. [*applause*] You appear not to care about gaining the love and respect of your subjects. Yet a nation which loved its authorities would be full of enthusiasm for work, for sacrifices and for creating a better future for our country. I have finished. [*applause*]

Wałęsa: I suggest we have one short speech more and then have a break, if the Prime Minister agrees.

Jagielski: I would rather continue without an interval, going straight on to further points. I can say to the previous speaker that my attitude, as Chairman of the Commission, towards problems of belief was expressed unequivocally. I fully understand your pain and bitterness and feel for you in what you experienced. The forms of address used by 'dignitaries' or speakers do vary but there is no intention to divide. 'Compatriots' is used. I used it myself on television yesterday. I didn't say 'us' and 'them', 'some' and 'others', but simply 'Esteemed Citizens, Inhabitants of the Coast'. Since this particular instance you mentioned so emotionally also touches my emotions, I am even ready to propose, well, I simply request that my colleagues here look at this question carefully. My general attitude towards this question has already been expressed.

Voice from the Hall: Comrade Chairman, perhaps this matter should be examined and the findings published.

Jagielski: That's what I propose.

Gwiazda: Prime Minister, High Commission!

I have already spoken of the fear in society. I now want to document it more fully by showing how the law operates: not lawlessness, but law itself. Let us suppose that a manager dismisses an employee without notice – a 'disciplinary' dismissal – groundlessly. The employee has the right of appeal to a local Appeals Tribunal. The case drags on in this tribunal for two or three months. He loses the case. He then appeals to the Labour Court which eventually decides that the dismissal had been groundless and orders reinstatement. Such a hearing can take six months. In all, the employee wrongfully dismissed has no wages for nine months. Even if he does get his job back, he is only entitled to one month's pay. The manager, by contrast, loses nothing. How can a man support his family for eight months? No one will compensate him. If he receives a disciplinary dismissal, he knows that there is no alternative except to look for work at lower pay elsewhere, taking with him the burden of humiliation and injustice.

Once he does take other work, we know from experience what the local tribunal and Labour Court will decide: 'Although he was wrongfully dismissed he has since found work. In order not to disturb him he should be left where he is.' His old position is not restored. This is also something people fear. They know there is no appeal against a manager's decision. Theoretically it exists, but the vast majority cannot use it. Thank you.

Jagielski: Well, you also give us a specific example, generalised to some extent. Dismissal without notice is an extraordinary case. I think that every manager must think very seriously before doing it. He really must! If such a dismissal was found to be groundless by the Labour Court then of course he must be reinstated, and if wrongfully dismissed, with full satisfaction.

Voice from the Hall: And compensation!

Jagielski: Yes, yes, of course. And if there is such a loophole in the legal system, we shall find it. It must be found and filled, so that such cases will not occur.

Krzywonos: One of our colleagues was very dishonestly treated. Janusz Skorek, a worker from the Gdańsk Shipyard, was detained on 24 August in Morąg, in Olsztyn province, and held for forty-eight hours. 10 978 złotys – part of the public fund donated for construction of a monument to the shipyard workers killed in 1970[16] – was confiscated from him. The militia asked why he doesn't put up other monuments. Many witnesses here confirm these facts. How is it, Prime Minister, that you assure us of full respect and safety for strikers and their supporters, while the facts belie it? In the light of the above, can we regard your further confirmation of our safety as plausible? [*applause*]

Jagielski: You put a question to me. I have already stated that we should observe the law at all times, base ourselves consistently on the Constitution. If there are instances of law-breaking, those responsible should be brought to account. What more can I say? If we are to proceed on this level, we will have to examine every single case. You cited one from Mrągowo[17] didn't you? I don't know if there was such a case but [*Protests from the hall*] well all right, I'm not saying I disbelieve you. I am only saying that I concentrated on the basic problems as they were presented here. One can multiply examples, can't one? But then we would be concentrating on specific cases not on ways to resolve the problems. After all, our intention was to find a constructive agreement. Unless there isn't one, in which case we won't find it.

Pieńkowska: I want to return to the cases of Zadrożyński, Jan Kozłowski and Marek Kozłowski. The Deputy Premier promised a review of their sentences. But do we have any guarantee that this will be conducted according to the law? At the trial of Błażej Wyszkowski, in Gdańsk in June 1978, the judge, Sułkowski, did not allow defence witnesses.[18] This is illegal but he got away with it. That is why we demand the release of Jan Kozłowski, Marek Kozłowski and Zadrożyński.

Jagielski: I dealt with this as well, unequivocally.

Zieliński: This way of reasoning suggests that every case should be referred – well I don't know – to the International Court in the Hague, because there is no justice in this country. I didn't want to raise this matter [*laughter*] . . . Wait a moment! Wait a moment! I didn't want to raise this matter in order not to spoil the atmosphere. But I do want to say this: I don't know all three cases mentioned, I don't know the business with the Kozłowskis. I didn't have time. But on my last visit to Warsaw I found out about the Zadrożyński business from the appropriate authorities, the Ministry of Justice. It turns out that this man has been convicted several times in recent years under the same article of the penal code. Was the trial fixed every time he came up on a theft charge? It is said he appealed: I don't know because I had no chance to check. It is said the sentence is not yet enforced: I don't rule it out. Listen, you can never tell with people. I don't know what he got up to. Some social activists run foul of the law for other reasons. Let's drop this. The higher court can look at it calmly. Maybe this court will also be packed with cads and bounders who want to wring Zadrożyński's neck, what?

Jagielski: Mr Chairman, I would like to get on with today's agenda: constructive discussion of the remaining problems. Our purpose is to exchange views and then nominate the working groups which will sit down after today's meeting. It doesn't seem to me that experts were necessary for what we have discussed so far. They can simply sub-edit the points we have already agreed. That way, we will move forward. But . . . well, if you think experts are necessary, let them be present. Right, let them be there.

Gruszecki: Deputy Premier, Esteemed Commission!

It is no wonder all these people have spoken so sincerely and so sorrowfully on this subject. The Commission should take that as an indication of what injustices came into our life. In my view, the Commission cannot claim ignorance of such facts. It should believe that we are speaking the truth here and that we are concerned deep in our hearts, that such things should not be repeated. I think that a constructive solution would be reached if the Commission could cite some guarantees that they will not recur, that the working man will have some means of defence against all the wrongs done in the name of law. Thank you.

Jagielski: I do believe you and take every fact to heart just as you do. I spoke of guarantees, about all possible guarantees under the Constitution and laws stemming from it. Where necessary, they must be changed. Let's make a note of this. I propose changes in laws relating to problems of work and work safety, to problems of strikes and to the personal safety for those on strike. This relates, as it were, to the conception of a law which should regulate this matter. Because strikes are regulated by law the world over. It is laid down when, how, in what way and with what – so to speak – consequences for both sides. We too must regulate these matters properly.

Wałęsa: The general feeling in this room and in the hall is that you, Prime Minister, and the Government Commission do not, or did not know that such things take place. It's just a feeling. I think, though, that you do know how things stand and what the observance of law is like.

Jagielski: We got to know some particular examples.

Wałęsa: But these examples could be multiplied. We didn't do that because you really would sit here for a week, a month, or even longer. Andrzej Gwiazda will speak now and maybe bring this matter to a close.

Gwiazda: Prime Minister. We did go into detail here, but it is only through details that one can see the law in operation rather than just on paper. Minor details, small human injustices reveal the workings of the law most precisely.

I have been handed a statement on the radio transmission and press coverage of the Primate, Cardinal Wyszyński's homily at Jasna Góra, during the central ceremony in honour of the icon of St Mary of Częstochowa, on 26 August:

'The Press Bureau of the Polish Episcopate is empowered to announce that the published text was neither complete nor authorised. The author was not asked for his consent to publication in the Polish mass media. The authorised text is in the possession of the Polish Episcopate.'

Jagielski: I will clarify this matter with the central authorities. I was here throughout and do not know about it. I cannot reply to what you said because I don't know the text of the statement. I will make enquiries and then may be able to reply.

Gwiazda: Prime Minister, we do not expect you to know the details of every transgression and explain them. But we do intend that a picture of life as it really is should emerge from them. Life as experienced by an ordinary person.

Jagielski: I do understand.

Wałęsa: Prime Minister, I propose we prepare the communiqué and announce an interval. As for the homily, the public feeling is that they really were just excerpts, with bits of other sermons, and not what it should have been. So I suggest we clear this up, take the break and issue the communiqué.

Jagielski: I would rather go on. I will clear it up, but I must first get in touch with the appropriate authorities in Warsaw. I don't know whether I will get through. But I will clear it up. I will speak to them, find out about this and explain.

Lis: We will continue, won't we? The break is only for an hour?

Wałęsa: We agreed that we would continue to discuss only Points Three and Four today. They must be worked out, so we won't find ourselves in a vacuum later because someone said something. They must be finalised, so we have facts to stand on.

Jagielski: What other points are to be discussed?

Wałęsa: Only Three and Four. But in a final form initialled and signed. So we don't have to come back to them. Simply to get them out of the way.

Fiszbach: And will today's session end with that?

Wałęsa: No. After the break we will go back to Point One because we want to deal with that too. Now, quickly, Points Three and Four. They are less important points.

Jagielski: Just a moment, just a moment. You mean we have discussed Points Two, Three and Four? What are we to clear up? What am I to do now?

Wałęsa: Finalise them, signatures included. So these points won't come up again. Settled definitely . . .

Lis: In a written protocol?

Wałęsa: Yes, yes. Done with, we sign, that's it.

Jagielski: I understand that we agree the following procedure: Points Two, Three and Four will be finalised by members of the Commission, sitting with experts. I will go and clarify this other matter. Perhaps you can give me some hard information since it is new to me. May I ask about the text Mr Gwiazda read out: was it the original? Please pass it to me. Whose text is this? Who issued it? What is the legal status of this document?

Gwiazda: I was just given it for information.

Jagielski: I ask because we can only proceed on the basis of established fact.

Gwiazda: I suggest we make you a clean copy, so there is no confusion.

Jagielski: Gentlemen, why should we explain? We won't accept this text. We must be meticulous throughout. I will explain when you have a signed text. [**Voice from the Hall:** It was unsigned.] Then I will explain. If this text is by the Episcopate, I will explain everything.

Mr Chairman, may I make a suggestion? I have conducted

various negotiations in my life, mainly economic ones, or rather on economic cooperation. But I have never negotiated Polish affairs in front of foreign correspondents. Who are those people down there? Are they all Polish?

Wiśniewski: They are friends.

Jagielski: I am not saying they are not friends. I am only asking who they are. There is no practice of negotiating Polish affairs in the presence of foreign correspondents. We are discussing national affairs! Polish affairs! If they are accredited Polish journalists, all right. But not if they are foreign journalists and others. When I go abroad no one gets into the talks. No one! I present the views of the Polish side. A press spokesman meets the journalists and tells them that at such and such a meeting, so and so was discussed.

Wałęsa: I must point out this came about because there was no information and we could not agree how to provide it.

Jagielski: All right, that's why I have not raised this before now.

Wałęsa: That's why this communiqué should be really thorough, so we can overcome the problem. [**Jagielski:** All right.] I suggest we work out the communiqué jointly, or unilaterally if you want and issue it as soon as we have checked that all is in order. How long should the break be, Prime Minister?

Jagielski: What is the time now? Let's agree how to get in touch. You should make sure your telephone is not engaged for too long. We sometimes ring you but your line is engaged.

Wałęsa: I also spent nearly two hours trying to get through to you.

Jagielski: So we are leaving now. I will contact Warsaw. Two or three hours should suffice, provided you finalise the text. Who from our side . . .

Wałęsa: Surely two groups are needed, Prime Minister [**Jagielski:** Yes, yes.] with experts on each point. So we can finalise them, sign them and get them out of the way. They can stay behind and work. They will hand them over at the start of the next meeting, so that we can get rid of these points. [**Jagielski:** Yes.] So, only the experts from each side should stay behind. They should finish work by 5 p.m. Let's meet then to sign them and get them out of the way. Then we'll come back to Point One.

Jagielski: Fine, 5 p.m. We will try to finalise Points Two, Three and Four.

Wałęsa: Jointly?

Jagielski: Jointly. We will recommence at 5 p.m. Agreed?

Wałęsa: Yes. There is still the communiqué. I would ask that it should simply be reassuring.

Jagielski: Yes, the communiqué. I suggest that one of my colleagues hands out the communiqué.

Wałęsa: I don't think we quite understand each other. I mean the statement signalling that occupation strikes are not desirable because we are already winning. Winning is too strong a word. Because we are coming, yes coming, to an agreement. We just ask for solidarity. They can set the condition that if we don't get what we want, they may stop work then. But stopping now is undesirable for the economy and for the country.

Jagielski: All right, let's try to write such a statement. Perhaps as you suggest. The central authorities must be consulted on some matters. We shall do so promptly. In a moment we shall agree who will come next. I understand you only want to negotiate within the shipyard?

Wałęsa: Yes.

Voices from the Hall: We invite you here . . .

Voices: But not all of you!

Jagielski: We're only joking. Members of our Commission and experts will come and do the work. We shall meet at 5 p.m. to continue the talks.[19]

Wiśniewski: We building workers request the Minister of Building comes.

Wałęsa: Fine, but he is not needed today. We only have the three points. Maybe for later points, when we discuss these matters.

Wiśniewski: We building workers do have views to express. We would simply like a private meeting.

Jagielski: I can't bring him today. I may possibly reach him in time for tomorrow, but I'm not sure because I think Minister Barszcz has to go off to sign a contract. It will be his deputy.

Wałęsa: Let's not prolong this because we want a quick settlement. The meeting is closed.

FOURTH MEETING (30 AUGUST)

Wałęsa: I welcome the government delegation for the fourth time. I want to start settling these points, as planned. The trouble is, Point One is still being typed. We are signing things as fast as lightning – the typewriter can't keep up. So we have about five minutes before we can start discussing Point One. We are a bit behind – there's no typed copy yet.

Jagielski: Then you can use ours . . .

Wałęsa: It might be better if it's ours. Anyway, that's not a problem. I suggest we discuss Point Two until the text of Point One arrives. Have you got Point Two?

Jagielski: I have it in front of me.

Wałęsa: Our attitude to the unions will be presented by Andrzej Gwiazda.

Gwiazda: I now have the draft protocol relating to Point One:

1. Trade unions in the Polish People's Republic have not lived up to the hopes and expectations of employees. It is necessary to form new, self-governing trade unions, as authentic representatives of the working class. The right to remain in the present unions is not questioned and we envisage cooperation between unions.

2. The Interfactory Strike Committee declares that these new, independent, self-governing trade unions will accept the bases of the Polish Constitution. The new trade unions will defend the social and material interests of employees and do not intend to act as a political party. They accept the principle of the social ownership of the means of production on which the existing socialist system in Poland is based. While acknowledging the leading role of the Polish United Workers' Party in the state[1] and not questioning the established system of international alliances, their purpose is to provide working people with appropriate means for exercising control, expressing their opinions and defending their own interests.

    The Government Commission declares that the government will guarantee and ensure full respect for the independence and self-government of the new trade unions, both as to their organisational structure and to their functioning at all levels of their activity. The government will ensure the new trade unions have every opportunity to fulfil their basic functions of defending employees' interests and meeting their material, social and cultural needs. It also guarantees that the new unions will not be subject to any discrimination.

3. The creation and operation of independent, self-governing trade unions accords with ILO Conventions 87 on Freedom of Association and Protection of the Right to Organise and 98 on the Right to Organise and to Collective Bargaining, both ratified by Poland. The increase in the number of trade unions, and other bodies representing employees, will necessitate changes in legislation. In particular, the government undertakes to introduce appropriate amendments to the laws on trade unions and workers' self-management and to the Labour Code.

4. The existing strike committees are free to become bodies representing factory employees, such as: workers' or employees' committees, workers' councils or founding committees of the new, self-governing trade unions.[2] The Interfactory Strike Committee as the Founding Committee of these unions, has a free choice over which form of a single union or association on the Coast to adopt. The founding committees will continue to function until elections of new officials under their statutes. The government undertakes to provide conditions for registration of the new trade unions outside the Central Trade Union Council register.

5. The new trade unions should have a genuine opportunity to express their opinion in public on the major decisions which determine the living standards of working people: the division of the national product between consumption and accumulation; the allocation of the social fund amongst various sectors (health, education and culture); the basic principles for calculation and determination of wages, including that of automatic increases to compensate for inflation; long-term economic planning; the directions of investment and price changes. The government undertakes to provide conditions for fulfilment of these functions.

6. The Interfactory Committee is establishing a centre for social and professional studies. This will undertake objective research into the circumstances of employees, the welfare conditions of working people and ways in which employees' interests can best be represented. It will conduct detailed research into wage and price indexing and propose means of compensation. The centre will publish the results of its investigations.[3] The new unions will also have their own publications.[4]

7. The government will ensure observance of the 1949 law on trade unions which states in Article One, Paragraph One, that workers and employees have the right of free association in trade unions. The newly-created trade unions will not join the association represented by the Central Trade Union Council. A new law will incorporate this principle. Participation by representatives of the Interfactory Strike Committee or founding committees of self-governing trade unions and other bodies representing employees in drawing up this new law is assured.

Wałęsa: That's how we see this point. We now want to finalise it.

Jagielski: Ladies and gentlemen. The time has come to conclude our work. Negotiations have been long and difficult, but – let us not deny it – they dealt with major issues. We have to terminate a sharp social conflict and resolve problems of very great significance for the future of our country.

As you have said, Point One in your catalogue of proposals is the cornerstone of our agreement. It is also the most difficult to resolve. The remaining points are no less significant since the majority of them concern wages and conditions, and social demands made by the working class and other sections of society. Such problems cannot be regarded as peripheral, nor can they be resolved easily, even though it might appear that changes in this sphere – I refer to what you have suggested – could be made straightaway. However, our representatives and the experts on Point One had a particularly difficult task. I thank them sincerely. Perhaps some people became impatient with their protracted negotiations. But we should recognise that the view taken in this sphere is of a fundamental character and will undoubtedly influence the level of working-class activity, and that of other social strata, for years to come.

Ladies and gentlemen. We accept the formulations of the working group and experts, in principle, as the proper basis for the final decision to be taken here in this hall. In this connection, I would like to mention two basic matters. The first relates to defining what I would call the ideological and political profile of these trade unions. We called them 'self-governing trade unions and other bodies representing employees'. I observed with satisfaction that the Interfactory Strike Committee was unambiguous on this question. It was emphasised that these unions accept the principle of social ownership of the means of production on which the existing socialist system in Poland is based and acknowledge the leading role of the Polish United Workers' Party in the state and the established system of international alliances. Taken together, this means that they will stand, and do stand, on the basis of the Polish Constitution. [*applause*]

The second matter concerns the form of greater representation and of democracy which would meet your proposal for the most effective defence of employees and their interests. This should be performed by self-governing trade unions, conditions for whose registration should be created. We realise, of course, that a statute needs to be drawn up prior to registration. A founding committee of the new union must also be formed, or alternatively, existing strike committees may become bodies representing employees. There are various possibilities: workers' or employees' committees, workers' councils or founding committees. All this is acceptable. Of course, a semi-federal arrangement may emerge. That would ensure union representation in the expression of opinions on major policies determining the living standards of working people, the shaping of our social and economic policy and various others. I see they are all mentioned in this protocol. It talks about health, education, culture, and so on and so forth, and about the determination of wage policy.

In giving my approval to the solutions mentioned – which we all know were the core of your proposals – I want to emphasise that the difficulties in finding the appropriate formulations did not arise from any failure to appreciate the importance of union activity or of the need to satisfy peoples' aspirations for social activity. The difficulty in finding mutually satisfactory solutions stemmed from the fact that making new arrangements which involve genuine institutions and not just slogans, required resolution of political, normative, legal, organisational and technical questions. Merely to declare 'self-governing unions' was insufficient. Treating this seriously meant giving it an appropriate legal and sociopolitical form. You gentlemen have repeatedly raised the question of governmental guarantees for the proper, statutory functioning of the trade unions. I fully appreciate this and think that the agreements to be adopted have satisfied your aspirations.

Our Party will define its position, in principle, on the questions we are discussing at the Central Committee Plenum later today. I think, however, we have grounds for saying – and I have just been to Warsaw – that it is precisely this which will give the highest guarantee of political resolve to carry through the agreement. Some of you said 'Today the Commission is led by Jagielski. In a fortnight it may be someone else.' So it will not be Jagielski but the Party at today's plenum which takes a decision, in principle, on this matter. Mr Chairman, I propose we now both initial this point. I will initial it for the Government Commission and you will do the same on behalf of the Presidium or the whole hall. I will take the initialled points to Warsaw, where the plenum meets at 3 p.m. I will report this to them and come back here. I have one request. When I get back, let us sign everything else. Only three points are still outstanding: the so to speak political ones.

To tell the truth, I was sure we would come to terms. When they meet, the others, well, everybody else, will go through the agreement with a tooth-comb. I don't find that altogether surprising: I too am a professor and if I were up against the wall perhaps I would also weigh every word. But we want an overall settlement. Need we spend six or nine hours on these remaining points? I propose we initial Point One now and that you finish the remainder before our return. We shall sign the document this evening.

Wałęsa: Prime Minister, we have only completed Point Two, making two points in all so far. Three more are nearly finished.

Jagielski: Is Point Two ready?

Wałęsa: Yes.

Jagielski: We are agreed on Point Two. I am familiar with it.

Wałęsa: Yes. Only One and Two are ready. The rest still have to be finished.

Jagielski: Since Point Two is agreed and I am familiar with it, I hereby agree to accept it on behalf of the Commission.

Wałęsa: I suggest it is read out. So everything is clear.

Jagielski: Fine. Let's read it out.

Gwiazda: This is the joint position agreed by the working group on demand number two: 'To guarantee the right to strike and personal safety for strikers and their helpers.'

The right to strike will be guaranteed by the law on trade unions now in preparation. It should lay down the conditions for declaring and organising a strike, methods of resolving disputes and liability for breaches of the law. Articles 52, 64 and 65 of the Labour Code will not be used against strikers.

Prior to adoption of the law, the government guarantees the personal safety of strikers and their helpers, together with their present positions at work.

Jagielski: Mr Chairman, I have an objection. Before we finalise this point, do we need the term 'helpers'? Please consider it. I don't want your reply now. I only request you think about it.

Wałęsa: There will be legal definitions. They will make clear who this means. I don't think it's all that important. It can stay as it is. Eventually, in some legal document . . .

Jagielski: We accept, in order not to prolong this.

Gwiazda: Prime Minister, these are people who helped us out of goodwill.

Jagielski: I don't deny it. I even thanked them.

Wałęsa: Prime Minister, I don't quite understand. If we sign, does this mean it is all settled and will be implemented. Or is there still some doubt?

Jagielski: So far as the Commission is concerned there are no doubts.

Wałęsa: That means we can sign these two points and get them out of the way.

Jagielski: I have no doubts. I only want to give you guarantees from the highest political level.

Wałęsa: I for my part also sign with my modest hand and consider that these two matters are now finally settled. [*Prolonged applause.*]

Jagielski: What comes next? A document to initial?

Wałęsa: How many copies do we have?

Voice from the Hall: Enough!

Jagielski: Always in duplicate, you keep one, I keep the other. I am signing the second copy. What's the date today? 30/8/1980. [*To Wałęsa*]: Please sign here. Good.

Wałęsa: Prime Minister. Something here is still not quite right. 'To form new, independent, self-governing unions.' We have three terms. I suggest simply 'independent'. The same comes up in Points Two and Three 'independent, self-governing'. Really, the majority is for 'independent'. Yes, so as not to create problems, I propose 'independent trade unions', a shorter expression. [*applause*]

Jagielski: But we've already signed.

Wałęsa: And there are three terms in the protocol. [*Several voices at once.*] We couldn't shorten it? [**Voice:** It doesn't matter now.] So, let it be all three terms: 'new, independent, self-governing trade unions'.

Gwiazda: We will treat it as a description rather than a name.

Wałęsa: So, I repeat, 'independent, self-governing trade unions'. It stays as it is.

Jagielski: No, crossed out.

Wałęsa: No, no, Prime Minister, nothing crossed out. It stays as it is. And 'new' should be added there: 'new, independent, self-governing trade unions'. Yes, yes, this name stays, certainly.

Jagielski: All right. Now: Point Two. In duplicate. Are we signing?

Wałęsa: Yes we are. Please sign here: 30/8/1980. Good, that's that. We really do understand each other, Prime Minister. We do hope you will get back to us as quickly as possible . . .

Jagielski: Mr Chairman, I would like to make a statement.

The Commission will forward to the government all problems and proposals raised here by the Interfactory Strike Committee regarding: improvement of living standards, in particular improving the supply of goods, above all food; housing; social services such as crèches and nurseries; and proposals of the workforce regarding higher wages, their correction in relation to cost-of-living increases; and certain welfare proposals, including equalisation of family allowances, raising the lowest pensions and annuities, extension of maternity leave and increasing the number of free Saturdays, in order that a definite programme for their implementation can be worked out by 30 September 1980. This procedure has been accepted in Szczecin.[5]

I want to emphasise, in particular, that questions concerning wages will be settled in the spirit of discussion. Wages will be increased by degrees, starting with the lowest-paid. It was established that, as a rule, wages will be increased by individual factories and branches. They will amount, after taking into account the differences between the professions and branches, to increases of one point on the scale or corresponding increases in other components of pay. For white-collar workers in industry, the increase will amount to one point on the scale. There is the further suggestion of creating a Government Commission to oversee implementation of all matters raised here in the twenty-one proposals. We accept this. A mixed Governmental

Commission will be formed from representatives of both the government and the Interfactory Strike Committee.

I have the final communiqué in front of me, of course a draft that has still to be agreed. I have still to go to Warsaw, to the Central Committee Plenum and report Point One, by far the most fundamental, which we have initialled. Wouldn't it be a good idea, following both your suggestion, Mr Chairman, and what I have heard from Szczecin, to produce a communiqué indicating that we have reached agreement in principle and declaring that what most concerns us now is ending the strikes and a return to work? We have such a communiqué in draft and can leave representatives behind to edit the final version.

I will be back from Warsaw this evening, as early as I can, because I know it's Saturday today and people want to rest. I'm a farmer, and I know from experience that Saturday is a lucky day. [**From the Hall:** Our Lady's Day.] Well, Our Lady's Day. My parents used to start the harvest on a Saturday. [*Noise, shouts of approval.*] Well then gentlemen, either we go through point by point spending hours on each or we accept and proceed to implementation.

Wałęsa: Prime Minister. It really won't be too much to go through these most important points. They won't take long. We have waited all this time. Let's work on Saturday and Sunday to finish it and have it all in writing. You will come back and let us know what it looks like there. There's really no hurry here. Why should we rush into agreement? [*applause*]⁶ If all goes well, we really do want to go back on Monday. But we must have it in black and white.

Jagielski: It will be in black and white.

Wałęsa: Will be, but we want to have it.

Jagielski: After all, we have signed it today, haven't we?

Wałęsa: I think we have got 50 per cent agreed.

Jagielski: When something is written down in ink, it cannot easily be erased.

Wałęsa: But Prime Minister, we have so many things still not worked out. So many things . . .

Jagielski: In that case, I propose . . .

Wałęsa: I have a proposal of my own, Prime Minister.

Since we really have contacts, and have begun to understand each other, I propose someone uses his influence to halt arrests. There are now mass arrests, mostly in Warsaw, of – to put it simply – KOR people.[7] But these people are not to blame. They helped us but they were not here and didn't do anything. We really do appeal that no one should spoil our good work, because we are reaching an agreement. They should not spoil it. I request that arrests should stop and that these people are let out. If they are going to do wrong, even we will be in favour of reacting to it. But so far they haven't done any wrong. I propose and request their release.

Jagielski: I can only say this: soon after my arrival I heard there were some events in Wrocław. The matter was cleared up completely. They were only detained briefly.

Gwiazda: Three scientists![8]

Jagielski: They are at liberty. The matter is closed.

Wałęsa: We have a list. We can give it to you. There are mass arrests in Warsaw.

Jagielski: I would now like to read the draft final communiqué. This can be finalised while we are away.

1. As a result of talks conducted by the Government Commission (we can name the Chairman if you like), the Government Commission and the Interfactory Strike Committee have reached agreement on matters of vital interest to the workforces on the Gdańsk Coast. (That is Point One, we shall polish it.)
2. Demands put forward by the Interfactory Strike Committee in the Twenty-one Points and discussed, will be fulfilled in accordance with the Constitution of the Polish People's Republic and the country's economic resources.
3. There will be formed (the names will be given later) self-governing trade unions, based on a socialist platform, ensuring authentic representation of working people and protection of their interests.
4. Agreed problems of wages and social affairs will be forwarded to the government, which will by 30 September 1980 establish a timetable and procedure for resolving them, so far as circumstances allow.
5. In order to establish detailed methods and conditions for resolving problems which require further decisions, a mixed Commission is being formed including government representatives, regional authorities and the Interfactory Strike Committee.

6. In view of the above, the strike on the Gdańsk Coast is declared over. The Government Commission and the Interfactory Strike Committee call on all workforces now on strike to return to work immediately.
7. The Government Commission and the Interfactory Strike Committee agree that the major priorities at present are: calm, a resumption of the normal pattern of life and work, the unity of the whole society, and a general understanding that everything should be done for the good of the Fatherland.
8. We are convinced that every individual at his workplace, and all of us as a society, will do all that is necessary for the creation of prosperous living standards.
9. Let the agreement reached be of lasting value to ourselves, our families and friends. Let it stand as an expression of our determination to consolidate and develop the socialist principles of our social and political life.

That is our draft. We submit it for further work.

Wałęsa: We accept this and really will work on it. We do have minor reservations. We shall include them and agree. So I propose we do not prolong matters because the Prime Minister no doubt has much to attend to. We shall conclude now. The Commissions will stay behind and work, as quickly as they can, to finalise the remaining points. The Prime Minister will come back. We really do want him to come back. You will make the proposal about arrests when you are there? So that they will stop? Because we keep hearing about them and there's no need for it. Then I think we can settle the whole thing by Monday.

Jagielski: But I have the impression that the discussion should be completed today, when I return.

Wałęsa: Yes. If the experts can manage it. But I don't know if they can. They still don't know all these matters. If they manage it, if it's all as we agreed, then we will certainly do what we should.

Jagielski: Let's give a joint undertaking. As the Chairman of our Commission, I oblige all members of the Government Commission and our experts to do everything to finish matters in time for signing today. Now you.

Wałęsa: Prime Minister. They won't manage it. Tomorrow is Sunday. I don't think there is such a hurry. They can work all day, and in the evening if necessary. Sunday is not a working day. So we'll be all right. And on Monday we will go back to work. Let's finalise it just as we want. I promise we will.

Fiszbach: Mr Wałęsa, I have a four-year old grandson. I would like to see him. [**Wałęsa:** Me too.] I mean that I want to visit him on Sunday.

Wałęsa: These eight hours won't save us. We want to do everything properly – precisely – to the satisfaction of both sides. So we are really in no hurry. Let's not decide now. We may manage it. Let's not decide now.

Jagielski: So, let's not agree, let's not decide yet. Perhaps you gentlemen will work quickly and we shall finish.

Wałęsa: Prime Minister. When you come back from there we request that communications be restored. So that we can talk about everything, about everything that is not quite clear. Point Two is settled. We want to telephone people to inform them how things stand. We want to clear up misunderstandings.

Jagielski: Once again, I was busy the whole time in Warsaw . . .

Wiśniewski: I have a question for the Prime Minister. Can the two points already initialled be broadcast on the radio news? Simply to make known what we have agreed.

Jagielski: Let's wait.

Wałęsa: The meeting is closed.[9]

FINAL MEETING (31 AUGUST)

Wałęsa: Our next meeting is open.[1] We really hope that everything we have undertaken will be settled today to everybody's satisfaction. I propose the Prime Minister presents his position on all points outstanding including the detentions. Points One and Two of our proposals are now resolved beyond doubt. Those in this hall already know how the remaining proposals were received in Warsaw. But we would like to have a brief summary so that everyone else can hear how they were resolved. After that, we plan to sign these things, for everything is in fact dealt with. Then, three or four hours after we have signed the protocol, I will declare the strike over, by arrangement with the Prime Minister.

Jagielski: I, too, express my satisfaction that we are able to continue talks and am convinced that we will conclude them today. I accept the procedure you suggest, Mr Chairman: we will regard the points agreed as settled. I will omit those which remain to be discussed and go on directly to the last one – the matter you mentioned – about which a statement is needed. Later today we will sign a protocol to end these talks and issue a draft communiqué, an agreed one. The declaration you have mentioned will be made this afternoon, as suggested. Which of the Twenty-one Points have been agreed?

Wałęsa: Point Three is agreed. Point Four is accepted, but some things in it are not clear and we would like to read them out. Simply to run through them briefly. I also propose the Prime Minister gives us his views on these detentions. I have a list of them here. It's not a question of names but of the Prime Minister telling us how he sees the problem.

Jagielski: I would prefer to do that at the end.

Wałęsa: At the end. It can be at the end.

Lis: So I will read out the proposals agreed with the Interfactory Strike Committee Presidium and ready for signature. These are, Point Three:

1. The government will submit a draft law to the *Sejm* on the control of press and publications within three months.[2] It will be based on the principles that censorship should protect: the state's interests, that is preservation of state and economic secrets which will be more closely defined by law; matters of state security and its major international interests; religious feelings and those of non-believers; and should prevent dissemination of morally damaging material. The draft law will also provide a right of appeal to the Supreme Administrative Court against decisions taken by bodies controlling the press and publications. The right of appeal will also be incorporated into the Code of Administrative Procedure.

2. Religious associations will be granted access to the mass media as part of their religious practice once various essential and technical questions have been resolved between the organs of state and religious associations concerned. The government will allow the radio transmission of Sunday mass, in accordance with detailed arrangements to be made with the Episcopate.

3. Broadcasting, the press and publishing, should express a diversity of ideas, opinions and evaluations. They should be subject to social control.
4. The press, like members of society and their organisations, should have access to public documents such as administrative acts and social, economic or similar plans issued by the government and its subordinate organs. Exceptions to the principle of openness in administrative activity will be defined by the law in accordance with sub-point 1.

Jagielski: Agreed. I accept this point. [*applause*] Are we to sign it? Here you are.

Lis: Point Four: '(a) To reinstate all those dismissed for participation in the strikes of 1970 and 1976 to their previous positions and those students expelled from studies for their beliefs or opinions; (b) To release all political prisoners, including Edmund Zadrożyński, Jan Kozłowski and Marek Kozłowski; (c) To cease repression for beliefs or opinions.' The government will ensure:

(A) An immediate review of the grounds for dismissals from work after the strikes of 1970 and 1976. In all cases where injustices are confirmed, there will be immediate reinstatement if desired, recognising any qualifications gained in the meantime. This will also apply to the expelled students, where appropriate.

(B) The cases of persons mentioned in sub-point (b) will be referred to the Minister of Justice for review. He will take the necessary steps within a fortnight. Those persons named who are in prison, will be released pending completion of the judicial procedure. The bases for detention will be reviewed and persons named in the appendix will be released. (That is, in the appendix you have received, Deputy Premier.)

(C) Complete observance of freedom of expression and opinion in public and professional life.

Jagielski: As this point has been read out, I accept it, in the spirit of understanding the importance of this matter. I am signing this point. [*applause*]

Lis: Prime Minister, since we have only one clean copy, without corrections, I suggest . . . Is there another one?

Jagielski: Here you are. I will have the other one.

Lis: Prime Minister. You were given an appendix to Point Four, drafted yesterday. It lists the names of all those detained during the strike action in Gdańsk, Warsaw and Wrocław. You did receive it, didn't you? We request you give us your opinion on this straight away. It really is a burning issue and we would like some information on it.

Jagielski: I would rather express my views on the matter – just this moment presented to me – at the end, after discussing the Twenty-one Points.

Lis: All right. The Interfactory Strike Committee accepts that. We will go on to Point Five: 'To put information in the mass media about the formation of the Interfactory Strike Committee and to publish its demands.'³ This was not discussed by a working group but the content was decided today: 'This proposal will be met by publishing the present protocol in the national mass media.' In other words, the media will publish the protocol to be signed at the end of our talks.

[*Conversation outside the range of the microphone.*]

Wałęsa: Prime Minister, we really do want to know about these detentions. The whole hall and those outside demand to hear your views. Let's not put off this point about detentions. Let's get on to it now.

Jagielski: Gentlemen. If we are to act constructively, I request we discuss all these points first. I need time to consider this matter.

Voice from the Hall: You've had it since yesterday.

Jagielski: No, I received it just a moment ago.

Wałęsa: But the Prefect had it yesterday. I don't know why he didn't pass it on to you.

Jagielski: The Prefect informed me yesterday that he had passed it on to the public prosecutor. Therefore, gentlemen, all I can say is this. I am here as a representative of the government. This comes under the jurisdiction of the public prosecutor. If I am wrong about this, let the lawyers in the hall say so. I have carried out all my obligations so far, point by point. This matter has been referred to the public prosecutor. I may add that if we sign everything today, I will go back to Warsaw and report this matter just as it was presented here.

Walentynowicz: Do please realise that those now under arrest helped the families of workers sacked in 1976. Workers still remember it. That is why they have come out in support of the Gdańsk Shipyard workers. We request the immediate release of those arrested and detained in connection with the strike.

Jagielski: Once again, I declare with full sense of responsibility that I will go there this very day and report the matter just as you presented it here. I have no jurisdiction other than what I do on my own responsibility and conscience. No other jurisdiction. I am speaking to you frankly – that is all I can say.

Gwiazda: We believe in your goodwill, Prime Minister. However, the arrests continue. New names are being reported at this moment. Prime Minister, these are people who helped workers in 1976 and 1977. It was eventually acknowledged that they were right. They were released from prison in the end[4] and it was recognised that the offences they had committed were not in fact offences.

As my colleague Walentynowicz said, they helped workers who were wrongfully dismissed from the shipyard in 1976. We have just signed an agreement that they will reinstated. These workers helped to draw up the list of those arrested which I will give you.

Jagielski: I suggest we append this to our protocol. As I have said, I will do all I can to report the matter this evening. Regarding the list I have received, these names are unknown to me. I really cannot say much about it. I will append it to the protocol and report the matter. I propose we go on to the remaining points.

Wałęsa: Ladies and gentlemen. We must obviously settle these important matters, they certainly are very important. But we have the right to strike. We have a place in Wrzeszcz – Marchlewskiego 21 – to which our commission and plenary session will move. If these people are not released, we shall declare another strike. Now we should go on. If they are not released we shall do the same again. Of course we shall clear this matter up. So now we will go on to the next point. We'll see about this later.

Lis: We go on to Point Six: 'To take definite steps to lead the country out of its present crisis by (a) giving the public full information about the social and economic situation and (b) enabling all social groups to participate in discussion of a reform programme.

'We consider it vital to speed up work on economic reform. The authorities will define and publish the basic assumptions of this reform within the next few months. There should be wide public participation in discussing the reform. Trade unions should be involved in the preparation of laws on socialist economic organisations and workers' self-management. The reform of the economy should be based on a radical increase in the independence of enterprises and genuine participation by workers' self-governing institutions in management. There should be appropriate legislation to guarantee that trade unions are able to fulfil the functions defined in Point One of this Agreement.

'Only an aware society, well-informed about reality, will be able to initiate and implement a programme for putting our economy in order. The government will radically increase the range of social and economic information made available to the public, to trade unions, and to economic and social organisations.

'The Interfactory Strike Committee proposes further: creation of lasting prospects for the development of private peasant farming, the basis of Polish agriculture; equal treatment for the private, state and cooperative sectors of agriculture in access to all the means of production, including land; creation of conditions for the revival of rural self-government.'[5] Point Seven.

Wałęsa: Let's sign Point Six.

Jagielski: Let's sign.

Wałęsa: We are signing Point Six. [*applause*]

Jagielski: Here, if you will be so kind. We will sign in the same way, so that our names appear together.

Lis: Points Seven and Eight are not agreed yet. Our position is that all workers taking part in the strike should receive the equivalent of vacation pay for the strike period. We would like to hear the Government Commission's position.

Jagielski: Ladies and gentlemen. An instruction was issued by the Ministry of Labour, Wages and Social Affairs,[6] confirmed subsequently by the Council of Ministers. It is expressed clearly and you all know what it means. It applies to the whole country. A fixed advance of 40 per cent of the basic wage is made available to those on strike, according to their point on the wage scale. Following a return to work, employees will receive full pay for the strike period, according to their point on the scale.

Lis: Prime Minister. This position is not acceptable to us. Workers on piece-rates would loose greatly for these fourteen or even seventeen days on strike. Most piece-rate workers are very low on the wage scale. Only an average for the past three months can compensate them for this loss. Payment based according to the point on the scale will certainly give them too little.

Wiśniewski: I would like to convey what workers on strike feel about this. We get only two or three hours' sleep. We are not asking for overtime but we want to be paid the average for eight hours. Why? We all know these Gdańsk matters were particularly protracted through no fault of the strikers. We don't want to blame anyone. There were various complications. We do value the goodwill of Prime Minister Jagielski. But, I repeat, it was not the strikers' fault that matters dragged on, nor was the Interfactory Strike Committee to blame. It would create bad public feelings. People would see it as a reproach, a slap in the face. We understand what you said, but an average as for vacation leave must be paid.

Gwiazda: Prime Minister, the method of payment proposed by the government would amount to 12 or 13 per cent of normal wages for many employees and even less for drivers on some other scales.

Jagielski: Yet Mr Gwiazda, you are telling me the whole time I must abide by the law. I, too, am bound by certain rules and regulations. But I don't want to appear a formalist. I am actively considering the consequences for those on piece-rates, for drivers and others, especially those with children and large families. Perhaps I could take a decision on the spot and report it to the authorities later. Well, yes, let's deal with it like this. The matter can be settled between the director and the workforce by such means as greater economy, using fewer raw materials, increased productivity and making up the backlog. In other words, we shall pay in the way you wish.

Fiszbach: The average for eight hours!

Jagielski: Yes, as it was proposed.

Wałęsa: Let's sign this point: the average from three months, for eight hours, without overtime.

Jagielski: I propose we sign, providing we have an appropriate supplement, which can be written later.[7]

[**Voices:** Without the supplement.]

Sobieszek: As if everybody worked eight hours, without overtime.

[**Voices:** Yes, yes, the average for vacation pay.]

Jagielski: I've already said I'll go along with it. I have no authority to do this, but I do see the problem. Right, let's sign.

Wałęsa: Now the next point.

Lis: Point Eight is the next bone of contention.

'To raise the basic pay of every employee by 2000 złotys a month, to compensate for current cost of living increases.' Shall I read the whole thing?

'The wages of all groups of employees will gradually be raised, above all those of the lowest paid. It was agreed in principle that wages will be raised by individual factories and sectors. They will continue to be implemented as at present, according to specific jobs and trades, by increases of one point on the scale or its equivalent in other elements of wage calculation. For white-collar workers in industry the increase will consist of one point on the scale. Increases still under discussion will be agreed according to sector and implemented by the end of September this year.'

The Interfactory Strike Committee did not accept this position and added the following: 'Instead of raising wages by one point on the scale or one grade, there should be a uniform increase of 1000 złotys for those earning up to 3500 złotys a month (this refers to the lowest paid, without overtime) and of 500 złotys for those earning more.' We think this is much fairer and should be accepted by the Government Commission.

Jagielski: I must ask you to consider what this would mean: not only for Gdańsk, but for the whole country. We worked it out. If we allowed an average rise of 400 złotys for those on the minimum wage, at present 2000 złotys, this would amount to an annual expenditure of 12 000 million złotys. An increase of 1000 złotys would cost the country around 40 000 million złotys. That's the first point. If we are to implement the second suggestion, taking 40 or 45 per cent of employees, from a total of eleven million, then it would amount – please correct me if I am wrong – to 35 000 million złotys. Such a decision would cause instant inflation and completely ruin the economy. So I suggest we adopt our proposal not yours – that is the one originating with us which we worked on together yesterday. One of you put it very wisely; I still remember your words. They seemed to me an indication of great maturity and political and state culture: 'We, too, understand what inflation means, what the consequences are.' Suppose we had agreed. Is it only money wages that count or is it also important that money keeps its value and that you can buy something with it?

Let me add this: the experts and representatives on our side have considered the material position of the lowest paid. They believe that I will be in a position by 30 October 1980 to state: 'After consultation with trade unions, the government will present a programme for raising the wages of the lowest paid, to come into force on 1 January 1981.' This applies, of course, particularly to large families. I was in a position to cite figures because I knew about these proposals and asked for them to be calculated on the basis of employment and the wage fund, in order to determine what the consequences for the state would be. We must take them into account and make decisions with, so to speak, national responsibility.

Wałęsa: Prime Minister, we realise that money can't be produced without something to back it. But we would like to suggest where the money is: in the swollen state apparatus. It can be taken from them – not all in a rush but by an acceptable date. I will propose one. We have our unions, free independent unions. They can deal with this, saying where the money is to be found, and how to take it.

If it is not taken away, then, we have the right to strike. After the deadline, we will use it. [*applause*] I think we can accept the point like this.

Lis: One further comment. The fifth point on the scale does not include white-collar workers.

Wałęsa: We accept one point on the scale for the time being. If it's still bad, if it's not taken away from the state administration as we said, then we shall go on strike. We shall demand to know why they take money that should be ours. So, let's not rush. We shall deal with it later.

Jagielski: I have signed. Now we must consider where to get the money. It must be thought out properly.

Wałęsa: Let's go on to Point Nine.

Lis: We are not signing Point Eight now, are we?

Jagielski: We shall sign it with an amendment. We can sign the amendment and leave it to you. I am signing it.

Lis: Point Nine: 'To guarantee automatic wage increases that keep up with price rises and a fall in the value of money.'

'It was deemed necessary to halt price increases on basic goods through greater control over the socialised and private sectors and in particular by putting a stop to "hidden" inflation. The government will do research into determinants of the cost of living. Similar studies will be conducted by trade unions and research institutes. The government will work out a method of compensation for cost of living increases by the end of 1980. After public discussion and acceptance, this will be implemented. The method chosen should take into account the *social minimum*.'[8] The problem was discussed and accepted by both sides.

Jagielski: Accepted. I am signing. Two copies.

Lis: Points Ten, Eleven and Thirteen were taken together: Point Ten 'To supply sufficient food for the domestic market, exporting only and exclusively the surpluses', Point Eleven 'To abolish commercial prices and sales for hard currency in shops for *Internal-Export*' and Point Thirteen 'To introduce ration cards for meat and meat products – food coupons – until the market is stabilised.' I will now read what was agreed:

'It was established that meat supplies will be improved by 31 December 1980 as the result of greater incentives for agricultural production, reduction of meat exports to a minimum, additional meat imports and other measures. A programme for improved meat distribution, including the possibility of introducing rationing, will be presented by the same date'. It was agreed that 'foreign currency shops [PEWEX] will not stock Polish products in short supply. Information will be published about decisions and measures taken in regard to market supplies, by the end of the year.'

We offered various amendments to this point, including the additional statement, 'The Interfactory Strike Committee proposes that commercial shops should be closed and the price of meat and meat products be regulated and standardised at an average level.' This proposal is to be considered by the government. Our point here is that ordinary butchers' shops have nothing in them, while the few commercial shops have queues miles long.

Jagielski: I gather this is something for the government to consider.

Lis: Yes, for examination and consultation. There may be a variety of views.

Jagielski: So, all right, I shall discuss this afterwards with whoever made the proposal. Later, outside the hall. We are now signing Points Ten, Eleven and Thirteen.

Lis: And now Point Twelve: 'To introduce the principle that people in leading positions are chosen on the basis of qualifications rather than Party membership. To abolish the privileges of the militia, security service and Party apparatus by equalising family allowances and closing special shops, etc.

'It is accepted that people in leading positions will be selected on the bases of qualifications and ability, whether they are Party members, members of allied parties or unaffiliated. The government will present a programme for equalising the family allowances of all professional groups by 31 December 1980. The Government Commission states that shops and cafeteria for their employees are identical to those at other workplaces and offices.'

There was an amendment to this point. It concerned the abolition of the *nomenklatura*.[9] Perhaps, Prime Minister, you would . . .

Jagielski: No. Since we are speaking plainly, I propose we do not introduce the problem of the *nomenklatura* here. We accept the proposal as it stands. This determines selection, doesn't it? I think there is a matter of principle here and we are upholding it.

Zieliński: May I request, Prime Minister, that the phrase 'privileges of the Party apparatus' be struck out?

The Party apparatus does not have any privileges. It has no family allowances other than those received by society as a whole. There are no special shops: simply the same cafeteria as at other workplaces. What is all this talk about privileges of the Party apparatus?

Wałęsa: I see only one solution. We trade unions will investigate. We'll see if there are!

Krzywonos: But there's nothing to investigate! After all, this is quite normal. The army and militia have their own cafeteria. While I may leave work at 8 p.m., they can buy food at any time.

Voice from the Hall: Just like the Party apparatus!

Krzywonos: You have your cafeteria here too, and access to everything.

Zieliński: The same as in every enterprise.

Krzywonos: Not the same at all!

Wałęsa: We'll investigate as unions. We'll get to the bottom of it. Our journals will publish whatever is found. We'll clean it up! So let's not make it a problem now. We'll investigate!

Jagielski: We'll investigate! We are signing this point.

Wałęsa: If need be, we will appoint a special commission of our independent unions. A Commission of Investigation! That's it! We find out how things really stand.

Lis: Point Fourteen: 'To lower the retirement age for women to fifty and for men to fifty-five. To allow retirement of those who have worked in Poland continuously for thirty years for women and thirty-five for men, regardless of age.

'The Government Commission considers that this proposal cannot be fulfilled in the present economic and demographic circumstances. It may become a subject for discussion in the future.

'The Interfactory Strike Committee proposes this be investigated by 31 December 1980. The possibility of retirement five years early for those working in difficult or arduous conditions, after thirty years for women and thirty-five for men, should be considered. In the case of particularly arduous work, retirement should be advanced by at least fifteen years. Early retirement should take place only at the employee's request.'

Jagielski: I accept this proposal.

Lis: Point Fifteen of our demands: 'To increase pensions and annuities of the old portfolio to present levels.

'The Government Commission declares that the lowest pensions and annuities will be raised annually, within the limits of what the economy can afford and taking account of the increase in lowest wages. A government programme to implement this will be presented by 31 December 1980. The government is working out a scheme by which the lowest pensions and annuities will be raised to the level of the *social minimum*, defined by appropriate research institutes, whose findings will be made public, and subject to trade union control.

'The Interfactory Strike Committee emphasises the extreme urgency of this matter, reiterates its proposal for the increase of pensions and annuities of the old portfolio to present levels and adds that increases in the cost of living should be taken into account'.

Jagielski: So your side's appendix to what has been agreed would be that 'cost of living increases should be taken into account'?

Lis: Yes.

Jagielski: Fine. I will add that and sign.

Lis: Point Sixteen: 'To improve working conditions in the health service, so that full medical care can be provided for all employees.

'It is recognised that increased financial resources and capital investment, and improved supply of medicines and raw materials are urgently needed.' . . . [**Voice from alongside:** 'Improved supply of medicines through additional imports of raw materials.'] Ah, yes . . .

Pieńkowska: Perhaps I could read the correct text:

'It is recognised that an increase in the building capacity

available for health service investment, improved supply of medicines through additional imports of raw materials, higher wages for health service employees (a change in the pay-scale for nurses) and implementation of governmental and regional programmes for the improvement of public health, are urgently needed.' Other steps in this direction are set out in an appendix which was handed to the government.

Lis: Point Seventeen: 'To provide sufficient crèche and nursery places for children of working mothers.

'The Commission fully supports this proposal. The regional authorities will present the necessary programme by 30 November 1980.'

Point Eighteen: 'To grant paid maternity leave for three years while a mother brings up her child. An analysis of whether the economy can afford this will be carried out by 31 December 1980, in cooperation with trade unions. The size and length of paid maternity leave for mothers whose leave is unpaid at present will be determined. The Interfactory Strike Committee proposes the allowance be the equivalent of full pay for the first year and half pay for the second, but not less than 2000 złotys a month. The proposal should be implemented in stages from the first half of 1981.' The point was discussed.

Jagielski: We accept it.

Lis: Point Nineteen: 'To reduce the waiting-time for flats.

'The regional authorities will put forward a programme to improve the housing situation by shortening the waiting-time for flats, by 31 December 1980. The programme will be opened to general public discussion in the region. There will be consultation with such bodies as the Polish Society of Town Planners, the Association of Polish Architects and the Chief Technical Organisation (NOT). The programme should involve both full utilisation of existing housing factories and a further increase in the building industry's capacity.'

The Interfactory Strike Committee proposes to add that 'the same steps will be taken in the rest of the country'.

Jagielski: I accept this but not the addition. There will be a different building method in Nowy Sącz, yet another in Wrocław and so on.

Lis: Naturally, but the form is the same . . .

Jagielski: You gentlemen rightly pointed out in the course of our earlier discussion, correcting me in fact . . . [*short passage indis-*

tinct] We are not concerned here simply with these two housing factories, but with doing most useful and effective work for the Gdańsk Region.

Fiszbach: The first part of the proposal concerning this region does matter most. Our housing situation is particularly difficult . . . [*passage indistinct*]

Lis: Point Twenty: 'To increase travelling allowances from 40 to 100 złotys, plus compensation for separation from family.

'It was agreed that travelling allowances will be increased on 1 January 1981. The government will present proposals for this by 31 October 1980.' The Interfactory Strike Committee proposed the amendment that 'compensation for separation from family should be raised to 70 złotys'.

Jagielski: We have agreed that travelling allowances will be increased on 1 January 1981. We accept the amendment that there will be an addition for compensation. The government will present its proposal for this by 31 October 1980. We will know the budget by then.

Lis: Point Twenty-one: 'To make all Saturdays work-free. Employees on a three-shift and a four-brigade system will be compensated for the loss of free Saturdays by extension of annual leave or other paid days off. Ways of introducing a programme for paid, work-free Saturdays, or some other method of regulation to shorten working hours, will be drawn up and presented by 31 December 1980.[10] The number of paid, work-free Saturdays will start to increase in 1981. Other steps in this direction are included in the appendix to the Interfactory Strike Committee's proposals.' The appendix is mainly concerned with changes to the Labour Code.

Jagielski: I accept this point, the twenty-first and final one. We are now ready for the communiqué.

Pieńkowska: I want to insert a comment here. The Deputy Premier promised the personal safety of all strikers and their helpers. One of them came to the shipyard from Warsaw at the beginning of the strike and helped workers to produce the news-sheet *Solidarność*. He simply taught us the techniques because we are not printers or specialists in this field. This was Mirosław Chojecki.[11] He was sent back to Warsaw and arrested on a prosecutor's warrant. He was one helper of our strike and of the Interfactory Strike Committee. Deputy Premier, I would like to hear what you have to say on this.

Wałęsa: We have reached agreement. We are meeting tomorrow in Wrzeszcz, Marchlewskiego 21. By then we will know about this. We must agree which enterprises are to send delegates. The place is big enough for everyone. If these matters are still not settled we will prolong the strike. This is the only logical way out. But I think everything will turn out as we want because our matters were settled. We have settled our Twenty-one Demands. But implementing them depends on us. On our solidarity. On how we watch over the way they are implemented. It's all in our hands. We must watch over them. And I believe we will.

Jagielski: We have here a final draft communiqué. I propose we sign it now.

Wałęsa: I propose a ten-minute break.

Jagielski: I propose we end this kind of work. The communiqué is agreed. We can sign it.

Lis: It is not yet agreed.

Wałęsa: It is not yet agreed. So I propose a twenty-minute break. Perhaps you gentlemen would go to the director's office and have tea or coffee.

Lis: I suggest the break should be a bit longer, while the communiqué is worked out. The Prime Minister will find out, by telephone perhaps, how things stand in Warsaw with those arrested. When you come back the whole protocol could be signed in the big hall.

Wałęsa: We can go through with the Prime Minister for the signing itself. We needn't drag everyone through there. We'll sign it properly in the big hall, in front of all the delegates.

Bądkowski: As to the communiqué, you suggested to me that we enlarge the final point. This still needs working out.

Wałęsa: Once again, I propose a twenty-minute break.

[Government Commission leaves]

Wałęsa: *[to the hall]* You know the position, and the condition I took to the Prime Minister a moment ago. How does the Gdańsk Region regard our agreement? They accept it totally. Thousands are outside. They agree with everything on condition that the prisoners are let out and freedom guaranteed. So the Prime Minister is going to give us an assurance in writing that these people really will be released. Only then will we sign the final protocol. And we will get it – that's for sure. *[applause]*

Some people will not be satisfied. For what remains, we have our own place: Marchlewskiego 21. We are already moving there. Not all of us, there isn't room. We'll review them then. On Monday, someone should come there from every enterprise. After work, of course. We'll talk over the position and see if the conditions – the release of prisoners and others – are met. One from each enterprise should be there at 4 p.m. or 5 p.m. Anyway, we'll discuss all this later. They are just details. Despite everything, I am sure our conditions are going to be met.

We did back down on some points. Even if they do give us the 2000 złotys as planned, it still flopped badly. We know the security service and militia have too much. We'll have to watch that and get it under control. Our unions are going to set up a special commission to investigate how all this is implemented, where things are being blocked, where they have too much. We'll show where those billions are! But we cannot do it all at once, that's obvious. Everyone who thinks, knows this.

Now there's going to be an assurance by the Prime Minister, in writing, that all prisoners will be let out[12] and then we shall sign. We'll sign that our Twenty-one Points are settled and that the strike will be ended. In three or four hours' time, I'll go on television to say a few words: the strike is over, the proposals were accepted. If anyone from other enterprises has any doubts or objections, he can come to Marchlewskiego. I'll be there. I'll be explaining. And not just me. All of us! I think that after so many hard days, we managed to settle all we could. We all fought like lions. Not just me. All of us. That's very good, but it doesn't mean any of you is let off further work. This is the first stage. A small stage won. But the next stage is much more difficult. Everyone must take part in the next one. Everyone. If we mess up the next stage, we'll be back to square one. That's the truth. I think our first test will come when we meet under the crosses.[13] I'll be waiting there at 2.30 p.m. Maybe we'll know then how things stand. If I'm not there, something's wrong, so search for me. But I think I will be and you must be too. [*applause*] These will be the first fruits of what we have done. We'll talk it over: are we doing well or badly? Is everything going properly? There we can even try the next strike. So: not so long not so far. We shall see. In the end, we must have trust.

Tomorrow is 1 September. Children go back to school. The trams will be packed out, and all the usual troubles. Anyway, what's the use of telling you this, you all know what life is like. We

are going home now, worn out. What happens next, we shall see.
What we shall do, will be. Thank you.

Voices: Not yet!

Wałęsa: Not yet, not yet. There is still the official signing to show
that everything is accepted. The protocol and then the real end:
the statement on television that the strike is over: 'Thank you very
much' and all that. That's what it'll be like. One last thing. What
do you think as a plenum: did we do well or badly? Those who
think well, please raise your hands. [*applause, acclamation*] Who
thinks we did badly or bungled it? [*applause*]

Wiśniewski: Much work lies before us. Remember, we acted for
people who believed and trusted in us. We must have prudence,
prudence and yet more prudence. Tomorrow we shall start to
organise these independent, self-governing trade unions.
[*Speaker leads the singing of 'May he live a hundred years'.
Ovation. Acclamation.*]

[*Interval*]

Wałęsa: Prime Minister, High Commission.

This time we should finalise matters and conclude all this.
Before we do. I propose the Prime Minister speaks about these
detentions, as we agreed. So we can get rid of the question and go
on to the final act, which will bring satisfaction to us all.

Jagielski: Earlier today, this morning in fact, you gentlemen
wanted me to make a statement about the list of persons handed
to me here while our talks were in progress. Then I did not know
the matter, nor the list, but I would like to make a short statement
now.

First, I must reiterate what was put into our agreement: no one
will be punished for strike activity or for helping to organise it,
unless he committed a criminal offence. Second, in view of the
various misunderstandings which have arisen over certain issues,
I want to make a statement as follows:

The prosecuting authorities will reach a decision on the release
of those they have detained, whose names appear on the list
handed to me by the Interfactory Strike Committee in Gdańsk,
by noon tomorrow, 1 September 1980. I am certain that if
these persons refrain from acts contrary to the criminal law
in future, they will not incur the penalties which the law
prescribes.

I have done as you asked. My action was inspired by a profound conviction of the importance of what we are discussing. That is, still having these twenty-one proposals before us. I may add that the appropriate bodies in Warsaw have already started work on implementing them. With reference to the statement which I am passing on to the proper authorities, I would request Mr Chairman, that you kindly give me an undertaking that after the signing of the protocol, the issuing of my statement and the signing of the communiqués, the strike will end. I am responsible: I have to put documents in writing.

Wałęsa: Let's do it like this, Prime Minister. Since the delegates all want to see you, I want us both to move through to the big hall to sign our Agreeement. Let's go through now. I have the undertaking ready and will give it there.

THE FINAL CEREMONY

Wałęsa: Prime Minister. We are glad our talks, so difficult at first, were conducted later in a spirit of greater understanding, which sought the best way out of this difficult position for the country. It gives me satisfaction to say that our dispute has ended. When they want to, Poles can always reach agreement with Poles. This is a success for both sides. We shall remember that. We count on exact and full observance of what we signed. I am certain it is good for the country. And now I want to turn to all those listening to me.

My dears, we are going back to work on 1 September. We all know what this date means, what we think about on this day. We think of the Fatherland, the national cause, and the common interests of the family called Poland. We gave it much thought during our strike. Did we achieve all we wanted, fulfil all our longings and our dreams? I always speak my mind frankly and sincerely and I will do so now. Not everything. But we all know we have gained a lot. Trust me now, as you have all along. We got all we could in the present situation. The rest will be achieved because we have what matters most: our independent, self-governing trade unions. That is our guarantee for the future.

We were not fighting only in our own interests but for those of the whole country. You all know the great solidarity of the working people of the whole country with our struggle. On behalf of the enterprises on strike, I want to say to all those who supported us: we fought together, we fought for you too. By winning the right to strike, we gained some guarantees for ordinary citizens. Above all, we won the right to independent trade unions. All working people have the guaranteed right of voluntary association in independent, self-governing trade unions. And now, showing the same solidarity and prudence with which we went on strike, we return to work. Tomorrow, our new trade unions will start their life. Let's make sure they always remain independent and always self-governing, working for all of us, for the good of the country, for Poland. I declare the strike over. [*Applause. The speaker leads the singing of 'So that Poland should be Polish'. All join in.*]

Wałęsa: Are the papers ready? We are going to sign them in the hall. Please give us the documents: the concluding ones.

Ladies and gentlemen. I would like to use this interval to thank the Prime Minister and all those in power who did not allow this to be resolved by force. We really have reached agreement as Pole with Pole. Without the use of force. Solely by discussion and negotiation, exchanging minor concessions. This is how it always should be because applying force is neither simply nor easily done. We now know there is, after all, a mutual, shared concern. We must together gather up everything that has been spilled. And we must make up some backlog, that's a fact. We really must. Above all, we must feel we are masters of this land. This we shall feel and set to work.

I, whom you trusted and believed, promise to do everything to bring this about. I know you will help me. We will manage it together. That is why this settlement is so truly great. There was no force used here. Everything was settled as it should be. How was it – really thanks to our awareness – that those who sought a way out through force did not win? It was a victory for common sense and prudence, represented here, as we all know, by Premier Jagielski and some group that was reasonable enough. Thank you. [*applause*]

Jagielski: Esteemed audience, I regard it as my duty to add a few words. Our joint work has ended as the Chairman said. It really was not easy. The talks were difficult and demanded great effort. But they were concerned with vital issues. They concerned problems of employees, both those present here and those who are not, of their families, their wives and children, friends and colleagues at work. We tried throughout to understand the aims that prompted you. Sharp words were addressed to us. We used some ourselves. We tried to show the practical limits of what we could undertake and actually implement. I reiterate and confirm what has been said: we talked as Poles should talk to one another: as Pole with Pole. [*applause, acclamation*]

I strongly confirm one final thing: we should take from this hall the same spirit that accompanied us throughout the negotiations. There are no winners or losers: no victors and no vanquished. What matters most is that we have reached agreement. We came to an understanding. The major guarantee of implementing our Agreement will be work and its results. Only effective work can produce the goods which we then share out. The whole country is watching us. Let us set an example of selfless, reliable work. We will manage it together, as just stated. I am profoundly convinced that this will be the best proof of our patriotic, Polish, civic intentions. It will prove that we want, to the best of our abilities, to serve the cause of all working people, of our nation, of our socialist Fatherland: the Polish People's Republic. [*applause, noise, renewed applause*]

Wałęsa: Then we shall discover, surely we shall find something greater, that suits us even better. For the moment, though, this is enough. It is already a great deal. [*applause*]

I would like to remind you that the news-sheet we have published here – *Solidarność* – will become the journal of our unions. [*applause, acclamation*] I want to thank the Government Commission, for they have other business to attend to. We thank them very much. The shipyard can go home now. We delegates will sort out what remains. We shall talk things over for another half an hour and then go home too. Thank you.

Experts and the Working Group

TADEUSZ KOWALIK

THE FORMATION OF THE GROUP OF EXPERTS

On the afternoon of 23 August, Bronisław Geremek telephoned me in Warsaw from the office of Director Gniech in the Gdańsk Shipyard – all other lines were disconnected – to report that Wałęsa and the Interfactory Strike Committee had requested the formation of a Commission of Experts. Geremek and Tadeusz Mazowiecki proposed to include Bohdan Cywiński, Waldemar Kuczyński, Jadwiga Staniszkis, Andrzej Wielowieyski, Tadeusz Kowalik and 'a good lawyer'. He accepted my suggestion of Leszek Kubicki of the Institute of Law at the Academy of Sciences. All agreed to go to Gdańsk and if I had some difficulty in convincing them, this was not of the usefulness of this initiative, but of the authenticity of my information (Cywiński's reaction was: 'Tadeusz, you must be drunk, sleep if off and ring me later'). I did not speak to Staniszkis who had already gone to the shipyard on the suggestion of someone there. The rest of us were due to leave the following morning, Sunday 24 August, at 9.00 a.m.

One must state at the outset that we did not regard ourselves as a 'Commission of Experts' but simply as a group of advisers helping to attain a Gdańsk Agreement. No one had a monopoly of wisdom in this situation. My impression is that the choice of the term 'experts' was made by the strikers themselves, perhaps influenced by some myth of intellectual 'expertise'. This could be seen from the selective way in which the Interfactory Strike Committee communiqué of 24 August, announcing the formation of the 'Commission of Experts', presented the members' qualifications. Apart from economics and sociology,[1] the stress was laid on law – believed to be essential for the conduct of negotiations. This emphasis was justified only in that at least two (Kowalik and Mazowiecki) had studied law. None, however, had actually practised for quite some time. History (Geremek) and philosophy (Cywiński) were omitted. Although it has been stated that the team was 'in constant touch with other specialists throughout the country', this was true only in the most general sense that the country's sympathy for the striking shipyard workers was so great that every request of the Interfactory Strike Committee and even its team of experts met a positive response in specialist circles. However, we did not go to Gdańsk entirely unprepared. On the eve of our departure, a number of specialists in various fields brought us material prepared overnight on self-management, compensation for inflation, censorship and on trade unions. Their authors all later worked for Solidarity.

According to Geremek, the Prefect (Kołodziejski) had promised to reserve six seats on the 9.00 a.m. flight to Gdańsk, but when we reached the airport it transpired that no bookings had been made and that nobody knew anything about it. We noticed an extra number of militiamen and secret policemen, attributing this at first to the general situation in the country. But as we passed through the departure gates after buying tickets, each of us was searched and taken to a room under the guard of a cheerful militia sergeant. We were held there for two hours. Then a Colonel from the Ministry of the Interior arrived – that is how he introduced himself – and apologised for keeping us. The delay, he said, was due to a misunderstanding. Wishing us useful work for the good of the 'socialist state', he said we were free to go. We did not board the next flight, however – a relief plane – wrongly thinking it would be a 'special flight', but took the next scheduled departure, an hour later.

The atmosphere at Gdańsk airport was just the opposite: calm and goodwill prevailed. Airport employees helped us to ring the Interfactory Strike Committee, which sent two 'strike' taxis for us. Geremek was waiting a few yards in front of the shipyard and advised us to walk the rest, in case we were mistaken for representatives of the authorities. Some hours later Leszek Kubicki, who had earlier expressed reservations about our status, declared that he had come on the understanding that he would be advising both sides – strikers and the government. Since this was not to be the case, he withdrew from the Commission and left.

Several other persons arrived in the shipyard after the Commission of Experts had been formed including the author and sociologist, Jan Strzelecki, and Jerzy Stembrowicz, Professor of Law at Warsaw University, both members of the discussion club 'Experience and the Future' (DiP), as was Wielowieyski. Mazowiecki did not want to set a precedent by 'coopting' new members, so both served as consultants to the Commission.

Stembrowicz took an active part in working on Point Three (questions of censorship) and his ideas were incorporated into the final draft of the Gdańsk Agreement. Two local lawyers also helped the Interfactory Strike Committee: Lech Kaczyński and Jacek Taylor (who worked on Point Four – political prisoners). Two other lawyers arrived from Warsaw at the end of the week: the renowned advocate Jan Olszewski and Andrzej Stelmachowski, Professor of Law at Warsaw University.

WORK ON POINT ONE

We knew from the beginning that the demand for free trade unions was most crucial, though we did not realise that it would so overshadow all the rest. Almost all members of the Commission arrived in Gdańsk with grave doubts about the feasibility of this point. When I raised the question, Mazowiecki emphasised that the experts' status did not permit them to change the content of the strikers' demands; Geremek advised us newcomers to form our opinion after talking to the workers on strike. Holding such conversations and taking part in the Strike Presidium meeting that evening, made us realise that the workers' resolve was too great to admit of any concession. I was one of those, however, who considered that experts should make contingency plans for less favourable developments and have milder versions of this demand in reserve. A joint meeting of Presidium members and experts was held discretely in a distant part of the shipyard (in a disused canteen) to discuss whether the Strike Committee would be satisfied with a radical reconstruction of the old trade unions, so-called Variant B. We presented a short paper on the subject. It was categorically rejected by all who spoke. I must add that during the course of a whole week's negotiations, I did not meet a single striker or delegate who was willing to compromise on this issue.

After the second meeting (26 August) the Government Commission and Interfactory Strike Committee formed a 'working group' to prepare the ground for further talks. Initially, our participation gave rise to some distrust on the part of the government – even though the Prefect had promised to facilitate our journey to Gdańsk. This was expressed by Deputy Premier Jagielski (whom I had known well more than twenty-five years ago) during the negotiations. He mentioned to our representatives (Bogdan Lis and Bądkowski) that the presence in the negotiating hall of experts, some of whom had connections with KOR, might put him in a difficult position. We were willing to make concessions. Mazowiecki suggested that only two of us (himself and Kowalik) should be present, while the others withdrew to an adjoining room. But when Wałęsa heard about this, he rejected it completely, insisting that we all be present in the negotiating room. The atmosphere improved thereafter. A member of the Prefecture, Tadeusz Bruski, mentioned to Mazowiecki that Staniszkis could also be present and others joined later.

On his arrival for the second meeting (26 August), Jagielski had declared loudly 'I see there are experts present. So, let ours be called. Please tell Professors Pajestka and Rajkiewicz that I have sent for them.' They appeared a few minutes later, accompanied by a Professor of Labour Law from Gdańsk University, Czesław Jackowiak. At the end of the session dealing primarily with Point One, Jagielski stated loudly that he and Wałęsa had agreed to the formation of 'working groups', with three from each side. These were duly constituted after the meeting, under Kołodziejski for the government and Gwiazda for the strikers, together with Bogdan Lis and Kobyliński. Mazowiecki named the following as members of a working group: himself, Kowalik and Geremek. Staniszkis then asked to be included, stressing her qualifications as a sociologist and her deep interest in the issue. Mazowiecki was hesitant, not I think from personal animosity but rather preferring someone more reserved, who would know how to keep quiet when necessary, but Geremek withdrew in her favour.

The first meeting of the working group, held later that day (26 August), was devoted to a preliminary exchange of views and to determining the range of problems to be included in the Agreement. The following differences of opinion then emerged. Our side stressed that the formation of free trade unions was the only way to resolve the Polish crisis. We argued that this should be agreed during the strike and that the necessary legal adjustments could be made later. The government team tried to convince us that the strike should end with a public undertaking by both sides to hold democratic elections of delegates for a union congress and to discuss the form of future trade unions, on which binding decisions would be taken at the congress.

I had the distinct impression throughout that the government representatives did not regard their own proposals as realistic. They seemed simply to be dutifully presenting the position of those 'above' and also attempting to discover what they were up against. I thought they soon realised that the workers' position on the question of creating new trade unions was categorical and there was no point in deluding oneself that half-measures would be accepted.

Most of the talking at this first meeting was done by experts. This was partly because most of them came from the same Warsaw intelligentsia milieu, knew each other personally, or had heard of one another, but also because legal and procedural matters were in the forefront of discussion. Professor Jackowiak was particularly prominent. He seemed to be multiplying procedural difficulties over Point One, less perhaps as a negotiating tactic than from professional habit.

In contrast to the relaxed atmosphere of 26 August, the next was a crisis day. The second scheduled round of negotiations did not take place. Instead, Deputy Premier Jagielski attempted to hold talks at the Prefecture with a few representatives of the Strike Committee (needless to say without experts). The Strike Committee rejected his proposal. However, a second meeting of the working group was held at the shipyard – almost as a substitute. The discussion at this meeting took on a political character and was by no means so amicable as before.

Kołodziejski made the first speech. He explained that the government delegation had failed to attend the morning's meeting because it wanted first to obtain 'certain explanations' from a narrower group. He then proceeded to outline the government's position under three headings. First, he referred to the division of the international trade union movement and demanded that – should various Polish unions come into being – they would have only one representative abroad. His next point was an explicit delimitation of the new trade unions to the Coastal region. Lastly, and principally, he referred to the necessity of a clear and unambiguous political declaration by the Interfactory Strike Committee on the 'inviolability of the system and the leading role of the Party', and on the need to define the ideological character of the future trade union. He stated that such a declaration was a precondition for 'the centre's acceptance' of an Agreement. Following this, the government delegates and experts all made additional points about the political declaration. Rajkiewicz tried to prove that such a declaration would counter-act foreign propaganda which was presenting the strike as an attempt to make fundamental changes in the system. Pajestka observed laconically 'everything that goes from us to the West returns to us from the East'. He warned that someone who swallows too much too fast can choke.

Gwiazda replied that the leading role of the Party meant, in practice, its monopoly over economic decisions, which are put above criticism. This led to 'damaging campaigning': 'Large-scale enterprises? Everyone in favour'; 'Housing factories? Everyone for them'. The root of such 'campaigning' was the *nomenklatura*,[2] which, he said, precluded any challenge to the policies of the centre. Kobyliński made the same point: 'We don't want to attack the Party or intervene in its internal affairs, but we are concerned that the names of candidates, at least for low-level positions, should not be "brought in a brief case". Appointments should be made on the basis of professional qualifications and honesty.' He also gave an assurance that, once the strike was over and its root causes resolved, people would return to work willingly. Kołodziejski interjected at this point that he had no fear of working people whom he 'knew well'. This sounded like an attempt to counterpose workers to the intelligentsia and, more specifically, the strikers to their 'helpers', especially the experts.

During the debate, a split arose between the experts on our side, at first unnoticed. Mazowiecki and Kowalik remained fairly quiet, considering that the lead in questions of this type should be taken by the workers' representatives. Staniszkis, however, spoke several times. The upshot of her remarks was a rejection of the need for the political declaration. I did not pay much attention to her comments at the time, nor to her early departure from the session. The reason for them became apparent only later, when I saw her outside in the shipyard. She was telling a group of journalists that she had left the working group and withdrawn from the team of experts in protest against their agreement to the 'leading role of the Party' formula.

We related the proceedings of the working group and the statement made by Kołodziejski to a meeting of the Strike Presidium that evening. Mazowiecki was the principal rapporteur. I do not remember whether Staniszkis was there. I do recall, however, my own astonishment that this cardinal point did not give rise to much interest at the plenum. Much greater interest was shown in lesser matters, such as the appearance of a feuilleton in the Strike Bulletin critical of Jagielski.[3] However, we did come from the Presidium meeting convinced that we had its mandate to work out a text containing a broadly positive attitude towards the government's propositions.

This text was drawn up by our group of experts, headed by Mazowiecki. It was his idea to adhere to a 'symmetrical political formula', according to which both sides would undertake certain obligations. The Interfactory Strike Committee would undertake to observe the Constitution, to accept the common ownership of the means of production as the basis of the system, and not to question the leading role of the Party or its international alliances. There followed a series of undertakings on the government's side: to guarantee the complete independence and self-government of the new trade unions, to provide conditions for fulfilment of its basic functions and to introduce appropriate changes of legislation.

There was a further meeting of the Strike Presidium and experts on Thursday morning (28 August), devoted to preparing the text on Point One. The draft which Mazowiecki read out at this meeting was virtually identical to that of the final Agreement. We already employed the dual formulae 'independent and self-governing' (the former being suggested by Mazowiecki and the latter by myself), although the more neutral term 'new' was also used. One of the more substantial alterations made later was the inclusion of an undertaking that the union would not 'play the role of a political party', proposed by the government expert Pajestka. Once again, the text did not encounter any opposition from the Strike Presidium. One change of substance was proposed by Florian Wiśniewski: to replace the delimitation of the new unions to the Coast with the phrase 'in the whole country'. I recall reacting very sharply to his proposal for which I immediately apologised. No one spoke in support of Wiśniewski's proposal and it was rejected.

The discussion of procedure was more lively. Wałęsa proposed reading out the text to the delegates' plenum straight away. Mazowiecki advised against doing this so soon, lest the text 'get out to the world' through the foreign correspondents and make talks with the government delegation more difficult. Wałęsa accepted this point and so, it seemed, did the other Presidium members, who remained silent. Their consent may have been more apparent than real, however, in view of what happened later. There were, moreover, rumblings of disquiet from those outside about the lack of information.

When returning to the shipyard with Mazowiecki and Cywiński after spending the night at the Pallotynes' monastery, we spoke to an old shipyard worker who had taken part in the December 1970 demonstrations. He told us that people were worried by the shortage of information and hence open to rumours. Of course, we agreed with him. But our position was difficult. Should we not have agreed to the working groups? Should we perhaps have admitted they were to some extent used as a substitute for plenary sessions, under public control? On the other hand, it had been agreed that they were only to prepare draft documents which would not be binding. They met in a small room, without journalists, in order to facilitate purposeful discussion, rather than speaking 'to the microphone'. Had it been otherwise, even the experts might have become 'political' and paid more attention to the public reaction than to the merits of the case. Nevertheless, we did decide to make a small improvement in the supply of information. We issued a communiqué on the previous day's working group, mentioning the subjects discussed, but the most important point – which was to give rise to so much passionate debate later on – was summarised in the phrase 'the attitude of the new trade unions towards the existing system in Poland'. Everyone knew what was meant, however, since it had been mentioned in general terms at the second meeting.

Following the suggestion of the old worker to 'give the strikers something to do, for instance a survey to answer', we quickly drafted a questionnaire on the subject of the future trade union (what should it be called, what should its chief functions and organisation be?). Mazowiecki, though, advised strongly against it, suggesting, I think, that there would be the possibility of smuggling in bogus 'responses' from outside. This was undeniable. Documents were vanishing before our very eyes. We kept those not currently in use under our feet.

Let us return now to the negotiations and the work of the experts. The Presidium meeting on Thursday morning (28 August) had decided that the plenary sessions would proceed to discussion of further demands, while the working group continued with Points One and Two. It met that afternoon – on the government side, Kołodziejski, Bruski, Jackowiak and L. Starosta (a Reader in Law at Gdańsk University); on ours, Gwiazda, Bogdan Lis, Kobyliński, Mazowiecki, Geremek and Kowalik – but there was little further mention of Point One. Attention turned to the right to strike and to censorship.

The government side presented a written statement of their position on the question of strikes. It proposed: 'the right to strike will be guaranteed by the law on trade unions now in preparation. It should lay down conditions for declaring and organising a strike, methods of resolving disputes and liability for breaches of the law.' In the course of discussion, this formula was extended and agreement was quickly reached on a statement that Articles 52, 64 and 65 of the Labour Code would not be used against strikers. However, differences arose on two further matters: guaranteeing the personal safety of strike helpers and the transition period between signing the Agreement and the enactment of the new law. It was agreed to add the following sentence: 'Prior to adoption of the law, the government guarantees the personal safety of strikers and their helpers, together with their present positions of work.' We did not agree to the addition of 'with the exception of those whose activity contravenes the law' Gwiazda and Lis pointed out that so general a formulation would be open to various interpretations.

Despite the previously-agreed agenda, we then proceeded to discuss Point Three. There were also some small changes in the composition of the working group, notably the inclusion of Bądkowski, our spokesman on censorship at the plenary session and Professor Jerzy Stembrowicz. The government team again surprised us by producing a prepared statement on this point. This one was highly unsatisfactory, above all in its assertion that censorship should prevent publication of materials 'hostile to socialism'. One of us observed ironically that all we needed to do now was decide who will determine which statements are 'hostile'. In the course of discussion at this meeting and the next, four points emerged. On the suggestion of our side, it was established that a draft law on censorship would be submitted to the *Sejm* within three months and that there would be a right of appeal against decisions by the censorship to the Supreme Administrative Court; the government would agree to the broadcast of mass; there would be access for a plurality of opinion to the mass media, which would come under social control, and the principle of accessibility of public documents was recognised. In the light of later experiences, it appeared we failed in one respect. Retention of the censorship's right to protect the state's 'major international interests' was too broad. It allowed the authorities to make arbitrary decisions as to what constituted its 'international interests'.

On Friday 29 August discussion on Point One unexpectedly resumed. As on Wednesday, the government delegation failed to turn up for the plenary talks, scheduled for 12.00 noon, informing us that they were not yet ready for them. They proposed a meeting of the working group instead. Reporting this to the delegates' plenum, Bogdan Lis remarked 'The Government Commission is taking us for a ride.' Gwiazda spoke in the same vein. When the working group met, an hour later, Kołodziejski declared that there still remained certain matters to 'clarify' concerning Point One. Professor Rajkiewicz then spoke. His highly personal speech contained the position of the government side, probably agreed earlier, on the following points:

1. Toning down the negative assessment of the existing trade unions. Replacing the sharpest phrase about their being compromised with a statement that their conduct had 'not lived up to the hopes and expectations of employees'.
2. Attempting to blur the impression of a clear-cut choice between the old and new unions by listing a number of alternatives. Consequently, the fourth paragraph of Point One (somewhat unrelated to the previous three) refers to the possibility of reshaping strike committees 'into bodies representing employees such as: workers or employees' committees, workers' councils or founding committees of new self-governing trade unions'. It was also left open whether the founding committee would opt for a single union or some new association, limited, however, to the Coast.

3. Regarding registration of the new trade unions, Rajkiewicz mentioned the authorities' preliminary agreement to their registration in court. The point of disagreement was: which court? We insisted on the Supreme Administrative Court, while their side favoured a public court. Hence came the general formulae in the final text: 'the government undertakes to provide conditions for registration of the new trade unions outside the existing Central Trade Union Council register'.

Our overall impression was that we were close to obtaining the authorities' agreement to new trade unions. The Government Commission seemed mainly concerned with reducing the impression that the strikers had won a victory. The point was already being made that the Agreement was a victory for a particular line of policy, rather than for one side. This was the origin of the phrase 'there are no victors or vanquished', reiterated at the Final Ceremony.

On Saturday, our working group met for the last time. We worked on Point Four both in the morning and afternoon. I don't have any notes on the question of political prisoners, perhaps because I was now giving more attention to the delegates' hall and the shipyard itself, than to the working group. I have noted only that Adam Łopatka arrived after lunch – he had taken part in the Szczecin negotiations. I also recall the constituting of a second working group (possibly on Saturday morning) to work on the social and economic demands. On our side, the most active Presidium members were Florian Wiśniewski and Alina Pieńkowska: I think the third was Kobyliński. The most prominent of our experts were Waldemar Kuczyński and Andrzej Wielowieyski.

Kuczyński was chief author of the text of Point Six in the Agreement: on methods of bringing the country out of its economic crisis. The point was based on greatly increasing the availability of information on the state of the economy and on permitting a wide public discussion of a reform programme. There were also proposals about agriculture (creating lasting prospects for private peasant farming, equal treatment of the state, private and cooperative sectors in access to the means of production and the revival of rural self-government). These were not disputed and regarded as summarising generally-held views. The question of worker self-management was an entirely different story. A majority of the advisers Mazowiecki had assembled were inclined to favour economic reform based on decentralisation and self-management. The views of the government experts, Pajestka and Rajkiewicz, were not too dissimilar. An interest in self-management was taken by all those disenchanted with the economic bureaucracy they had observed at close hand. Seeing it as the main obstacle to reform, they searched for support from workers who would want to base reform on self-management. Workers themselves, however, showed no such inclinations. There were two reasons for this. One was that the existing Conferences of Workers' Self-management were utterly passive institutions, which people identified with self-management in general, completely compromising the idea. A second, perhaps more substantial, was the familiar dislike of workers for all official institutions, for politics and for collaborating with the authorities even at the lowest levels. An enterprise director was generally regarded as representing the state authorities. The fact that the final Agreement states that the way to attain economic reform is not only 'a radical increase in the independence of enterprises' but also 'genuine participation by workers' self-governing institutions in management' was not the result of the workers' demands, but rather the outcome of influence exercised by the advisers of both sides.

THE PARTY'S LEADING ROLE AND POLITICAL PRISONERS

Friday 29 August had been a crucial day. Most of those on strike knew that the drafting of an agreed text on Point One was essentially complete. Both sides had copies. The Government Commission had received theirs on Thursday, but were not ready to publish it, evidently waiting for approval from Warsaw. This, though, meant further delays. As Giełżyński and Stefański noted, 'Both in the Prefect's office and at the Shipyard, there appeared to be an impasse. No one knew when talks would resume or what the outcome might be. Overall uncertainty and disorientation.'[4] The fact, moreover, that the only place where work still continued was the experts' room, drew attention to us and aroused ill-will. As the reporters put it, 'An increasing number of talks take place in groups and sub-commissions. Does this mean the Strike Presidium is being by-passed? Gwiazda explained to the delegates that negotiations in the small room, without loudspeakers, were unimpeded, without the worry that every word about Polish affairs would be broadcast to the world. Not everybody is convinced.'[5] This was putting it mildly.

The basic source of the strikers' frustration was uncertainty. It was compounded by fresh attacks in the national and neighbouring press on 'anti-socialist' forces. There was great concern about a rumoured raid on the shipyard and at the enclosing encirclement of the military and special services around Gdańsk. Nor were these simply rumours. The number of arrests was rising, particularly amongst members of KOR, editors of *Robotnik* and of those in circles connected with the strikers. The widening scale of arrests inevitably produced the impression that the authorities were insincere in negotiations. Indeed, strike participants, and especially the leaders, had every reason to be afraid that they too would soon become victims of repression. It was no wonder that some of the strikers' frustration was directed not only against the experts, but against the Strike Presidium, including Wałęsa.

Presidium members were themselves subject to abrupt changes of mood. What appeared reasonable only the day before, now seemed doubtful. Reservations about the 'leading role of the Party' formula started to appear. The rationale for making this concession was brought into question by the continuing arrests, which seemed to destroy the symmetry of the mutual undertakings. While the authorities declared that they intended to resolve conflicts within the framework of law, by negotiations and by political means, they were simultaneously acting outside the law. There emerged not only feelings of solidarity with those arrested, but also voices saying that there should be no further negotiations with the authorities – or signing of an agreement – until the prisoners were released. Moreover, there developed a tendency which advocated 'taking the law into our own hands', i.e. founding new unions without waiting for sanction from the authorities. Those 'strike helpers' who had wagered on reaching an agreement began to be trusted less than others who had expressed their distrust of the authorities from the outset.

We suddenly noticed that the Strike Presidium had split into two parts. One was cooperating with the experts, and betting on an agreement with the government. The other was conferring with lawyers in another building, on the statute of the new union. The latter group favoured a speedy founding of the new union, to present the authorities with a *fait accompli*. A preliminary list of founder-members of the new union began to be circulated amongst the strikers. We took the view that such conduct might erode the government's confidence in the Interfactory Strike Committee as a partner to negotiations, since the prepared Agreement was based upon the observing of a legal framework. Given that the authorities had emphasised their desire to resolve conflicts through agreement, we argued that one should attempt to exhaust this possibility first, and only later – should this fail – proceed with the policy of *fait accompli*. Of course, even we were not entirely unprepared for the possibility that the policy of negotiations might break down. We were strongly convinced, however, that such an option should eventually become a common decision of the whole Presidium, rather than let it split into two competing factions.

We brought about a meeting between these two groups – late on Friday evening – at which the policy of negotiations was openly opposed by some 'strike helpers': editors of the Strike Bulletin. Members of the Strike Presidium said little. One of the editors declared that he had hitherto limited himself to providing an information service for the strikers, but that since it was now apparent that negotiations were not bringing results, he had decided to take action to ensure that the strikers would not leave the shipyard empty-handed. He attacked Mazowiecki and his colleagues directly, stating that we practised politics 'behind closed doors', replacing the masses, and declared himself in favour of a policy of social movement and revolutionary activity. I argued in reply that the phrase 'behind closed doors' could not be used to describe negotiations within the shipyard, where the Interfactory Strike Committee alone could take binding decisions, plenary meetings were open and the Strike Presidium and experts could only prepare the bases for final decisions. It was negotiation which offered the chance for a mass movement, whereas the method of *fait accompli* could only provide the impetus for a narrow union, embodying thousands of members instead of millions.

This nocturnal wrangle continued at the next morning's meeting of the Strike Presidium, in which two experts (Cywiński and Kowalik) took part. Experts were blamed for the lack of results so far in negotiations. Those Presidium members who took part in our working group remained silent. Cywiński then blew up and said: 'In that case, we having nothing left to do except issue a short statement and leave.' It did not come to this, however, as luckily, a moment later, secret news arrived that 'Warsaw accepted' the text of Point One of the Agreement. This brought about a general relaxation. The attitude towards the experts radically improved. But not for long. I was amazed how quickly in the course of that Saturday the wave of satisfaction that negotiations were bringing results subsided, to be replaced by further waves of dissatisfaction that the Agreement gave too little, that the Interfactory Strike Committee had conceded too much, above all on the question of the political declaration.

I found to my astonishment that our formula had not been understood. We used the phrase 'the leading role of the Party in the state', which in our view protected social (non-state) organisations from Party interference. We thought the formulation used in the Constitution went further: referring to the leading role of the Party in the construction of socialism, in which the whole society is engaged. We intended the formula to mean simply that we do not question the domination by communists of political power irrespective of the degree of support the Party might enjoy within society. In return, the Party undertook not to exceed its powers in social life beyond what genuine influence and credibility it might obtain as the result of its members' behaviour. This would mean that the Party apparatus would have no authority with regard to the new union.

In retrospect, I think we made a mistake in trying to compress this problem into half a sentence. There should have been a clear separation of the two points: distinguishing the privileges of the communists in the apparatus of power from that of the leadership of social organisations. Acceptance of the former should have been clearly separated from the phrase about the independence and self-governing of the new trade union. No one would then have been able to play on the entirely natural and understandable fear of many honest and moderate workers by suggesting that the 'leading role of the Party' formula would be interpreted as potentially subordinating the new union to the Party.

During Saturday afternoon, the working group on Points Three and Four was interrupted by a young girl, evidently from the intelligentsia, who burst into the room and started shouting at us – obviously intending the experts on our side – for betraying the workers. She shouted something about Judas's hands. In the shock of it all, I don't recall everything she said, but she did refer to the damnable compromise with the 'leading role of the Party'. We sent her to Wałęsa. It transpired later she was a journalist from KPN.[6]

Following this incident, I tried to spend more time in the delegates' hall, to get to know the mood. I also compared it with the atmosphere outside and watched how Wałęsa was received when he spoke to the crowd outside Gate Two. My general impression was that the delegates' hall was becoming more and more overcrowded and intemperate. The number there had swelled to one thousand or more. Less rigorous checks at the entrance let in many local residents. There were many members of the local intelligentsia including, I discovered, collaborators of KOR, *Robotnik*, the Young Poland Movement[7] and KPN. I could not tell which group predominated, but their general character was easily observed. Not only was the proposed political compromise questioned and the freeing of prisoners loudly demanded, but also personal allegations were being made about the Presidium being too soft, isolating itself from the delegates and strikers. Wałęsa was said to manipulate, conceal and even betray, and the experts were held to negotiate 'behind closed doors', to be 'in collusion' with the authorities. There was also discord amongst the Strike Presidium. Some were now emphasising their links with the hall and 'the masses' and distancing themselves from those who were conducting the talks. Wałęsa, Gwiazda and Wiśniewski did their best to persuade people and to calm them down, but it became steadily harder. Even Wałęsa was in growing difficulty. Only the moments spent in front of the great crowd outside Gate Two gave him the feeling of enthusiastic support.

Shortly before the signing ceremony was due, I pushed my way through the hall. I noticed a loud group of potential trouble-makers and caught the smell of alcohol for the first time in the whole week. It was disturbing that one could see great tiredness on the faces of the delegates – as though the news of reaching an agreement had put paid to their ability to endure calmly. Full of forebodings – not helped by the words of the young journalist whom I saw several times in animated conversations with delegates – I rapidly reviewed the alternatives. Entering the working group, I saw a desperate Wałęsa who was saying to those nearby 'the hall is boiling: we must do something to cool it down'.

I stated: 'Today is hopeless. We cannot even take responsibility for the safety of the government delegation. We must put off the signing until tomorrow.' Wałęsa immediately agreed. Jagielski and Kołodziejski were telephoned to say that we were not yet ready for the signing. There was astonishment and dissatisfaction at their end: the Szczecin Agreement had already been signed.

Wałęsa added that the hall should be cleared of suspicious characters. Passes had to be changed and checks at the door increased. He even said to some members of the Presidium: 'You must stand at the entrance.' So it came about that the next day was much more peaceful, despite the continuing debate about the 'leading role' and the political prisoners.

Sunday was similarly a day of fluctuating moods. Admittedly, the strict checks on those entering the hall had their effect, but more radical attitudes duly appeared later on. The matters in dispute were, as before, the leading role of the Party and the release of political prisoners. It was expressed even in the Strike Presidium, where attacks on Wałęsa were intensified by colleagues who accused him of indifference to the fate of those who had previously been strike helpers.

Wałęsa favoured signing the Agreement at once, regardless of whether those recently arrested were to be released under the terms of the Agreement or whether the strikers obtained some public assurance from the government that they would be released as soon as possible after the Agreement. The experts on our side were also of the same opinion and advised the Presidium accordingly. In view of the growing tiredness and nervous exhaustion of the delegates – in contrast to their quiet determination at the start of the week – it seemed to us dangerous to protract the negotiations on this one issue. We also saw the prepared Agreement as an act of great historical significance which seemed almost certain to determine the subsequent political atmosphere in the country. It seemed to us that the continued detention of those whom the authorities had arrested, in order to isolate them from the strikers at a moment of great tension, would no longer be possible. Naturally, we regarded the rulers' conduct as unreasonable. We saw this, however, as an indication that the most conservative among them opposed signing the Agreement.

The debate about those arrested ended, as is well known, with Jagielski's promise that they would be released on the day following signature of the Agreement. The master hand of Wałęsa as a politician can be seen in this. There were several critical moments over that weekend, one of which has remained clearly in my memory. While chairing a session of the delegates' plenum, he received a motion proposing the suspension of negotiations until those arrested had been released. Although he was against such an ultimatum, he put it to the vote and it was carried by a large majority. A moment later he read out – to great applause – a letter of thanks to the Pope which began with the words 'Dear Holy Father, in a day of ending our strike . . .'. After this, Wałęsa had no difficulty in pushing through a proposition tacitly disavowing the previous ultimatum: the Agreement would be signed only once Deputy-Premier Jagielski had given a written undertaking that those arrested would be released in the shortest possible time. Nobody would have wanted to disappoint the Polish Pope by not ending the strike as promised.

THE COMPARISON WITH SZCZECIN

It has sometimes been suggested that the Agreement reached in Szczecin was in certain ways better than that at Gdańsk. Ascherson, for instance, states that the points raised by strikers in Szczecin 'were in effect subsumed into the Gdańsk Agreement. But in a few respects the workers at Szczecin had gained more and conceded less.'[8] Yet to illustrate this thesis he mentions only that the 'formula' of the leading role of the Party was absent from the Szczecin Agreement.

As in Gdańsk, the government delegation in Szczecin attempt-ed to ensure that negotiations were directed towards improve-ment of the existing trade unions. Prior to signing the Szczecin Agreement, on 29 August, Vice-Premier Kazimierz Barcikowski, Chairman of the Government Commission, stated on television:

The question that has aroused most passion in the Strike Committee is that of trade unions. From the very beginning of the talks, this issue has been the most difficult to resolve. For the purpose of a detailed examination of the problems in-volved, including legal and social aspects, we today established a joint team of experts, some of whom are scholars with outstanding expertise in labour law. The work of the team of experts is being conducted in a business-like atmosphere. We believe that the work of the team, which by its very nature must be detailed and prolonged as any legal work is, should not delay the ending of the strike. It can be done while work at industrial enterprises goes on and the proposals that the team put forward can be submitted to the workers for their comment as soon as they are couched in the necessary legal form . . . I have repeatedly stated in the talks that we fully share the opinion on the need to broaden the powers of the trade unions as the representatives of the working class, both in the workplace and in the state. We share the view that the role of the trade unions should be regulated by new legal provisions to ensure, among other things, greater influence of the self-government cells in the work of enterprises, and in the choice of management personnel. A new law on trade unions is also necessary to ensure . . . [9]

It is notable that there is not a word here about the real demand of the strikers for new, different, independent trade unions. On the contrary, it is suggested that both sides agree that the power of the existing trade unions should be extended and that difficulties arose principally with the legal aspects of this issue. Much legal work would be required, but the strike must be terminated first. The matter could be discussed later.

One wonders whether this was designed only to be heard beyond the Baltic Coast or also at the negotiations? Here, it may be helpful to consider the agreed documents, as it transpires that those constituting the Szczecin Agreement were not one but three.

In the basic document – the published protocol – the trade union issue was covered in two sentences:

It has been agreed that, on the basis of the opinion of experts, self-governing Trade Unions may be created, which will be socialist in character, according to the Polish Constitution and based on the following principles: as soon as the strike ends, Strike Committees will become Workers' Commissions, which will organise, if necessary, general, direct and secret elections to Trade Union leaderships. Work will continue on drawing up a law, statute and other documents, in accordance with ILO Convention 87, Article 3. A timetable will be established for this purpose.

How would a lawyer evaluate this Agreement? His attention would be drawn to the fact that the *Interfactory* Strike Committee vanishes from the protocol, as though its role terminates with the Agreement. There remain only Strike Committees at particular enterprises. The Interfactory Strike Committee is mentioned only in the heading to the Agreement, in the final clauses and signature. Even where the formation of Mixed Commissions is mentioned, it is declared that it will be 'workers' and not Interfactory Strike Committee representatives who take part in them. Consequently, the acceptance of free elections could only refer to those within enterprises, not at higher levels.

Could self-governing unions be created before the new law comes into force? In regard to a further point (about the repression of political activists), we find the sentence that 'creation of the organisation can take place in accordance with the legal framework of the Polish People's Republic'. Given that work on the new law remained to be completed, did this not mean postponing the date of creating new trade unions until the new law came into force? It will be 'On the basis of the opinion of experts.' This is puzzling given that on the night of 29 August both sides initialled 'propositions concerning an end to the strike' which stated that 'legal opinion is the basis for creating self-governing Trade Unions'.

The problem is that, so far as I know, this opinion was never made public and that the journalist who attempted to discover it in September 1980, learned only that it is kept in the safe of the Warski Shipyard management (where the negotiations were held). Some sentences, though, were quoted recently by the former Party Secretary in Szczecin, Janusz Brych. He said that 'In Point Five of this opinion it was stated, *inter alia*':

> The opinion has been established that there is no legal obstacle to recognition of a trade union if it fulfils the following conditions:
> 1. The socialist character of the trade union. It accepts the basic principles of the political and socio-economic system, contained in the Polish Constitution.
> 2. The legal character of the trade union. Legality is based on accordance of its statute with (a) the Polish Constitution, (b) Polish law and (c) conventions ratified by the Polish People's Republic.

3. Principles of representation of the occupational, professional, social and cultural interests of employees.
4. Trade unions can act (in the last resort by strikes) in cases of breach of the collective or individual interests of employees.[10]

From this seemingly incomplete fragment of the opinion, it is impossible to judge the whole. Yet, strictly speaking, we have here the same vagueness as in the published protocol. It is not stated whether self-governing unions can emerge on the basis of already existing legislation; nor is there anything about departing from the principle of organisational unity of trade unions, on which existing legislation was based. Without the words 'of pluralism' or 'of uniformity' following the word 'principles', the third sentence is meaningless. Finally, one of the most important agreements between the strikers and the Government Commission, the decision as to where the new unions would be registered, was placed outside the main document—that is the agreed protocol. Only in the 'propositions concerning the ending of the strike' initialled by the Strike Presidium and the Government Commission on the night of 29 August and in the 'opinion of experts' is found the agreement that the new unions are to be registered in the Central Trade Union Council – the Central Council of the existing trade unions, according to Brych's account. The role of the Central Council in management is not restricted: it was to decide the extent to which the self-governing unions would diverge from existing ones, determine the level and territorial extent over which they will have the right to organise, and also judge whether they have a socialist character. Leaving these tasks to the Central Trade Union Council was, in fact, indirect recognition that on the national level, it remains the highest body representing the interests of employees. Even Ascherson calls this 'a dangerous concession'.[11]

It is hardly surprising, therefore, that the three documents of the 'social contract' in Szczecin were brought up again by one of the signatories, writing in a government publication, three days before the final delegalisation of Solidarity. The author claims that the Szczecin Agreement 'opened the way to giving a new character to trade unions', and expressed his regret that the Szczecin Agreement 'although signed first, was later kept in the shadow of the Gdańsk Agreement'. The same point was made even more categorically by the main expert of the team at Szczecin, Adam Łopatka: 'For a long time, even to this day, there has been one-sided publicity for the Gdańsk negotiations and agreement, while those in Szczecin are overshadowed. This is wrong. We should stop this in order to give proper value to Szczecin.'[12]

THE GDAŃSK AGREEMENT

The Gdańsk Agreement also contains some imprecise phrases which could be open to several interpretations. Compared to the Szczecin Agreement, however, they are a model of clarity.

A number of matters were agreed beyond any doubt:

1. The acceptance by the authorities of the creation of new, independent and self-governing trade unions. 'The government will guarantee and ensure full respect for the independence and self-government of the new trade unions, both as to their organisational structure and to their functioning at all levels of their activity.'

2. Defining the role of the Interfactory Strike Committee and agreement of the government to ensure the complete independence of new unions from the existing ones. 'The government undertakes to provide conditions for registration of the new trade unions outside the Central Trade Union Council register.' 'The newly-created trade unions will not join the association represented by the Central Trade Union Council. A new law will incorporate this principle.'

3. The bases for creating new unions were existing legislation, international conventions and the Gdańsk Agreement. Existing legislation would not be used to prevent union pluralism. The Agreement refers to an article which guarantees the right to association in trade unions: 'The government will ensure observance of the 1949 Law on trade unions, which states in Article One, Paragraph One, that workers and employees have the right of free association in trade unions . . . Participation by representatives of the Interfactory Strike Committee or founding committees of self-governing trade unions and other bodies representing employees in drawing up this new law is assured.' The government

also undertook to introduce new legislation to accommodate 'the increase in the number of trade unions and other bodies representing employees'.

4. The transformation of the Interfactory and other Strike Committees into Founding Committees is guaranteed, ensuring their continued existence until new officials are elected under their statutes. This clearly indicated who would organise the new trade unions. 'A free choice over which form of a single union or association on the Coast to adopt' was guaranteed. This is the only place where the intention to restrict the territorial extent of the new trade unions to the Coast is mentioned. Of course, the Katowice Agreement, a few days later, did extend the Gdańsk Agreement to the whole of Poland.

5. The government was obliged to create conditions enabling the new trade unions not only to have 'every opportunity to fulfil their basic function of defending employees' interests' at the workplace, but also to have 'a genuine opportunity to express their opinion in public on the major decisions which determine the living standards of working people'. Almost all the major macroeconomic decisions were mentioned: the division of the national product between consumption and accumulation; long-range economic planning; the direction of investment; changes in prices; the allocation of the social fund; and the basic principles for calculating and setting wages, in particular that of automatic correction of wages in conditions of inflation.

6. The government would guarantee the right to strike in a new law on trade unions, as well as the personal safety and existing working conditions of strikers and their helpers, before the new law came into force. Articles of the Labour Code would not be used against strikers.

In exchange, the Interfactory Strike Committee accepted, on behalf of the future trade unions, not only general obligations to observe principles of the Polish Constitution, and stated that they did not intend to play the role of a political party, but also three other explicit undertakings. They stated unequivocally that the new unions would accept 'the principle of the social ownership of the means of production on which the existing socialist system in Poland is based'. The final sentence of the declaration did, though, give rise to many accusations, being open to various interpretations. These state that 'while acknowledging the leading role of the Polish United Workers' Party in the state and not questioning the established system of international alliances their purpose is to provide working people with appropriate means for exercising control, expressing their opinions and defending their own interests.'

According to Jadwiga Staniszkis:

> During the Gdańsk negotiations, it was possible to get concessions from the government side on this question . . . At worst, they [the rulers] would have accepted some formulation which accepted the Constitution, as happened at Szczecin . . . Mazowiecki and all the experts knew that the government side was in a panic because of the miners' strike . . . one could have negotiated on that. But there was no negotiation over the substance, just refinement of the form. The government got more than they expected.[13]

Staniszkis also recalls that 'it was a dramatic moment when Jagielski spoke and paraphrased Point One: he spoke of what it meant to him, how happy he was that we had given our approval to his Party and so on. It was at this moment that the workers understood what this formula, that had been so neatly packaged for them, really meant.'[14]

Leaving details aside, let us consider whether the strikers' spokesman could defend the essential content of this formula. Defend in the obvious sense that the leading role of the Party provokes a negative reaction from being associated principally with the practice of the omnipresence of the Party apparatus. It is the ideological basis for the *nomenklatura*: the Party's usurpation of nominations for its own people, not only in the ruling apparatus but also in social organisations, through concealing particular directives for appointments from the public. The workers, of course, had every reason to distrust this constitutional formula, since the Party apparatus commandeered the trade unions and so-called 'Workers' Self-management' institutions, in practice removing them from social control. In these circumstances, two ways of meeting the workers' fears existed. One was to pass over the formula in silence, assuming this would be an indirect way of denying its fundamental character. The other was to renegotiate in order to limit it. Here there is no need to resort to mémoires, since analysis of the sentence itself in which the formula appears does indicate that it was the subject of negotiation and that it was restricted in two respects: though unfortunately in too general a form and, therefore, not noticeable enough.

First, unlike the Constitution, where the Party is called the leading force *in society*, this is restricted in the Gdańsk Agreement to the leading role *in the state*. Although this is not, perhaps, the most fortunate definition of the ruling Party, it does imply that the Party will not necessarily play the same role with respect to social organisations, and trade unions in particular. Put this way, it could become the basis for a demand that the *nomenklatura* be restricted, and that the Party's directing of social organisations be abolished. In the Gdańsk Agreement, the government had undertaken to respect the full independence and self-government of trade unions.

Secondly, when the first and last parts of the sentence are taken together, it becomes apparent that the new trade unions are presented here as a counterbalancing force in relation to the Party. The Agreement seems to say: 'Leading role of the Polish United Workers' Party in the state? We accept this, on condition that working people will have adequate means of control, freedom to express their opinion and to defend their interests.' In an oblique form, this states that – from the workers' point of view – the Party does not fulfil the function of representing workers' interests, nor of controlling those in power. Indeed, the leading role of the Party takes on a different meaning when it has to coexist with independent trade unions, which moreover – in the same Agreement – have the guaranteed right to express their opinion in public on key decisions of Party and state. As a compromise between the authorities and the workers, this is not insignificant. It is no accident that Jagielski repeated these two sentences of the political declaration word for word, omitting the last part, which mentions why the new trade unions are needed. It is a pity that none of the negotiators of the working group attempted his own interpretation of this declaration in its full edition. That would, perhaps, have helped to calm the workers and prevented other, arbitrary, interpretations.

The Agreement

Subsequent to consideration of the Twenty-one Demands put forward by the workforces striking on the Coast, the Government Commission and the Interfactory Strike Committee have reached the following decisions:

With regard to Point One: 'To accept free trade unions, independent of the Party and employers, in accordance with ILO Convention 87 concerning free unions, ratified by Poland', it was established:

1. Trade unions in the Polish People's Republic have not lived up to the hopes and expectations of employees. It is necessary to form new, self-governing trade unions, as authentic representatives of the working class. The right to remain in the present unions is not questioned and we envisage cooperation between unions.
2. The Interfactory Strike Committee declares that the new, independent, self-governing trade unions will accept the bases of the Polish Constitution. The new trade unions will defend the social and material interests of employees and do not intend to act as a political party. They accept the principle of the social ownership of the means of production on which the existing socialist system in Poland is based. While acknowledging the leading role of the Polish United Workers' Party in the state and not questioning the established system of international alliances, their purpose is to provide working people with appropriate means for exercising control, expressing their opinions and defending their own interests.

   The Government Commission declares that the government will guarantee and ensure full respect for the independence and self-government of the new trade unions, both as to their organisational structure and to their functioning at all levels of their activity. The government will ensure the new trade unions have every opportunity to fulfil their basic function of defending employees' interests and meeting their material, social and cultural needs. It also guarantees that the new unions will not be subject to any discrimination.

3. The creation and operation of independent, self-governing trade unions accords with ILO Conventions 87 on Freedom of Association and Protection of the Right to Organise and 98 on the Right to Organise and to Collective Bargaining, both ratified by Poland. The increase in the number of trade unions and other bodies representing employees, will necessitate changes in legislation. In particular, the government undertakes to introduce appropriate amendments to the laws on trade unions and workers' self-management and to the Labour Code.

4. The existing strike committees are free to become bodies representing factory employees, such as: workers' or employees' committees, workers' councils or founding committees of the new, self-governing trade unions. The Interfactory Strike Committee, as the Founding Committee of these unions, has a free choice over which form of a single union or association on the Coast to adopt. The founding committees will continue to function until elections of new officials under their statutes. The government undertakes to provide conditions for registration of the new trade unions outside the Central Trade Union Council register.

5. The new trade unions should have a genuine opportunity to express their opinion in public on the major decisions which determine the living standards of working people: the division of the national product between consumption and accumulation; the allocation of the social fund amongst various sectors (health, education and culture); the basic principles for calculation and determination of wages, including that of automatic increases to compensate for inflation; long-term economic planning; the directions of investment and price changes. The government undertakes to provide conditions for fulfilment of these functions.

6. The Interfactory Committee is establishing a centre for social and professional studies. This will undertake objective research into the circumstances of employees, welfare conditions of working people and ways in which employees' interests can

best be represented. It will conduct detailed research into wage and price indexing and propose means of compensation. The centre will publish the results of its investigations. The new unions will also have their own publications.

7. The government will ensure observance of the 1949 Law on trade unions, which states in Article One, Paragraph One, that workers and employees have the right of free association in trade unions. The newly-created trade unions will not join the association represented by the Central Trade Union Council. A new law will incorporate this principle. Participation by representatives of the Interfactory Strike Committee or founding committees of self-governing trade unions and other bodies representing employees in drawing up this new law is assured.

With regard to Point Two: 'To guarantee the right to strike and personal safety for strikers and their supporters', it was established:

The right to strike will be guaranteed by the law on trade unions now in preparation. It should lay down conditions for declaring and organising a strike, methods of resolving disputes and liability for breaches of the law. Articles 52, 64 and 65 of the Labour Code will not be used against strikers. Prior to adoption of the law the government guarantees the personal safety of strikers and their helpers, together with their present positions at work.

With regard to Point Three: 'To uphold freedom of expression and publication as guaranteed by the Constitution, not to suppress independent publishing, and to grant access to the mass media for representatives of all denominations', it was established:

1. The government will submit a draft law to the *Sejm* on the control of press and publications within three months. It will be based on the principles that censorship should protect: the state's interests, that is preservation of state and economic secrets which will be more closely defined by law; matters of state security and its major international interests; religious feelings and those of non-believers; and should prevent dissemination of morally damaging material. The draft law will also provide a right of appeal to the Supreme

Administrative Court against decisions taken by bodies controlling the press and publications. The right of appeal will also be incorporated into the Code of Administrative Procedure.

2. Religious associations will be granted access to the mass media as part of their religious practice, once various essential and technical questions have been resolved between the organs of state and religious associations concerned. The government will allow the radio transmission of Sunday mass, in accordance with detailed arrangements to be made with the Episcopate.

3. Broadcasting, the press and publishing should express a diversity of ideas, opinions and evaluations. They should be subject to social control.

4. The press, like members of society and their organisations, should have access to public documents such as administrative acts and social, economic or similar plans issued by the government and its subordinate organs. Exceptions to the principle of openness in administrative activity will be defined by the law, in accordance with sub-point 1.

With regard to Point Four: '(a) To reinstate all those dismissed for participation in the strikes of 1970 and 1976 to their previous positions, and those students expelled from studies for their beliefs or opinions; (b) To release all political prisoners, including Edmund Zadrożyński, Jan Kozłowski and Marek Kozłowski; (c) To cease repression for beliefs or opinions', it was established:

(A) There will be an immediate review of the grounds for dismissals from work after the strikes of 1970 and 1976. In all cases where injustices are confirmed, there will be immediate reinstatement, if desired, recognising any qualifications gained in the meantime. This will also apply to the expelled students, where appropriate.

(B) The cases of persons mentioned in sub-point (b) will be referred to the Minister of Justice for review. He will take the necessary steps within a fortnight. Those persons named who are in prison, will be released pending completion of the judicial procedure.

(C) The bases for detention will be reviewed and persons named in the appendix will be released.[1]

(D) There will be complete observance of freedom of expression and opinion in public and professional life.

With regard to Point Five: 'To put information in the mass media about the formation of the Interfactory Strike Committee and to publish its demands', it was established:

This proposal will be met by publishing the present protocol in the national mass media.

With regard to Point Six: 'To take definite steps to lead the country out of its present crisis by (a) giving the public full information about the social and economic situation and (b) enabling all social groups to participate in discussion of a reform programme', it was established:

We consider it vital to speed up work on economic reform. The authorities will define and publish the basic assumptions of this reform within the next few months. There should be wide public participation in discussing the reform. Trade unions should be involved in the preparation of laws on socialist economic organisations and workers' self-management. The reform of the economy should be based on a radical increase in the independence of enterprises and genuine participation by workers' self-governing institutions in management. There should be appropriate legislation to guarantee that trade unions are able to fulfil the functions defined in Point One of this Agreement.

Only an aware society, well-informed about reality, will be able to initiate and implement a programme for putting our economy in order. The government will radically increase the range of social and economic information made available to the public, to trade unions, and to economic and social organisations.

The Interfactory Strike Committee proposes further: creation of lasting prospects for the development of private peasant farming, the basis of Polish agriculture; equal treatment for the private, state and cooperative sectors of agriculture in access to all the means of production, including land; creation of conditions for the revival of rural self-government.

With regard to Point Seven: 'To pay all employees taking part in the strike wages equivalent to vacation pay for the duration of the strike, out of Central Trade Union Council funds', it was established:

Members of the workforces on strike will receive 40 per cent of normal wages for the duration of the strike and, on return to work, additional amounts equivalent to 100 per cent of wages for vacation pay, calculated on the basis of an eight-hour day. The Interfactory Strike Committee appeals to the workforce to increase productivity, to economise on raw materials and energy and to improve labour discipline at all levels, in cooperation with the directors of enterprises, workplaces and institutions, once the strike has ended.

With regard to Point Eight: 'To raise the basic pay of every employee by 2000 złotys a month, to compensate for current cost of living increases', it was established:

The wages of all groups of employees will gradually be raised, above all those of the lowest paid. It was agreed in principle that wages will be raised by individual factories and sectors. They will continue to be implemented as at present, according to specific jobs and trades, by increases of one point on the scale or its equivalent in other elements of wage calculation. For white-collar workers in industry, the increase will consist of one point on the scale. Increases still under discussion will be agreed according to sector and implemented by the end of September this year.

After analysing all sectors, the government, with the agreement of trade unions, will present a programme for increasing the wages of the lowest paid, with particular attention to large families. This will be put forward by 31 October 1980 and come into force on 1 January 1981.

With regard to Point Nine: 'To guarantee automatic wage increases that keep up with price rises and a fall in the value of money', it was established:

It was deemed necessary to halt price increases on basic goods through greater control over the socialised and private sectors and in particular by putting a stop to 'hidden' inflation. The government will do research into determinants of the cost of living. Similar studies will be conducted by trade unions and research institutes. The government will work out a method of compensation for cost of living increases by the end of 1980. After public discussion and acceptance, this will be implemented. The method chosen should take into account the *social minimum*.

With regard to the related points: Ten, 'To supply sufficient food for the domestic market, exporting only and exclusively the surpluses', Eleven, 'To abolish commercial prices and sales for hard currency in shops for *Internal-Export*'; and Thirteen, 'To introduce ration cards for meat and meat products – food coupons – until the market is stabilised', it was established:

Meat supplies will be improved by 31 December 1980 as the result of greater incentives for agricultural production, reduction of meat exports to a minimum, additional meat imports and other measures. A programme for improved meat distribution, including the possibility of introducing rationing, will be presented by the same date.

Foreign currency shops (PEWEX) will not stock Polish products in short supply. Information will be published about decisions and measures taken in regard to market supplies, by the end of the year.

The Interfactory Strike Committee proposes that commercial shops should be closed and the price of meat and meat products be regulated and standardised at an average level.

With regard to Point Twelve: 'To introduce the principle that people in leading positions are chosen on the basis of qualifications rather than Party membership. To abolish privileges of the militia, security service and Party apparatus by equalising family allowances and closing special shops, etc.', it was established:

It is accepted that people in leading positions will be selected on the bases of qualifications and ability, whether they are Party members, members of allied parties or unaffiliated. The government will present a programme for equalising the family allowances of all professional groups, by 31 December 1980. The Government Commission states that shops and cafeteria for their employees are identical to those at other workplaces and offices.

With regard to Point Fourteen: 'To lower the retirement age for women to fifty and for men to fifty-five. To allow retirement of those who have worked continuously in Poland for thirty years for women and thirty-five years for men, regardless of age', it was established:

The Government Commission considers that this proposal cannot be fulfilled in the present economic and demographic circumstances. It may become a subject for discussion in the future.

The Interfactory Strike Committee proposes this be investigated by 31 December 1980. The possibility of retirement five years early for those working in difficult or arduous conditions, after thirty years for women and thirty-five for men, should be considered. In the case of particularly arduous work, retirement should be advanced by at least fifteen years. Early retirement should take place only at the employee's request.

With regard to Point Fifteen: 'To increase pensions and annuities of the old portfolio to present levels', it was established:

The Government Commission declares that the lowest pensions and annuities will be raised annually, within the limits of what the economy can afford and taking account of the increase in lowest wages. A government programme to implement this will be presented by 31 December 1980. The government is working out a scheme by which the lowest pensions and annuities will be raised to the level of the *social minimum*, defined by appropriate research institutes, whose findings will be made public and subject to trade union control.

The Interfactory Strike Committee emphasises the extreme urgency of this matter, reiterates its proposal for the increase of pensions and annuities of the old portfolio to present levels and adds that increases in the cost of living should be taken into account.

With regard to Point Sixteen: 'To improve working conditions in the health service, so that full medical care can be provided for all employees', it was established:

It is recognised that an increase in the building capacity available for health service investment, improved supply of medicines through additional imports of raw materials, higher wages for health service employees (a change in the pay-scale for nurses) and implementation of governmental and regional programmes for the improvement of public health, are urgently needed. Other steps in this direction are appended:

1. Introducing a Charter of Rights for health service workers.
2. Providing an adequate supply of cotton protective clothing.
3. Reimbursing the cost of purchasing protective clothing, from the material cost fund.
4. Awarding special bonuses from the wage fund to all those who distinguish themselves at work.

5. Granting progressive wage supplements to those who have completed twenty-five and thirty years' service.
6. Making extra payment for work in difficult or unhealthy conditions and introducing a bonus for non-medical shift workers.
7. Restoring the supplement for work with patients suffering from contagious diseases, or with contagious biological material and increasing the rate of pay for nurses on night duty.
8. Classifying spinal ailments as an occupational disease of dentists.
9. Allocating high-quality fuel to hospitals and crèches.
10. Paying nurses who lack complete secondary education bonuses equal to those received by nurses with diplomas.
11. Introducing a seven-hour working day for all specialist employees.
12. Introducing free Saturdays which do not have to be made up later.
13. Paying double time for Sunday and holiday duties.
14. Supplying free medicines to health service employees.
15. Enabling part repayment of housing loans from the social fund.
16. Increasing the number of flats allocated to health service workers.
17. Allowing single nurses to be allocated flats.
18. Converting the bonus fund into a thirteenth monthly salary.
19. Granting six weeks' holiday for those with twenty years' service and granting them paid leave for health improvement, like teachers.
20. Allowing four weeks' paid leave for those doing doctorates and two weeks' for those training to become specialists.
21. Guaranteeing doctors the right to a day off after an all-night duty.
22. Five-hour shifts for employees in crèches (as in kindergartens) and free food.
23. Allocating cars to employees of the basic health service and paying a mileage allowance or lump sum for professional journeys.
24. Nurses with higher education are to be regarded and paid the same as other employees with higher education.

25. Forming special maintenance teams in Area Health Authorities to protect health service buildings from further deterioration.
26. Raising the spending-limits on pharmaceuticals from 1138 złotys to 2700 złotys per hospital patient since this is the real cost of treatment, and raising the food allowance.
27. Issuing food coupons for the chronically sick.
28. Doubling the supply of medical vehicles in order to meet already existing needs.
29. Ensuring clean air, soil and water, especially along the Coast.
30. Opening new housing estates with health centres, pharmacies and crèche facilities already provided.

With regard to Point Seventeen: 'To provide sufficient crèche and nursery places for children of working mothers', it was established:

The Commission fully supports this proposal. The regional authorities will present the necessary programme by 30 November 1980.

With regard to Point Eighteen: 'To grant paid maternity leave for three years while a mother brings up her child', it was established:

An analysis of whether the economy can afford this will be carried out by 31 December 1980, in cooperation with trade unions. The size and length of paid maternity leave for mothers whose leave is unpaid at present will be determined.

The Interfactory Strike Committee proposes the allowance be the equivalent of full pay for the first year and half pay for the second, but not less than 2000 złotys a month. The proposal should be implemented in stages from the first half of 1981.

With regard to Point Nineteen: 'To reduce the waiting-time for flats', it was established:

The regional authorities will put forward a programme to improve the housing situation by shortening the waiting-time for flats, by 31 December 1980. The programme will be opened to general public discussion in the region. There will be consultation with such bodies as the Polish Society of Town Planners, the Association of Polish Architects and the Chief Technical Organisation (NOT). The programme should involve both full utilisation of existing housing factories and a further increase in the building industry's capacity. The same steps will be taken in the rest of the country.

With regard to Point Twenty: 'To increase travelling allowances from 40 to 100 złotys, plus compensation for separation from family', it was established:

Travelling allowances and compensation for separation from family will be increased from 1 January 1981. The government will present proposals for this by 31 October 1980.

With regard to Point Twenty-one: 'To make all Saturdays work-free. Employees on a three-shift and a four-brigade system will be compensated for the loss of free Saturdays by extension of annual leave or other paid days off', it was established.

Ways of introducing a programme for paid, work-free Saturdays, or some other method of regulation to shorten working hours, will be drawn up and presented by 31 December 1980. The number of paid, work-free Saturdays will start to increase in 1981. Other steps in this direction are included in an appendix.[2]

After the above had been agreed, the government undertakes:

to guarantee the personal safety and present working conditions of participants in the present strike and their helpers;
that the ministries concerned will consider the specific problems of the branches put forward by the workforces on strike;
immediate publication of the full text of the present Agreement in the mass media (press, radio and television).

The Interfactory Strike Committee undertakes to end the strike on 31 August 1980 at 5 p.m.

Interfactory Strike Committee Government Commission
Presidium

Chairman:	*Chairman*:
Lech Wałęsa	Mieczysław Jagielski
Deputy Chairmen:	Vice-Chairman of the Council of
Andrzej Kołodziej	Ministers of the Polish People's
Bogdan Lis	Republic

Members:	*Members*:
Lech Bądkowski	Zbigniew Zieliński
Wojciech Gruszecki	Member of the Secretariat of the
Andrzej Gwiazda	Central Committee of the Polish
Stefan Izdebski	United Workers' Party
Jerzy Kwiecik	
Zdzisław Kobyliński	Tadeusz Fiszbach
Henryka Krzywonos	Chairman of the Regional
Stefan Lewandowski	People's Council in Gdańsk
Alina Pieńkowska	
Józef Przybylski	Jerzy Kołodziejski
Józef Sikorski	Prefect of the Gdańsk Region
Lech Sobieszek	
Tadeusz Stanny	
Anna Walentynowicz	
Florian Wiśniewski	

Notes and References

The notes that follow are intended both to clarify some of the important issues arising in the text and to summarise the principal developments taking place offstage during the negotiations. Biographical information concerning persons mentioned in the talks is provided here. Profiles of the speakers themselves are placed in an alphabetically arranged appendix.

PROLOGUE

1. The backcloth to negotiations was the delegates' plenum, in almost constant session throughout the strike. This meeting was held in the early afternoon of 23 August, as strikers anxiously awaited the outcome of 'working contacts' with the government announced in the opening statement.
2. *Professor Geremek*. A distinguished historian of the Middle Ages whose work includes a study of Parisian craftsmen in the thirteenth to fifteenth centuries, translated into several languages. In 1973, he became head of a research team on Medieval Culture at the Polish Academy of Sciences, with the title of Reader (*docent*) in history. During the late 1970s he helped to organise the 'flying university'. Following the Gdańsk Agreement, he became a respected adviser of Solidarity, taking part in many of its negotiations with the government.
3. *Appeal of the Sixty-four*. This influential declaration by members of the Warsaw intelligentsia first appeared on 20 August. It subsequently obtained several hundred signatories, including a total of fifty-one full professors:

> The present moment may be crucial for our country. No one, though, can claim to be surprised by what has happened. There was no lack of indications that an economic and political crisis was coming. The signals were ignored, however, and the crisis came. Its causes were: ill-conceived economic policies over many years; the authorities' blind confidence in their own infallibility; broken promises and efforts to suppress the crisis; and a scorn for civic rights. Yet again, it has been proven that the Polish nation cannot be governed without listening to its voice. Polish workers are fighting, with maturity and determination, for the right to a better and more dignified existence. The place of the entire progressive intelligentsia is at their side. This is both a Polish tradition and the present requirement.
> Everything now rests upon which way out of the present crisis is chosen.

We appeal to the political authorities and to the striking workers to choose the path of negotiation and compromise. Nobody can be allowed to resort to lawlessness or acts of violence nor to throw down any challenges. The tragedy of ten years' ago must not be repeated: there must be no more bloodshed. The overriding national interest at present is the immediate opening of negotiations between the Government Commission and the Interfactory Strike Committee elected by workforces on the Coast. Even an hour's delay is inadmissible as it can create irreversible or dangerous facts.

In addition to considering their material demands and guaranteeing the personal safety of those on strike, it is essential to recognise the right of employees to elect genuine union representatives. Freedom of association in trade unions without external interference is a fundamental right of working people and must be respected under every social system. Most dire consequences will flow from the present crisis unless the public is given full information about the state of the country, inaugurating a truly nation-wide discussion and providing conditions for a mutual search for methods of improving it. The rulers and the ruled must both be guided by the good of Poland. The situation must not be inflamed, nor society divided, by thoughtless words and insults. There have been sufficient slanderous hate campaigns within living memory. Everyone should learn to respect the dignity of others.

We now need restraint and imagination. This crisis can only be overcome by an abandonment of the dogma that every call for political reform – however essential – is inimical to the state and threatening to its very foundations. Restraint is also needed in society's well-justified struggle for its rights and for improved living conditions. An appreciation of the country's difficult situation is required. Only prudence and imagination can lead to an agreement which is in the interest of the whole nation. History will not forgive anyone who attempts some solution other than agreement. We call for this course to be taken. We call for prudence and imagination. We are convinced that nothing is more important for Poland at this moment.

4. *Blockade*. Besides the telecommunications rupture, a police cordon was thrown around both the shipyard and Gdańsk itself, intended both to intimidate the strikers and to 'seal them off' from the rest of the country. While intimidation failed, the 'sealing off' was rather effective. An entire delegation from the Wrocław Interfactory Strike Committee, which set out for Gdańsk on 26 August, was arrested *en route*. Warsaw airport had refused to sell tickets for Gdańsk from 15 August. The blockade became international when a group of Hungarian intellectuals was prevented from flying to Poland on 27 August. The main exception was a delegation from the Szczecin Strike Committee which reached the shipyard on 22 August. They came in a regional Party car and were accompanied by a Deputy Minister, Białkowski, 'to guarantee their safety'.

5. *Preparatory talks*. The Strike Presidium had drawn up an eight-point list of matters for discussion. We have an account by Lech Bądkowski of the government's response:

(1) 'Reestablishment of telephone connections with the whole country.' Telecommunications with Szczecin were restored at 11.30 a.m. Further links would be restored as the situation in Gdańsk improved. The authorities were also interested in restoring communications, because their absence resulted in chaos on the market, panic-buying of foodstuffs and serious family problems, such as parents cut off from children away at holiday camps.

(2) 'Freedom of movement for strikers and their supporters.' Restrictions on movement applied only in certain places. They were made necessary because the militia had observed criminal elements assembling at particular points, in particular in the vicinity of the Gdańsk and Gdynia Shipyards. In the event of Interfactory Strike Committee members being detained, intervention by telephone was possible. The Strike Committee Presidium could ring the Prefect's office to discover the facts and receive an immediate explanation ('we are trying to secure the freedom of movement of strikers').

(3) 'Reopening of the Oil Products Centre (CPN) station, at least for essential enterprises.' Petrol delivered to the province amounted to only 100 000 litres per day. This was insufficient, but there was no possibility at present of increasing it.

(4) 'Allowing experts to come to Gdańsk (a list of names suggested by Tadeusz Mazowiecki).' There was nothing to prevent experts coming from Warsaw. He simply requested the list of names, so that those suggested by the Strike Presidium really would be ensured a free passage.

(5) 'Access of Strike Presidium representatives to television, if need be simply a press and television bulletin which mentioned the term "Interfactory Strike Committee" – some public acknowledgement of its existence.' Today's 'Panorama' programme on television might issue a text agreed by both sides. A suitable press release might be published when talks between the Government Commission and the Strike Presidium began.

(6) 'Talks with the Government Commission not to be construed as a break in the strike.' To be transmitted to the Government Commission.

(7) 'The termination of the strike to be announced by Wałęsa as Chairman of the Interfactory Strike Committee.' He would rather have a joint communiqué, but agreed that it would be read out ('physically') by Wałęsa on behalf of the Strike Committee.

(8) 'Other matters arising to be dealt with during the talks.' Noted.

There was an additional demand that: 'Andrzej Kołodziej, leader of the Strike Committee at the Gdynia Shipyard, should be allowed to get through to the Gdańsk Shipyard.' Nothing was known about the possible detention of Andrzej Kołodziej, but he would do all he could to 'settle the matter positively'. *Zapis* (Warsaw and London) no. 17 (January 1981) pp. 79–81.

FIRST MEETING (23 AUGUST)

Negotiations opened at 8.00 p.m. after the arrival of a distinctly nervous Government Commission by bus. Their reception was lively: 'on your knees' and other, more colourful, expressions were addressed to the authorities. Passing through the gauntlet of striking workers was a novel experience for these dignitaries, one of whom was overheard to mutter 'savages . . . animals . . . the wild East'.

1. *Smaller room.* Negotiations were conducted in a small room adjoining the delegates' conference hall, linked to it and to the rest of the shipyard by loudspeakers. Although the crowds listening outside did not impinge directly on the conduct of negotiations, their permanent presence was a powerful support to the Strike Presidium and on one issue at least – political prisoners – perhaps a decisive influence.
2. *Government Commission.* This consisted of ten Party and state officials under the Chairmanship of Mieczysław Jagielski, in his capacity as Vice-Chairman of the Council of Ministers. The ordinary members were: Tadeusz Fiszbach, Chairman of the Regional People's Council in Gdańsk (and First Party Secretary in Gdańsk); Jerzy Kołodziejski, Prefect of the Gdańsk Region; Andrzej Jedynak, Minister of Heavy and Agricultural Machine Industry; Zbigniew Zieliński, Head of the Central Committee Department of Heavy Industry, Transport and Construction (and a Central Committee Secretary) and five Deputy Ministers: Michał Zubelewicz (Administration, Local Government and the Environment); Krzysztof Kuczyński (Machine Industry); Tadeusz Żyłkowski (Foreign Trade and Maritime Economy); Stanisław Wyłupek (Communications) and Tadeusz Bielski (Domestic Trade and Services).
3. *Sejm.* The Polish parliament, elected on a single 'slate' of candidates but which, at times of political crisis, has sometimes ceased to play its normal role of 'rubber stamp' for communist rule.
4. *Polonia.* The Polish emigration, mostly in North America, catered for by an 'Association for links with Polonia abroad', founded in the mid-1950s in Warsaw.
5. *Mass.* Radio broadcast of mass, which ceased in 1949, was renewed on 20 September 1980.
6. *Polityka.* A political and social weekly founded in 1957 by Professor Stefan Żółkiewski and subsequently edited by Mieczysław Rakowski who became a Deputy Prime Minister in February 1981 and remained so under martial law.
7. *Edmund Zadrożyński.* A 'social activist' in Grudziądz (near Toruń) who helped to collect funds for the families of workers dismissed in 1976. He joined the editorial board of *Robotnik* and drew up a petition, signed by almost 1000 citizens, protesting to the *Sejm* about food shortages and inadequate social facilities in Grudziądz (*Robotnik*, 32 (30 April 1979)). He was arrested and held without charge in Toruń gaol. At his trial, a series of false charges were brought against him (see Third Meeting, note 13 below) and he was given a three-year prison sentence.
8. *Jan Kozłowski.* A construction supervisor and former Party member who gave up his career in 1974, to look after his mother's farm in Stalowa Wola. He was a founder member of the Peasants' Self-defence Committee in his region and co-editor of the independent farmers' journal *Placówka*. The state responded by expelling his son from the military training college in Dęblin and his daughter from a teacher training college in Kielce. Attempts

to have him confined in a psychiatric clinic failed. His arrest in October 1979 aroused strong protests, both amongst peasants and intellectuals. Fifty persons were detained during his trial. Statements in his defence were signed by many public figures: Andrzej Burda (a former Procurator-General); Professor Edward Lipiński (a founder of KOR); former leaders of the pre-war peasant movement; and the writer Jan Józef Szczepański. It was all to no avail. He was sentenced to two years' imprisonment.

9. *Marek Kozłowski*. A young locksmith from Słupsk, who approached KOR in June 1979 with information about conditions in prison, where he had served a total of six and a half years. As a result, KOR's Legal Intervention Bureau successfully prosecuted two militiamen for assaulting prisoners. Kozłowski then received death threats from the police and was beaten up by militiamen, who afterwards arrested him on the charge of threatening them with violence. In June 1980, 7500 leaflets were distributed in front of churches in Słupsk demanding his release. Shortly afterwards, he was sentenced to nineteen months' imprisonment. The judicial process is described in the Third Meeting, note 14 below.

10. *'Elektromontaż'*. An electrical equipment enterprise in Gdańsk. In January 1980, fourteen employees – including those with long service – were due for dismissal or transfer. A dozen of those singled out had connections with the Free Trade Unions, notably Wałęsa. He took part in a Workers' Commission for their defence. They called a general meeting (not a strike) which the management picketed and only sixty workers got in. By next morning, when workers presented their demand that the dismissals be rescinded, the enterprise was encircled by militia and secret police. The management confirmed the sackings and closed the enterprise for the weekend. The following Monday they announced plans to reduce the workforce by one third – making a further 137 redundant.

Wiśniewski's recollection is not correct in every particular: Wałęsa worked at 'Elektromontaż' for only nine months. He had six children.

11. *Trybuna Ludu*. 'A group of extremely irresponsible people, who had nothing to do either with the shipyard or workers, did not hesitate to misuse national symbols dear to us, nor to spread false information and abuse the lack of experience of young people.' Editorial, 22 August 1980.

12. A reference to Joanna Duda-Gwiazda, wife of Andrzej Gwiazda, and co-founder of the Free Trade Unions of the Coast. A member of the Strike Presidium, she suffered a nervous collapse and spent the last ten days of the strike in hospital.

13. *Jan Szydlak*. The attitude of the official trade unions (CRZZ) towards the strike was expressed by Jan Szydlak, their Chairman, in a speech to carefully selected 'activists' in Gdańsk on 19 August. He delivered the strongest attack so far upon the strike–'the product of hostile forces and terror'–and issued a memorable assertion of the Party's determination to retain political monopoly: 'We will not give up power, nor will we share it with anyone.'

The Interfactory Strike Committee replied: 'Although he considers himself to be representing workers, he in fact represents the institution which is responsible for the current situation in the country.' It decided on an immediate withdrawal from the state-run unions. Statement No. 1, 20 August 1980.

14. *Health.* Alina Pieńkowska, who had formulated this point, responded in writing: 'The Deputy Premier referred to heart disease and cancer as the modern social diseases. They are the current European problems. For us, the most dangerous illness at present is – as in the nineteenth century – tuberculosis. Between 1968–76, it was brought under control. Since then it has increased alarmingly amongst the 23–35 age group. The figures are published in specialised medical journals, but the censorship prohibits all mention of them in the mass media.

'Besides tuberculosis, of which we have the second highest rate in the world, there are stomach ulcers (a fact revealed at the last gastroenterological congress). The increase in such illnesses is evidence of the living conditions of employees: overcrowding, scandalously poor food, total lack of meat for infants (a protein essential for their development). Beef is unobtainable. Chickens are fed on hormones. This leads to the enfeeblement of our people.' *Solidarność*, 8 (28 August 1980).

15. *Four-brigade system.* In an effort to increase the output of Poland's major export item, coal, miners were put on a new shift system in the late 1970s. Four brigades alternated on three eight-hour shifts: six days on and two days off. The change met strong protests from the Polish Episcopate, who criticised Sunday working, and from *Robotnik* whose 'Charter of Workers' Rights' called for an end to weekend working for miners.

16. The session ended with an anodyne communiqué, read out by a government representative. It said that both sides had met, the Government Commission had presented its position on the Twenty-one Demands, the Strike Committee had put forward additional arguments and that talks would continue. The Strike Bulletin was more forthright: 'The statement by the Chairman of the Government Commission was vague, platitudinous, inept in places and devoid of definite proposals.' It concluded that the government had intended no more than the initiation of formal contacts, prior to the Central Committee meeting next day. Even so, a confidential dispatch from the Gdańsk Party headquarters to Warsaw concluded 'the strikers considered the opening of negotiations to be a success'. *Solidarność*, 4 (25 August 1980).

SECOND MEETING (26 AUGUST)

The first meeting had ended with a decision to continue talks but without specifying a date. The following day (24 August), Jagielski returned to Warsaw for an important session of the Central Committee (note 1 below). Meanwhile, the strikers set two preconditions for resumption of talks: (i) immediate restoration of telecommunication links with Warsaw and Szczecin and with the remainder of the country as soon as possible; (ii) broadcast of the next plenary session on Gdańsk Radio; at least 20 minutes live, with a later hour-long edition, agreed in detail with Interfactory Strike Committee representatives. Talks about a resumption took place on 25 August. Bądkowski notes:

12.30. Instead of the Prefect, his assistant Tadeusz Bruski arrived. He said he was empowered by the Government Commission to settle the further procedure for making contact between itself and the Interfactory Strike Committee. I was dissatisfied with this lowering of rank and authority. Even so, I did present our points. He replied that he would personally transmit them to the Deputy Premier, who was expected back from Warsaw at 2.00 p.m.

6.35. After a telephone conversation with the Prefect, I came to the conclusion that the government side is stalling, counting on wearing out the strikers, especially psychologically. I reiterated our whole position as it had been given to Bruski. Asking whether restoration of telecommunications was a *sine qua non*, he said something about our escalating the demands. I replied that it was not us who cut Gdańsk off and that we emphatically demanded reconnection before resuming talks. I relayed this conversation to the Strike Presidium, who decided to put the proposal for resumption of talks without all conditions being met, to the delegates' plenum. They rejected it out of hand.

This determined mood of the Strike Committee began to have an effect. Lines with Warsaw were suddenly reopened. Bądkowski continues:

10.05 p.m. Meeting of the Prefect and Tadeusz Bruski with Bądkowski and Bogdan Lis:

Prefect: There is already a connection with Warsaw. Lines in further, particular directions will be reopened as the talks make progress.

B. Lis: With the whole country?

Prefect: The situation in the country is abnormal. Abnormal measures are thus required.

B. Lis: The country is given one-sided information about events taking place here. That is why we insist communications be restored.

Bądkowski: The abnormal situation was not created by us, but by the authorities. It is they who are protracting it and making it more serious.

Prefect: If negotiations do resume, the Deputy Premier can begin by giving some information on the progress made and anticipated in reconnecting with the country. Is that agreeable?

I suggested a break while Bogdan Lis went back to the Presidium for its decision. He went off. The three of us tried to make conversation – we had known each other for years – but none came. Fortunately the Prefect was called away to the telephone – Jagielski on the line. Bruski chattered away in a confidential and familiar tone, saying that the strike was already over, everyone was tired and wanted to go home. I said we would keep going. Then the others returned and work resumed.

B. Lis: The Presidium agrees to resume negotiations on 26 August at 10.00 a.m. It is expected that the meeting will begin with information from the Deputy Premier on restoring telecommunications. The session will have to end by 6.00 p.m. as there is mass in front of Gate Two at 7.00 p.m. and people will need to get ready.

Prefect: I set the condition that order and security be maintained. On our way in for the First Meeting there were disgraceful incidents, uproar, invectives and banging on the bus outside the Gate. This was a matter of the physical safety of the delegation, particularly as it entered the Shipyard.

The Prefect also mentioned that during the First Meeting, we had experts in the hall who were KOR sympathisers. They should not be there. The Government Commission was conducting the talks with goodwill. It could not act under *diktat*. We replied that we had lived under a *diktat* for many years. This was not a *diktat*: we would not give up our advisers. *Zapis*, no. 17 (January 1981) pp. 84–7.

1. *Three important days*. The Central Committee Plenum, on 24 August, removed a majority of Gierek's supporters from the Politburo: Babiuch, Łukaszewicz, Szydlak (replaced as head of the official trade unions on 25 August), Pyka, Wrzaszczyk and Żandarowski. The purge was obviously associated with the failure to end seven weeks' industrial unrest despite promised economic concessions and veiled threats of Soviet intervention. Those dismissed included everyone involved in the attempt to end the strike without negotiations, with the exception of Gierek whose departure was not yet announced. Even so, the main report was delivered by Stanisław Kania, his replacement as First Secretary two weeks later.

   There were many new appointments. Stefan Olszowski, a critic of Gierek's economic policy, returned to the Politburo, from which he had been removed six months earlier. A new Prime Minister was named, Józef Pińkowski and a whole gamut of governmental changes: new Ministers of Foreign Affairs and of Finance; new Chairmen of the Planning Commission and of Radio and Television; and a host of lesser appointments. This earthquake 'above' left the strikers unmoved. They had learned from previous reshuffles that changes of 'personalities' mattered less than institutional guarantees. New faces were not enough.

2. *Leaflet*. Early on 24 August, a leaflet distributed by the regional committee of the Front of National Unity (the state's electioneering body) in Gdańsk, accused the Interfactory Strike Committee of refusing to negotiate with the government 'despite being invited to do so'. This seemed to the strikers an act of bad faith. The Bulletin asked how this reflected on the professed willingness for serious negotiations with the Strike Committee expressed by Deputy Premier Jagielski in the shipyard a few hours earlier: *Solidarność*, 3 (25 August 1980).

3. *Journalists*. Besides the 200 foreign correspondents and television reporters present in the shipyard, there were journalists from all major Polish newspapers. Accounts published in Poland, however, bore scant relation to actual events. Thirty-six of the journalists, therefore, drew up a statement to the Press Department of the Central Committee, with copies to the Journalists' Association and Strike Committee:

   As Polish journalists present during the strike on the Coast, we declare that much of the information published thus far, and above all the commentary on it, is at variance with the real situation. This leads to disinformation. We are distressed by the telecommunications blockade and the impossibility of publishing articles that present a true picture of the situation. It prevents us from discharging our professional responsibilities. In our view, the only way to resolve conflict situations and to ensure the future development of society, is to provide the public with full information about what is happening in the country.

4. *Government experts.* Three entered the room at this point: Józef Pajestka, President of the Polish Economists' Association and former Vice-Chairman of the Planning Commission; Antoni Rajkiewicz, Professor of Social Policy at Warsaw University; and Czesław Jackowiak, Professor of Labour Law at Gdańsk University.

5. *Democratic elections.* Gierek's speech to the Fourth Plenum (24 August) had announced new procedures for trade union elections: 'These elections should be fully democratic, secret and with an unlimited number of candidates.' The Party thus dropped its prerogative of nominating 85 per cent of candidates. The formation of free unions, however, was still precluded.

6. *Representatives.* A direct quotation from Gierek's speech.

7. *Registration.* In the weeks after the Gdańsk Agreement, founding committees of the new unions sprang up all over Poland and made applications for legal registration. On 22 September, the first of these was refused. While certain small unions did soon achieve recognition, an application from the Gdańsk Founding Committee was deferred. The court made known that certain changes to the statute proposed would be required: allowing Party members to hold office within it and mentioning the 'leading role' of the Party more prominently. In a subsequent hearing at the Warsaw district court, the presiding judge inserted additional clauses into the proposed statute and limited the right to strike. Many weeks of bargaining followed between the leadership of Solidarity and the government before registration was accepted by the Supreme Court – amidst the threat of a general strike – on 10 November.

8. *Statute.* The draft statute of an 'Independent, Self-governing Trade Union' had been drawn up during the strike. It was followed by much discussion within Solidarity; particularly on the question of federation or centralism. In addition to the Committee of Experts, three lawyers took part: Wiesław Chrzanowski, Jan Olszewski (who had brought a rough draft to the shipyard on 25 August) and Władysław Siła-Nowicki. A draft was published in *Solidarność* (Special Supplement) (31 August 1980).

9. *Housing.* The 1978 census revealed the following position:

10 936 000 families
9 326 000 dwellings
1 610 000 shortfall

Demographic trends worsened the position. From 1976–9, demand for housing grew at twice the pace of increased construction. Less was built in 1979 than 1978. *Nowe Drogi* nos 10/11 (Oct–Nov 1980) pp. 49–5. The problem was not helped by the practice of Party and state officials building themselves villas.

10. *Strikes in the whole country.* By 26 August, the strike movement had spread to Wrocław (where an Interfactory Strike Committee had been formed), Łódź (transport strikes), Kraków (in the steelworks of Nowa Huta), Poznań (the Cegielski Works), and many smaller towns. A great majority were declared in solidarity with workers on the Coast and often with the Twenty-one Demands.

11. *The working group*. This is described in full by Tadeusz Kowalik.

THIRD MEETING (28 AUGUST)

Negotiations did not resume on 26 August, nor the following day when Jagielski returned to Warsaw for a Politburo meeting. Some notion of the substance of its deliberations may be gathered from the address by Jagielski on Gdańsk television that evening. The essence of the strike, he argued, was economic. The Government Commission was, therefore, concentrating on rectifying the material situation by improved supplies of all goods including meat, rationing of which was no longer ruled out. He also recognised a second set of demands concerned with freedom of expression and publication. The difficulty, he admitted, concerned trade unions. He recognised a 'crisis of confidence' and 'weaknesses' in the existing unions but insisted that they could be overcome within the present framework. 'The sick body can and must be cured, regardless of how painful the cure will be.' Independent unions were not mentioned.

1. *Experts on Point One*. See Kowalik.
2. *Gomułka*. Discussed in the Introduction.
3. *Poznań, 1956*. See Introduction.
4. *Wyszyński's sermon*. The seriousness of the crisis was indicated on 26 August, when Polish television broadcast a sermon by Cardinal Wyszyński – the first such appearance since the 1940s – immediately after the evening news. It called for calm and patriotism and appeared to underline the authorities' appeals for 'law and order'. While mentioning that the state had not been blameless in protecting the rights of citizens, he noted that workers themselves could not avoid their primary responsibility: for honest work. Strikes could be justified when all other remedies had failed, but they were costly. Even legitimate demands, he added, could be fulfilled only 'gradually'. There were small omissions (on the subject of atheism), but not substantial cuts, as rumoured. The statement was subsequently 'corrected' by the Episcopate and Wyszyński himself apologised to Solidarity, on its day of registration.
5. *Bishop Kaczmarek*. Born in 1909 in Poznań, where he entered a seminary. At the age of twenty he was chosen to study at the Gregorian University in Rome. He was ordained on his return to Poznań in 1936. He was consecrated a bishop in 1959, working in the Gdańsk diocese, and became Bishop of Gdańsk in 1971.
   In the first days of the strike, he was indefatigable: acting as a go-between with the authorities and keeping the Cardinal and Episcopate informed about events in the shipyard.
6. *Trybuna Ludu*. An article 'Renewal of the Trade Union Movement' on 28 August rejected the 'establishment of a rival union body' as a '*de facto* political movement' against the Polish state and its socialist system. Such a proposal emanated from 'enemies' who were seeking 'to destroy the unity of Polish workers, to foster internal faction-fighting and to encourage social anarchy'.
   The point was amplified in a confidential dispatch from the Central

Committee to the Gdańsk Party organisation that same day. Acceptance of 'free trade unions', it said, would split the trade union movement and the working class, paralyse the economy and establish a 'socioeconomic basis' for opposition. It would form a 'bridgehead for anti-communist, Western forces in our country', who were already directing and funding the strike movement. The text was published, without comment, in *Solidarność*, 10 (29 August 1980).

7. *Pyka's mission.* Tadeusz Pyka, a Party official in his native Silesia, was moved to Warsaw, by Gierek, in 1974 to be Deputy Chairman of the Planning Commission and later of the Council of Ministers. As Chairman of the Government Commission in Gdańsk, he attempted to divide the strike movement by reaching economic settlements with separate workplaces. See the Introduction.

8. *Sixth Congress.* Resolutions of the Sixth Party Congress, held in Warsaw from 6–11 December 1971, announced a target of 33 per cent growth over the next five years, much greater authority for the *Sejm* and its commissions, a 'growing role' for trade unions in both 'the functioning of the social system' and 'in shaping and implementing social policy' and consultation between the government and specialists in policy-formation. See: *For Further Development of People's Poland: Basic Documents* (Warsaw, 1972) pp. 241–341.

9. *Łódź strike.* On taking over, the Gierek team made a hurried announcement of financial compensation for price rises, but did not rescind the increases. On 13 February 1971, the women of thirteen textile mills in Łódź declared a strike in protest against poor working conditions and low rates of pay. The following day, Prime Minister Jaroszewicz, Szydlak, Tejchma and Kruczek – just appointed head of the Central Trade Union Council – were sent to face the strikers. After a series of confrontations, the delegation went back to Warsaw. The price increases were annulled the next day.

10. *Rule book on censorship.* Guidelines for Polish censors were made public by a young clerk employed in its Kraków office from August 1975 until March 1977 when he defected to Sweden with a mass of documents. He sent them to KOR. Many of the banned subjects turned out to be social: environmental pollution, road safety, alcoholism, shortage of housing and kindergartens, and inadequacy of student grants. Religious articles suffered from great interference and the Catholic *Tygodnik Powszechny* was the newspaper most heavily censored. Only a handful of items from the 700 pages of material had any real connection with state secrets. These were given in general outline when KOR duplicated the documents for distribution to prominent members of the Polish establishment and to the general public. The entire collection appeared in two volumes abroad: *Czarna Księga Cenzury PRL*, vol. I (1977), vol. II (1978) (Aneks, London). They await translation in full, but a selection may be found in George Schöpflin (ed), *Censorship and Political Communication in Eastern Europe* (London: Frances Pinter, 1983) pp. 33–102.

11. *Appeal.* The appeal had been suggested by Catholic intellectuals in Gdańsk. The Strike Presidium and experts had grave doubts about it, but agreed to the appeal, provided it was delivered on television. The government suggested a joint appeal, in which they took part. This was rejected. In the

end, Wałęsa simply made a verbal appeal in front of Gate Two, during a break in the negotiations.

12. *Lawyers.* The defence in all three cases was conducted by Władysław Siła-Nowicki, a distinguished lawyer who had been arrested in 1947 for political reasons and imprisoned for more than nine years. After his rehabilitation in 1956, he returned to the profession and acted in defence of political prisoners at many trials.

His brilliant appeal in the case of Zadrożyński and his submission to the Minister of Justice on behalf of Jan Kozłowski were published as appendices to the Polish Helsinki Committee's presentation to the Madrid review conference: *O przestrzeganiu praw człowieka i obywatela w P.R.L.* (On the Observation of Human Rights and Rights of Citizens in Poland) *Document No. 1* (Warsaw, November 1980) pp. 165–82.

13. *Zadrożyński's trial.* Edmund Zadrożyński, an editor of *Robotnik* in the town of Grudziądz was arrested on 1 July 1979, charged in September and eventually brought to trial on 25 February 1980. The court found him guilty on three counts:

1. Inciting his son Mirosław to steal car parts and profiting from this. The evidence here was his son's confession, which was withdrawn several times during the trial. A second son, Andrzej, not only denied the accusation but gave evidence of police methods used to make him testify against his father. A form of torture had been employed: tying him up with belts and then tightening them greatly.
2. Providing Ludomir Borowski with 90 000 złotys for the purchase of dollars. This was categorically denied: Zadrożyński stated that he did not know Borowski. Had he done so, he is unlikely to have trusted him with such a large sum of money: Borowski was a thief.
3. Bribing a garage mechanic to give him a new car body. Far from persuading the mechanic to damage his car, Zadrożyński had been to the garage on numerous occasions to pay the mechanic for repair work undertaken.

The court dismissed two further charges – of bribe-taking and of perjury – and sentenced him to three years in prison.

14. *Marek Kozłowski.* The long and tragic case of Marek Kozłowski began with his arrest on charges of attempting to steal coal for which he was sentenced to a year and a half in prison. On his release, he was asked to collaborate with the militia but refused. Militia Sergeant Terpilkowski threatened to 'finish him off'. A year later he was detained, charged and acquitted. He was then accused of threatening behaviour, but the district court quashed the case for lack of evidence. He was rearrested illegally on the same charge and held for seven months, while the case was transferred from one court to another. Eventually, the regional court sent him to prison for seven months. Later, he was arrested on charges of petty theft. The investigation was conducted by Sergeant Terpilkowski. It was shown in court that the stolen item had been taken by someone else from another place, yet the regional court sentenced him to five years imprisonment. He served the sentence in full.

In April 1980, he was tried for causing a public disturbance, for which the police prosecution demanded a three month sentence. The court imposed a 2000 złotys fine. He was rearrested on 26 April on serious charges of hooliganism, threatening the militia and interference with their performance of normal duties. He was given a further nineteen months in prison.

15. *Wałęsa's reinstatement.* His successive dismissals were from the Gdańsk Shipyard (March 1976); ZREMB (November 1978); and 'Elektromontaż' (February 1980). On the second day of the strike, the Director of the Gdańsk Shipyard issued the following certificate: 'In connection with the undertaking by Lech Wałęsa to observe work regulations, the management of the Lenin Shipyard enrols the citizen in work as from 15 August 1980, in his capacity as electrical engineer in the Transport Section, pay grade IX.' A postscript added: 'continuity of employment is recognised'.

16. *Monument.* A monument in memory of those killed by the authorities in December 1970 was proposed and accepted on the first day of the strike. Its proportions were to be huge: thirty metres' high, consisting of four crosses (to symbolise the first four workers to fall in front of Gate Two) with anchors suspended from them to denote hope. A flame burns beneath the monument which was built entirely by public subscription.

17. *Mrągowo.* Mishearing by Jagielski.

18. *Błażej Wyszkowski.* A gold medallist for sailing in the 1966 Olympics. He was arrested after a joint meeting in Gdańsk between students, the editors of *Robotnik* and the Free Trade Unions of the Coast, of which his brother Krzysztof was co-founder. On 30 May 1978, he was sentenced to two months' imprisonment for 'causing a public assembly'. His defence lawyers and family were prevented from entering the court and he was not permitted to call witnesses.

19. Discussion did not resume that day, nor did the Government Commission arrive the following morning. The Strike Bulletin commented: 'In our view, it is high time the Government Commission showed greater understanding of the strikers' demands at a moment when the country stands on the brink of a general strike. The avalanche set in motion by the workers on the Coast, can only be contained by a radical change in the attitude of the authorities towards working people. The time has come when the government can no longer remain deaf to what society is saying and demanding. We hope they have realised this by now.' *Solidarność,* 9 (29 August 1980).

FOURTH MEETING (30 AUGUST)

1. *Leading role.* The doctrine of the 'leading role' of the Party in a communist state has never been defined clearly. Proposed incorporation of the phrase into the Constitution was widely debated by Polish intellectuals in the winter of 1975-6. A referendum on the changes was proposed. Though none was held, concessions were made to these protesters, including the weakening of the clause which mentioned relations with the Soviet Union. The Party's role was defined in the new Constitution as 'the leading force in society in the construction of socialism'.

During the Gdańsk negotiations, the authorities began to use the argument that free trade unions would be incompatible with the

Constitution, since they would be independent of the Party – the 'leading force in society'. The official line – and perhaps fear – was that free unions would develop into a political opposition. *Dziennik Bałtycki* commented on 28 August: 'Nowhere in the world are workers' organisations unaffiliated to a definite political movement or ideology with party political content.' Experts on the government side proposed that safeguard clauses should be written into the Agreement: that the new unions would accept the 'leading role' of the Party, observe the Constitution and 'do not intend to act as a political party'. See Tadeusz Kowalik.

2. *Workers' Committees.* Despite the profusion of terminology, the labour force opted overwhelmingly for new institutions, the largest of which, Solidarity, had enrolled 9.5 million members by the end of 1980.

3. *Research Centres.* A centre for Social and Professional Studies, based in Gdańsk and Warsaw, was created by Solidarity's National Executive Committee (KKP) under Andrzej Wielowieyski. Its functions were twofold: to provide the National Executive with 'research, analyses and predictions needed for the work of the Union' and pedagogic: to produce educational material for union courses. A second centre, for Social Research, attached to the Solidarity Warsaw Branch (Mazowsze), published a series of important papers between March and December 1981. These included works by Stefan Kurowski and Jacek Kurczewski, and collective reports on the economy, health and housing.

4. *Union publications.* A plethora of publications appeared in the following months. Among the most important were the censored newspapers *Jedność* (Szczecin) and *Tygodnik Solidarność* (Warsaw). The information bulletin of the Solidarity Press Agency in Warsaw, *AS*, is also indispensable for an understanding of the movement. It included a systematic review of the regional press of Solidarity and reprinted the most significant articles.

5. *Szczecin.* The Interfactory Strike Committee in Szczecin reached an Agreement with a Government Commission headed by Kazimierz Barcikowski on 30 August. It provided for trade unions that were to be 'self-governing' and 'socialist in character' conforming to the Constitution, but neither their 'independence' nor the 'leading role' of the Party were mentioned. The right to strike was not included, though the safety of those then on strike was assured. Most other issues were referred to the government for resolution within three months. Only on one issue was it more specific than the Gdańsk Agreement: family allowances – providing targets and time-limits for the levelling of payments of the militia and other groups. Professor Andrzej Tymowski assisted in drawing up this clause.

Unlike Gdańsk, Szczecin strikers had little contact with the intelligentsia or oppositional milieu. They shunned publicity and treated the negotiations as a private affair. Every sentence negotiated had to be ratified by delegates of all the Strike Committees and in turn approved by their workplaces. These numbered 740 by the last day of negotiations.

6. *Rush.* The evident haste of the Government Commission to reach a settlement caused the strikers considerable anxiety. Some nineteen points still remained to be accepted. The news of the miners' strike in Silesia and the threat of steelworkers in Kraków and Katowice to extinguish the blast furnaces had been received, but was yet to be confirmed, so strikers could

not be sure that this was the cause of Jagielski's haste. They feared, rather, some mistake on their part. Anna Walentynowicz recalled: 'Afraid that we had overlooked something, we called for an adjournment and went through the Agreement point by point for the whole night. When the miners' strike was confirmed, we sighed with relief. It was not some oversight on our part which had made the government so pressed for time.'

7. *KOR people.* On 28 August, the Prosecutor's Office in Warsaw had issued a number of arrest warrants, including those for members of KOR: Seweryn Blumsztajn, Mirosław Chojecki, Wiesław Kęcik, Jacek Kuroń, Jan Lityński, Adam Michnik and Zbigniew Romaszewski. Many other people, including editors of *Robotnik*, were being held on unknown charges. The relationship of KOR to the Strike Committee was indirect. As Wałęsa put it on 22 August: 'These people are not our leaders – because we lead ourselves – but they are offering us assistance, as they did before.'

The question of political prisoners (Point Four) was pursued most energetically by Andrzej Gwiazda (who had formulated it) and Alina Pieńkowska.

8. *Wrocław.* The Interfactory Strike Committee in Wrocław had contacts with local scholars, three of whom – Professors Mirosława Chamcówna and Roman Duda (a mathematician), and Dr Jan Waszkiewicz –were detained by the militia.

9. After the meeting, Jagielski returned to a Central Committee Plenum in Warsaw. In his absence, intense debate broke out amongst the strike delegates, on two main issues. One concerned the political prisoners. Wałęsa's proposal to accept verbal assurances from Deputy Premier Jagielski that they would be released was rejected by the plenum. Delegates insisted on a written pledge. Feelings on this issue ran very high. The threat of a prolonged strike was mooted. Walentynowicz reported the public mood to be: 'We will strike for another week if necessary: we won't abandon the political prisoners.'

The other worry concerned Point One. At the last stage of the strike, many delegates appear to have had second thoughts about what had already been initialled and to feel that, after all, they had been cheated. One source of anxiety was the geographic extent of the future union. Summarising the work in committee on this issue, Gwiazda stated 'They wanted a Union that was only regional, but we refused to accept this. As a result, however, we had to accept a certain vagueness in the text.' He pointed out that workplaces all over the country were now taking up the Twenty-one Demands and that no one would be able to prevent one region collaborating with others. As the evening wore on, there came rumours from Warsaw that Gierek would be replaced as First Secretary by Stefan Olszowski, with a much harder policy. The inclusion of the 'leading role' of the Party clause began to take on a new light.

Wałęsa took the view that 'If the Party is hoping to impose its views on the Union and to run it, they are mistaken. The Agreement is clear. These free unions will be those we elect democratically. It's all up to us. We will each have the Union we ourselves create.' He appealed for calm: 'We know that there are provocateurs in our midst . . . people who don't like what is happening. They will not be given a chance. We must prevent them from acting. We might still loose. We must not miss our chance of winning.' These debates are described by Jean-Yves Potel, *The Summer Before the Frost* (London: Pluto Press, 1981) pp. 167–71 and by Tadeusz Kowalik.

FINAL MEETING (31 AUGUST)

The events of the final day were as follows:

11.00 Government delegation arrives
11.30 Final Meeting opens
 1.20 Wałęsa addresses the delegates' plenum
 4.30 Final Meeting reconvenes – Jagielski's undertaking
 4.40 Signing Ceremony
      Government delegation leaves
      Thanks to the experts
 5.55 First session of the Founding Committee of Solidarity

1. After the strikers had celebrated Sunday mass, Jagielski reappeared with the Central Committee's acceptance of the Gdańsk Agreement. Its deliberations remain a close secret: Gierek's speech was not published and even the stenographers were removed from the hall. It seems that two arguments had proved decisive: that an agreement had already been signed in Szczecin – which may cast new light on the haste shown there by government negotiators – and that there was no alternative. The latter may have been argued by the service chiefs and by Stanisław Kania, head of internal security. Persistent rumours suggest that this had been a minority view within the Politburo until the last moment. Plans for the declaration of a 'state of war' and strike-breaking by force were undoubtedly well advanced.

2. *Censorship statute.* A new law eventually materialised in autumn 1981. It published guidelines for censorship activity and afforded a system of appeal against censorship decisions – both great changes from previous practice. In other respects, it fell short of the Gdańsk Agreement. See: *Tygodnik Solidarność*, 30 (23 October 1981).

3. Publication of demands had taken place in the Youth Union paper *Sztandar Młodych* on 27 August. The Agreement itself appeared in *Głos Wybrzeża* (Gdańsk) on 1 September and in *Życie Warszawy*, *Głos Pracy* (organ of the official unions) and dailies of other regions the following day.

4. *Released in the end.* In the third week of May 1977, a number of KOR members were arrested and charged with 'anti-state' crimes: Seweryn Blumsztajn, Mirosław Chojecki, Jacek Kuroń, Jan Józef Lipski, Jan Lityński, Antoni Macierewicz, Adam Michnik, Piotr Naimski and Wojciech Ostrowski, together with KOR associates. Hundreds of persons signed a protest letter to Gierek. The prisoners were amnestied shortly afterwards.

5. *Rural self-government.* The Government Commission did not offer any observations on the organisation and future of Polish agriculture. The Strike Committee, by contrast, sought to encourage initiatives that had already taken place.

An independent farmers' movement revived in 1978, when 500 000 peasants withheld contributions from a new pension scheme introduced by the state. On 8 May, a meeting of peasants in the district of Ostrówek, near Lublin, discussed possible means of self-defence. Two forms subsequently emerged: peasants' self-defence committees in Kolonia Góra (30 July), Zbrosza Duża (9 September) and Rzeszów (12 November) and Provisional Committees of Independent Agricultural Trade Unions formed near Radom (10 September). The latter's programme called for a union 'independent of Party authorities and the state', for the revival of a peasants' self-government movement and for cooperation between peasants and workers. A number of newsheets appeared: *Wieś Rzeszowska, Rolnik Niezależny, Gospodarz* and *Placówka*. The arrest of Jan Kozłowski failed to halt this movement.

The Gdańsk Agreement initiated a fresh stage of independent activity. Independent unions were quickly formed, beginning with *NSZZ Rolników 'Solidarność Wiejska'* (September 1980). Solidarity tried unsuccessfully to raise the question of their legal registration at talks with the government in October 1980 and January 1981: *Robotnik*, 73 (7 Feb 1981) p. 2. The unions realised that unification was their only chance of success. On 12 February, they amalgamated in Warsaw to constitute *NSZZ Rolników Indiwidualnych 'Solidarność Wiejska'*. Government acceptance of this institution was given in the conclusion of the 'Bydgoszcz crisis' (March 1981) and the union was legally registered on 12 May.

6. *Instruction*. Workplaces in Gdańsk, Elbląg, Szczecin, Słupsk and Koszalin received a telex from the Deputy Minister of Labour, Wages and Social Affairs on 28 August which stated:

   1. Strike Committees and directors of workplaces on strike should be informed that we are proposing to make partial compensation of wages for workers on strike.
   2. The matter will be resolved in talks between directors and the workforces concerned.
   3. Payment should take place immediately following a return to work.
   4. Strikers have the right to compensation according to their position on the pay scale. If the pay-day fell during the strike, strikers should be paid 40 per cent for the period of stoppage, according to their point on the scale.

The text and commentary were carried in *Solidarność*, 11 (30 Aug 1980). It pointed out that the telex contradicted a promise made by Jagielski – a more senior official.

7. *Supplement*. This stated: 'The Interfactory Strike Committee appeals to the workforce to increase productivity, to economise on raw materials and energy and to improve labour discipline at all levels, in cooperation with the directors of enterprises, workplaces and institutions, once the strike has ended.'

8. '*Social minimum*'. The Polish Government estimates a subsistence minimum for family budgets, adjusted annually. It assumes availability of goods and services at the lowest prices. The assumption was tested by the

sociologist Andrzej Tymowski in 1970 who found that, in practice, one family in five lived below the official 'minimum'. See his *Próba określenia minimum spożycia* (Warsaw: Instytut Handlu Wewnętrznego, 1971). The position improved in the first half of the 1970s but declined thereafter, with the fall of living standards recorded in 1978 and 1979 and 10 per cent inflation. In the autumn of 1980, he argued that the 'social minimum' should become a central concern of Solidarity. He advocated a radical increase in family allowances (as specified at Szczecin); pension reform and elimination of specially privileged groups (both mentioned in the Gdańsk Agreement) and much greater usage of the 'social fund': 'an indispensable instrument of levelling and of social development'. See: *Polityka* (4 October 1980) and *Więź*, 11/12 (1980) pp. 23–30, 252–4.

9. *Nomenklatura*. See the Introduction.
10. *Free Saturdays*. This problem is left vague under the Gdańsk Agreement. By contrast, the settlement in Jastrzębie (Upper Silesia) on 3 September 1980 was unequivocal. These negotiations were conducted in a large hall filled with miners. They concluded as follows:

> **Deputy Premier Kopeć:** Miners! If we decide to make all Saturdays free from 1 January 1981, will you go back to work? [*General applause. Acceptance. All stand and sing the 'Internationale'*] *Czas* (Gdańsk), 39 (28 September 1980).

After this, the remainder of the labour force wanted the same.

The government made its first proposal on 10 November: a 42.5 hour week (8.5 hour day), setting 20 November as the deadline 'for discussion'. Solidarity's executive rejected the proposal. On 23 December, a second government proposition offered twenty-five free Saturdays (nine more than in 1980) and an eight-hour day. Time for discussion over Christmas was effectively nil. The government declared that the first, third and fifth Saturdays of January 1981 would be free. When Solidarity's national executive discussed the matter on 7 January, less radical speakers such as Jacek Kuroń proposed a referendum on the subject, but were overruled by mandated delegates – including those from Jastrzębie. Solidarity declared all Saturdays free.

There was nationwide absenteeism on Saturday 10 January, and following reprisals against employees, a warning strike in Warsaw, where the city transport stopped for four hours. There followed stoppages in Poznań, Legnica, Częstochowa, Krosno, Kalisz, Wałbrzych, Radom and other cities. The dispute was rapidly getting out of hand by 21 January, when the government at last agreed to discuss the problem. Nothing came of talks, however, despite a compromise suggested by Solidarity: a 41.5 hour week (three free Saturdays a month with the fourth as a six-hour day). The proposals were now 0.7 hours (42 minutes apart). Nevertheless, it took a twelve-hour meeting on 31 January to bring the two sides to agreement.

11. *Mirosław Chojecki.* Founder of the independent publishing house NOWA, and member of KOR, who was dismissed from work at the Institute of Nuclear Research in November 1976. During the next four years he was detained forty-four times, and arrested three times on a Procurator's

warrant. On 25 March 1980 he was arrested on a trumped-up charge of stealing a duplicator. After a national and international outcry and a hunger strike in a church at Podkowa Leśna (outside Warsaw), he was released. By then, Chojecki himself was on the thirty-third day of a fast in prison. Charges, however, were not dropped, and he received a suspended sentence on 12 June. He informed the court that he regarded the trial as political.

In August 1980, he went to the Gdańsk Shipyard and – together with Konrad Bieliński and Mariusz Wilk – helped organise printing for the strikers. The first issue of *Solidarność* appeared on 23 August and it continued (fourteen numbers in all) until the end of the strike. Chojecki, however, had been detained by the security service, who sent him back to Warsaw, where he was arrested. He was released on 1 September in accordance with the Gdańsk Agreement.

12. *Assurance.* The Government Commission was extremely reluctant to offer anything more than verbal promises on the question of political prisoners, continually emphasising the independence of the judiciary. The Strike Presidium was equally adamant: without a written undertaking there could be no end to the strike. To break the impasse, the delegates' plenum was consulted: it stated that the undertaking had to be in writing. Gwiazda then had four private discussions with Jagielski, after which this last point was also accepted. The prisoners were duly released by noon the following afternoon – with the exception of Jan Kozłowski, who remained in prison until 4 September.

13. *The crosses.* For several years after December 1970, official wreaths were laid at selected cemeteries to commemorate some victims of the shootings. Later, such ceremonies were banned. The idea of a memorial to the repressed, first mooted in 1971, was taken up by the Free Trade Unions of the Coast in 1978 who organised a ceremony in front of Gate Two of the Gdańsk Shipyard to mark the eighth anniversary of the killings. Despite police precautions mounted since dawn, a crowd of 4000 assembled at the appropriate time: 2.20 p.m. to sing the national anthem and Internationale, observe a minute's silence and hear speeches by Dariusz Kobzdej (of the Young Poland Movement), who read out a letter from Kazimierz Świtoń in prison, and by Bogdan Borusewicz. Police efforts to forestall the ninth anniversary by arresting more than 200 persons – including members of the Free Trade Unions, *Robotnik*'s editorial board and the Young Poland Movement – failed. The public took this as an admission of complicity in the shootings. As before, the problem of political prisoners was discussed; the question of Katyń was raised; Wałęsa introduced himself and spoke; there was a powerful appeal on behalf of free trade unions by Maryla Płońska. Both speeches appeared in *Robotnik*, 42 (20 December 1979).

With such symbolism behind it, the strike movement could not but make the call for a permanent memorial one of its primary demands. The opening of the monument, in December 1980, was a most extraordinary pageant, in which ordinary citizens and helmeted dockers stood alongside miners in traditional costume, high dignitaries of Church and state, and members of the armed forces. The spectacle, stage-managed by Andrzej Wajda, provided a brief moment of unity unique in modern Poland.

EXPERTS AND THE WORKING GROUP

1. Two members of the Commission were professional economists: Waldemar Kuczyński and Tadeusz Kowalik. Jadwiga Staniszkis is a sociologist.
2. This system is described in the Introduction.
3. An editorial in the Strike Bulletin, 'With whom are we talking?', *Solidarność*, 6 (27 August 1980) had attacked Deputy Premier Jagielski personally for his conduct of the Second Meeting. Its essence was expressed in the comment 'the more often the Premier mentions his sincerity, the more sincere laughter echoes in the conference hall'. The editors added that the whole previous experience of workers showed that the intention of the authorities is to cheat them. The Gdańsk negotiations, they wrote, were no exception.

   This article was subtly drawn to Jagielski's attention, with the suggestion that it had been inspired by Mazowiecki. That is how the matter stood during the working group on Wednesday. Jagielski returned to the subject twice on Thursday, once in conversation with Mazowiecki, when he commented 'such things are written about me here' and again during the Third Meeting, when he mentioned that he had seen it written that he was a diplomat and asked 'What kind of a diplomat am I?'

   Although the Bulletin's status was undefined, it was widely regarded by readers as representing the views of the Strike Presidium. Mazowiecki raised the question at the Presidium meeting on Wednesday, when he stated that whilst the authorities are a partner to negotiations they should be treated as such and not described in language which obliterates the notion that one is trying to reach an agreement. The fear was expressed that the future union might inherit the language of the independent journal, which would mean that the language of a small group – in some ways a sect – would become the language of a mass movement. But members of the Presidium rather liked the article. All who spoke in the discussion which followed, favoured maintaining the independence of the Bulletin from the Strike Committee.
4. W. Giełżyński, L. Stefański, *Gdańsk–Sierpień '80* (Warsaw, 1981) pp. 164–5.
5. Ibid., p. 167.
6. The Confederation of Independent Poland, founded in Warsaw in September 1979. See Peter Raina, *Independent Social Movements in Poland* (London: LSE/Orbis, 1981) pp. 410–17.
7. Formed in Gdańsk, July 1979. See *Who's Who – What's What in Solidarność* (Gdańsk, 1981).
8. Neal Ascherson, *The Polish August, The Self-Limiting Revolution* (Harmondsworth: Penguin, 1981) p. 168.
9. Quoted from Raina, *Independent Social Movements in Poland*, pp. 553–4.
10. Janusz Brych, 'Jakie związki zawodowe, Szczecin, sierpień 1980', *Rzeczpospolita* (5 October 1982).
11. Ascherson, *Polish August*, p. 174.
12. Conversation with *Prawo i Życie* (28 August 1982).
13. J. Staniszkis, 'Experts and the "Leading Role", a Participant's Account', *Labour Focus on Eastern Europe*, vol. 4, no. 46 (1981) p. 13.
14. Ibid.

THE AGREEMENT

1. Those arrested on a prosecutor's warrant on 28 August, in Warsaw alone, included: Jan Ajzner; Seweryn Blumsztajn; Andrzej Bulc; Mirosław Chojecki; Jan Cywiński; Ludwik Dorn; Mieczysław Grudziński; Stefan Kawalec; Wiesław P. Kęcik; Sergiusz Kowalski; Jacek Kuroń; Jan Lityński; Adam Michnik; Zbigniew Romaszewski; Henryk Wujec; Andrzej Zozula; Kazimierz Janusz; Leszek Moczulski; Tadeusz Stański. Source: *Tygodnik Solidarność*, 22 (28 August 1981) p. 4.

2. It is proposed that the government should consider the following appended points by 30 November 1980:

   1. To alter the Council of Ministers' decree on the method of calculating payment for holiday and sick leave in the four-brigade system. An average of thirty days is taken at present, although twenty-two days are worked each month. This method of calculation reduces the average daily payment in the case of short illnesses and lowers the equivalent for holidays.

   2. We demand a single statute (a Council of Ministers' decree) to regulate the principles used for calculating payment for a period of absence from work in every case. The ambiguity of existing regulations operates against employees.

   3. The lack of free Saturdays for those on the four-brigade system should be compensated by extra days off. At present, the greater number of days off under the four-brigade system than under other systems does provide rest from an exhausting work schedule, but does not amount to genuinely free days. The arguments advanced by the administration, that such compensation should only be granted after equal hours of work in both systems, do not seem correct.

   4. We demand that all Saturdays be made work-free, as they are in other socialist countries.

   5. We demand removal of Article 147 from the Labour Code, which permits extension of the average working week to forty-nine hours whenever additional free days occur, and also Article 148. Our working week is at present one of the longest in Europe.

   6. To increase the importance of contractual regulations over pay, by introducing changes in the Labour Code to specify that not only a change in pay scale, or components of pay, but also a change in the method of payment (a day's wages for piece-rates) requires prior notice from an employer. The rule should be introduced that the pay scale in the case of piece-rates is applied to all the employee's work. The problem of using young employees in accordance with their qualifications should also be regulated so that the above agreement does not become an additional barrier to professional advancement.

   7. To introduce a supplement within the shift-system for night work of up to 50 per cent of day wages and 30 per cent of actual earnings under piece-rates. We also demand a supplement for afternoon working (as in the chemicals industry).

Profiles

Bądkowski, Lech. A writer, born in Toruń in 1920. He took part in the campaign of September 1939, later escaping to England where he joined the Polish Navy. After the war he became a staff member of *Dziennik Bałtycki* (Baltic Daily) in Gdańsk but was transferred in 1953 and then banned from journalism 'for life' for political reasons. He published a number of historical and war novels and became President of the local section of the Writers' Union. On 21 August 1980, he took a resolution of support from Gdańsk writers to the shipyard. After reading it out, he received an ovation and was coopted onto the Strike Presidium. He was its spokesman on questions of censorship. Following the Agreement, he worked for Gdańsk Solidarity as its first Press Secretary.

Fiszbach, Tadeusz. A politician, born in Dobraczyn (now in the USSR) in 1935. After being a Youth Union activist, he joined the Party and attended its School of Social Sciences in Warsaw. He took a degree in economics at the Chief School of Planning and Statistics and entered the Party apparatus. He became a Secretary of the Gdańsk Party in 1971 and First Secretary in 1975. During the late 1970s, he sent reports to Warsaw about likely social tensions as a result of investment policies which modernised harbours but left living conditions much as before. His warnings were ignored. He went to the shipyard in the first phase of the strike and gave written guarantees of strikers' safety. During the negotiations, he broadcast to the region in conciliatory terms. He argued throughout that agreement was possible and that the tragedy of 1970 need not be repeated. He became a Deputy Member of the Politburo in December 1980 but was demoted the following July. He ceased to be First Secretary of the Gdańsk Party in January 1982.

Gruszecki, Wojciech. Born of a sailor's family in Gdynia in 1936, he was employed first as a fisherman. He graduated in chemistry at Gdańsk Technical University where he later received a doctorate, and joined its staff in 1964. After being, as he later described it, a 'silent oppositionist' in 1968 and 1970, he took an active part in the strike of 1980. He was a delegate to the Strike Committee and like Bądkowski, was coopted onto its Presidium. At the first meeting, he took the lead in pressing the Government Commission to address themselves to the strikers' demands. After twelve months as a leader of Gdańsk Solidarity, he did not stand in regional elections and returned to the Technical University.

Gwiazda, Andrzej. An engineer, born in Pińczów in 1935. He spent the war in Siberia and was repatriated to Silesia before settling in Gdańsk in 1948. Alone of his school, he did not join the Youth Union. Admitted to Gdańsk Technical University in 1953, he was soon expelled and called up for military service. He was allowed to resume studies in October 1956. After a decade of political difficulties, he managed, by changes of department and transferring to evening classes, to complete his degree. He was an assistant lecturer at Gdańsk Technical University until his dismissal in 1973 when he took work as an engineer at 'Elmor' in Gdynia.

On the eve of May Day 1978, he co-founded the Free Trade Unions of the Coast. He spoke out in support of KOR, led many unofficial discussion meetings and was frequently arrested. He led the strike at 'Elmor' in August 1980 and helped to formulate its demands. He took them to the Gdańsk Shipyard, where they formed the basis for some of the Twenty-one Points. During the strike, he was prominent in discussions, both public and private, on free trade unions and political prisoners. Afterwards, he was Vice-Chairman of Solidarity.

Jagielski, Mieczysław. Chairman of the Government Commission. Born in Kołomyja (now in the USSR) in 1924 of a peasant family, he joined the Polish Workers' (later United Workers') Party in 1948 and studied at the Party School in Warsaw. He became head of the Central Committee's Agricultural Department in 1956, and subsequently Minister of Agriculture, holding the position until 1970. With the advent of

Gierek, he became a full member of the Politburo and a key member of the new economic team as Chairman of the Planning Commission and Poland's permanent representative to the Council for Mutual Economic Assistance (COMECON), whose headquarters are in Moscow. He was regarded as a potential Prime Minister until his career was set back by a serious heart attack in 1975.

In July 1980, he was sent to settle the strike in Lublin, which he did in two days. On 21 August, he replaced Pyka as Chairman of the Commission in Gdańsk. After an unpromising start, he agreed to negotiations and managed to gain the trust of the Strike Presidium, while not forfeiting that of his Politburo colleagues in Warsaw. One striker commented: 'he came as a politician, but left as a statesman'. So close an association with the Agreement, and with the economic strategy of Gierek's early years, proved to be liabilities. He was removed from the Politburo in July 1981, and lost his position as Deputy Prime Minister.

Kobyliński, Zdzisław. A storeman at the State Transport (PKS) depot in Gdańsk and its delegate to the Interfactory Strike Committee. He was elected to the Strike Presidium and took part in the 'working contact' with the Prefect on 23 August. Though not vocal during the negotiations, he was vociferous at meetings of the delegates' plenum. On the final evening he urged that free unions could not be restricted to the Coast: 'our victory must apply nationwide'. He took part in the 'working group'.

Kołodziej, Andrzej. Born in Zagórze in 1959, he was trained as a locksmith in Sanok until 1977, when he was employed as a fitter at the Gdańsk Shipyard. He became one of the first members of the Free Trade Unions of the Coast. He was expelled from night school in November 1979 for political activities and from the Gdańsk Shipyard in January 1980 for the same reason. On 14 August 1980, he found work at the Gdynia Shipyard and led the strike there the next day. He became the youngest member of the Interfactory Strike Committee's Presidium, and its co-Vice-Chairman. During negotiations, he adopted a populist stance: proposing the broadcast of talks on radio and television and opposing the formation of 'working groups': 'behind four walls they are always stronger than us'. He was active in Gdańsk Solidarity until the summer of 1981 but did not stand for regional elections. He returned to the Gdynia Shipyard. Immediately after the 'state of war' had been declared, he was arrested in Czechoslovakia.

Kołodziejski, Jerzy. A Professor of Architecture at Gdańsk Technical University who became Prefect of the Gdańsk Region in 1979. He initiated the 'working contact' in the shipyard prior to negotiations, and subsequently chaired the government's 'working group' on Point One. He ceased to be Prefect in January 1982 and returned to Gdańsk Technical University.

Krzywonos, Henryka. A tram driver, born in 1955. A delegate of the Gdańsk urban transport workers to the Interfactory Strike Committee, she was the member of its Presidium responsible for arranging taxis and petrol for private cars during the strike – public transport was at a standstill. She was outspoken during negotiations and in the delegates' plenum.

Lis, Bogdan. A machine setter, born in 1952. After working as a mechanic with the Gdańsk Harbour Authority, he moved to 'Elmor' as a setter. He joined the socialist youth union (ZSMP) in 1974 and belonged to the Party from 1975–81. In 1978, he met Gwiazda and became involved in Free Trade Union activities. In March 1980, he helped to organise democratic elections to the 'Elmor' council, in which Free Trade Union supporters won 60 per cent of the places. In August, he was Chairman of the 'Elmor' Strike Committee and delegated to the Gdańsk Shipyard, where he became co-Vice-Chairman of the Strike Presidium. He spoke briefly during negotiations, and later played a prominent role in Solidarity as head of the Union's Commission on the economy and responsible for its international contacts. He escaped internment in December 1981, and became Solidarity's most senior leader in hiding.

Lis, Zbigniew. A strike organiser at the Gdańsk Shipyard, responsible for order and security, who made one intervention from the floor. Afterwards, he was a Solidarity activist at the shipyard.

Mazowiecki, Tadeusz. Catholic intellectual and chief adviser to the Strike Presidium. He was Chairman of the Students'

Publishing House from 1947 to 1948, when he was dismissed for 'clericalism'. In 1958, he founded *Więź*, a Catholic monthly which advocated pluralism of thought and opening of the Church to contemporary life. He was a 'Znak' deputy to the *Sejm* from 1961 but not allowed to stand again after his protests against the treatment of students in March 1968. He went to Gdańsk in December 1970 and attempted to establish a *Sejm* Commission to investigate the shootings, but in vain. In the 1970s, he continued to work in the Clubs of the Catholic Intelligentsia (KIK), with his journal and through the 'flying university', of which he was a co-organiser. On 22 August 1980, he took the 'Appeal of the Sixty-four' Warsaw intellectuals to the Gdańsk Shipyard and was invited to stay on, select and head the team of experts. Afterwards, he was founder editor of the weekly newspaper *Tygodnik Solidarność*.

Pieńkowska, Alina. A nurse, born in Gdańsk in 1952, who worked in the regional hospital before transferring to the emergency service at the Gdańsk Shipyard in 1975. In June 1978, she joined the Free Trade Unions and later published articles in *Robotnik Wybrzeża* on occupational diseases and accidents at work. She helped organise educational courses for workers and was frequently detained by the militia.

In August 1980, she took charge of food deliveries for the strike. It was her speech in front of Gate Three which persuaded workers to remain in the shipyard for the second phase of the strike. During negotiations, she spoke on Point Sixteen (health care) of which she was author, and on political prisoners. She led the occupation strike of the Prefect's office in November 1980 – to protest against non-fulfilment of Point Sixteen – and was responsible for Solidarity's medical bank, coordinating assistance from abroad.

Sobieszek, Lech. A metalworker, born in Wałbrzych in 1945. After working in Wrocław and Puławy he moved to the 'Siarkopol' Sulphur Plant in Gdańsk in 1970. He became Chairman of its Workers' Council, which was dissolved by management shortly afterwards. On 16 August 1980, he was delegated to the Interfactory Strike Committee, joined the Strike Presidium and helped to formulate its demands. He adopted a fundamentalist stance during negotiations and later in Solidarity.

Szablewski, Alojzy. A former officer who describes the consequences of his discharge from the army.

Walentynowicz, Anna. A crane driver, born in Wołyn (now in the USSR) in 1929. She moved to Gdańsk after the war and started to work in the shipyard in 1950, as a welder. She was a delegate of the Youth Union to a Congress of Socialist Youth, held in Berlin in 1951, but terminated her membership shortly afterwards. In 1965, she changed her job to that of a crane operator for reasons of ill-health. Her first dismissal from the shipyard took place three years later, after she had attempted to uncover malpractices in the trade unions. She took part in the events of December 1970 and was a member of the Strike Presidium which met Gierek at the shipyard on 25 January 1971.

She joined the Free Trade Unions in the early summer of 1978. Her first article for *Robotnik Wybrzeża* described a visit by Gierek to the shipyard in 1979: 'A Frank Discussion about an Entrecôte Steak'. Many meetings were held in her home. She was arrested innumerable times, searched and beaten. In the spring of 1980, she was transferred within the shipyard and put in 'quarantine' by the management, who barred her from using the canteen. Her dismissal on 9 August, which led to protests on her behalf, was the immediate cause of the strike. She made one eloquent intervention during the negotiations and was afterwards a founder member of Solidarity and a popular speaker all over the country.

Wałęsa, Lech. An electrician, born near Lipno on 23 September 1943. He studied at a school of agricultural machinery and worked as an electro-mechanic in garages at Łochocin. After military service from 1963–5, he moved to Gdańsk, as an electrician at the shipyard. He was a member of the Strike Committee in December 1970 and was arrested for the first time. He was not politically active again until February 1976, when he spoke out against the authorities – including Gierek by name – at a Works' Council meeting. A local appeals tribunal upheld his dismissal. He was taken on by an enterprise for construction machinery (ZREMB) in May 1976.

He joined the Free Trade Unions in the early summer of 1978, and took an active part in organising the December (1970) memorial meetings. He was dismissed from ZREMB in

December 1978. Five months later, he found work at 'Elektromontaż'. He took part in a Workers' Commission to defend those due for dismissal in January 1980. The defence failed and he lost his job. He remained unemployed until August 1980 when he entered the Gdańsk Shipyard through the fence and took charge of the strike. All three enterprises rapidly reinstated him.

On 17 September 1980, he was elected Chairman of Solidarity's National Coordinating Commission (KKP) and was reelected by the First National Congress of Solidarity in October 1981. He refused to make any statement to support the 'state of war' in December 1981, and was held in various places of detention, before his release eleven months later.

Wiśniewski, Florian. An electrical technician, born in Lubań in 1937. He joined 'Elektromontaż' in 1953 and rose to be a deputy section head. He was a branch secretary of the Youth Union (1951–5) and a Party member (1960–72). Thereafter, he began to be harassed at work for attempting to introduce democratic electoral procedures for trade unions and other factory organisations. He took part in the Workers' Commission to contest dismissals in January 1980 and helped organise democratic union elections at the enterprise in March. The factory council thus elected was coopted *en bloc* onto the Strike Committee in August 1980. He was elected to the Interfactory Strike Committee Presidium and acted as a spokesman for construction workers during negotiations and afterwards within Solidarity, when he prepared a proposal for making the Work Inspectorate independent of management. He left the Presidium of Gdańsk Solidarity in November 1980, and returned to 'Elektromontaż'.

Wyłupek, Stanisław. A government official, born in Upper Silesia in 1923. He worked for the Central Committee apparatus during the 1950s and took a degree in electrical engineering at Warsaw Technical University. He became a Deputy Minister, first of Machine Industry (in 1967) and then of Communications (in 1973).

Zieliński, Zbigniew. A politician, who was a Secretary of the Central Committee from April 1977 until April 1981. He was also head of the Central Committee's Department for Heavy Industry, Transport and Construction. At the Eighth Party

Congress (February 1980), he was put in charge of a working party on 'economic effectiveness in the light of new conditions'. In August 1980, he was included in the Government Commission. On arrival in the shipyard, he was heard to mutter 'savages . . . animals . . . the wild East'. Apocryphal or not, this is how he treated workers during the negotiations.

Index

Page numbers in **bold** type indicate passages of direct speech.